PREFACE.

PUBLIC interest in the work of popularizing cheap and good cookery has for some time been so marked, and so many applications for a book of this character are continually received at the N. Y. School of Cookery, that we feel quite justified in offering our special plan of instruction for the guidance of societies or individuals who wish to establish similar institutions elsewhere.

In presenting this text-book to the public, we desire to call attention to the necessity for accompanying technical instruction with some explanation of the principles of cookery as applicable to the preservation of the general health. A book of mere receipts would fail to accomplish the purpose we have in view, i. e., some intelligent comprehension on the part of the cook of the chemistry of food and the physiology of nutrition. Our present limits will not permit any lengthy exemplification of this point, but we have embodied the general features of our instructions in the appendix to this volume, and the student is advised to become well acquainted with them before beginning the actual practice of the cooking lessons. The knowledge thus obtained will be available in enabling tyros in the culinary art to realize the imperative necessity for careful study from the very outset of their work, and will

assist the more advanced pupils (1) to classify different
articles of food in accordance with their effect upon the
system; (2) to alter and improve the dietaries of persons
following stated pursuits, so as to satisfy their physical
and mental needs; (3) to detect the adulteration and de-
terioration of food. The scholars should be questioned
occasionally by their teacher, as the lessons progress, for
the purpose of arriving at their understanding of the subject; and, near the end of the course, they should be
thoroughly examined; in no case should a diploma or cer-
tificate of proficiency be given until the pupil has not only
mastered the principles specified in the appendix, but has
also given abundant evidence by practical demonstration
that the cooking lessons are clearly understood.

Every cooking lesson should consist of the actual preparation of certain suitable dishes by the pupils, if the class is
small, or by some of the number acting in turn as assistants. when the class is large; the marketing should be
done by them, or in their presence, in all possible cases;
the kitchen, the fire and the utensils, put in order for the
lesson by them, and the most capable of them should act
as pupil teachers, aiding their less expert associates while
practicing their own tasks. The expense of the lessons can
be considerably diminished by allowing the pupils, their
friends, or visitors at the lessons, to purchase the dishes at
about their cost.

Both reasons and facts are good things for the average
cook to comprehend; familiarity with the nature of the
different nutriments in common use enables persons of ordinary intelligence to compose a variety of nourishing

dishes from a limited market supply, and shows how greatly the appetizing nature of a meal depends upon its combination and seasoning. ·

The prime fact that the sole object of cooking is to prepare for nourishing the body should never be forgotten, and, consequently, the methods which are best calculated to serve this purpose are the proper ones to employ. Good cooking should not be regarded as an incentive to gluttony, or used as the means of tempting the luxurious to undue indulgence of appetite; it has a nobler purpose, the accomplishment of which demands foresight, care and patience. Its mission is to show how every scrap of untainted food, cheap or costly, can be made to yield all its nutrient properties; to decide how every available particle can best be converted into warmth and strength.

Economy in cooking is often miscalled meanness; but the desire of a conscientious cook to economise is proportionate with his or her mastery of the culinary art. A good cook will not waste food any more than a good workman will wantonly ruin his tools or his handiwork.

Some discussion may arise concerning the prices attached to the ingredients required in making the dishes composing the lessons. It may be well in this connection to state that we have, for the past three years, been collecting the retail price lists of foods from all parts of the United States, and from information already received, we feel quite confident that the prices herein quoted will be found to form an average sufficiently accurate for a standard in estimating the expense of giving a course of cooking lessons. The prices in Boston and Philadelphia seem to range higher than those in Washington and Chicago. The figures used in this work represent the rates current in such New York localities as those east of Third and west of Seventh avenues, and in Washington Market. But in any place the price paid for articles of food largely depends upon the knowledge and discretion of the purchaser.

Before concluding this preface we desire to express our earnest thanks to those friends of the Cooking School who have manifested such genuine interest, and given such substantial support to the institution. Foremost among them ranks the public press of the United States, which has invariably accorded its generous support and judicious endorsement to the enterprise. To the encouragement and influence of the press is due the success which has attended the work of the NEW YORK SCHOOL OF

CONTENTS.

CONTENTS.

PART IV.

CHAPTER I.

FIRST LESSON OF LADIES' COURSE IN MIDDLE CLASS AND ARTISTIC COOKERY.

CHAPTER II.

SECOND LESSON OF THE LADIES' COURSE.

CHAPTER III.

THIRD LESSON OF THE LADIES' COURSE.

CHAPTER IV.

FOURTH LESSON OF THE LADIES' COURSE.

CHAPTER V.

FIFTH LESSON OF THE LADIES' COURSE.

CHAPTER VI.

SIXTH LESSON OF THE LADIES' COURSE.

CHAPTER VII.

SEVENTH LESSON OF THE LADIES' COURSE.

PART I.

CHAPTER I.

THE DEMONSTRATION KITCHEN.

Choice and Fittings of Kitchen.—The room selected as the place where cooking lessons are to be given must be light, airy, and thoroughly ventilated; its size may be in accordance with the probable audience. When plenty of space is available, two rooms of different size are desirable; a small one for the practice-kitchen, and a large one for the demonstration lessons.

The practice kitchen must contain a stove or range in good burning order, a sink with a full supply of hot and cold water, a dresser for dishes, a light closet for pots and pans, three or four large, strong, unpainted wooden tables, and plenty of cooking utensils in good condition.

The large demonstration kitchen must contain a large stove or range, a sink with plenty of hot and cold water, a large, light pot-closet, a dresser for dishes and several strong tables of unpainted wood. A refrigerator for keeping food is a necessary adjunct, even in cool weather; for by using one all the various perishable supplies will necessarily be collected together, and being under the cook's observation constantly, can be properly utilized without waste. The refrigerator should stand at a distance from the stove in order to escape the heat of the fire, and near a window, for the purpose of insuring fresh air.

In front of these articles of kitchen furniture, and about six feet from them, a long table or counter should extend across the width of the room; a low platform, containing a lecturer's desk, should be placed at one end of the counter, in such a position as to command a full view of every part of the room without interfering with the prospect of the audience.   When practicable, a gas pipe should be run under the counter, and jets be projected through apertures in it, in such a manner as to permit the preparation of some of the smaller dishes within the immediate view of the audience.

In front of the counter rows of seats should be placed, each row being slightly elevated above the one in front of it, so as to insure an unimpeded prospect to every one attending the demonstration.

The bill of fare for the lesson should be written in large, clear letters upon a bulletin board placed in a conspicuous position.   The pupils present at a lesson should be provided with note-books and pencils, and should carefully record every useful hint and direction given by the demonstrator.   It is useless to hope to remember all the information imparted during a cooking lesson, and every scholar should bear in mind the fact that accuracy in receipts is the secret of that even excellence which stamps the work of the well-trained cook.

Accurate Weights and Measures.—The demonstrator should weigh or measure every ingredient used, and report its exact quantity to the audience; if the flavor does not suit individual palates, the necessary alterations may be made, but the proper amount once found should never be deviated from, if a uniform flavor is desired.   Very much of the excellence of a dish depends upon its seasoning, and it is well worth a little trouble to decide upon the palatable point, and a little care to abide by the decision.   We give below a few receipts for preparing seasonings.

Dried Herbs.—Rub the leaves of a bunch of dried herbs through a sieve, and bottle them tightly until needed for use; tie the stalks together and save them until wanted to make what the French call a *bouquet,* for a soup or stew. A *bouquet* of herbs is made by tying together a few sprigs of parsley, thyme and two bay-leaves. The bay-leaves, which have the flavor of laurel, can be bought at any German grocery or drug-store, enough to last for a long time, for five cents. The best herbs are sage, thyme, sweet marjoram, tarragon, mint, sweet basil, parsley, bay-leaves, celery seed and onions. If the seed of any of the seven first mentioned is planted in little boxes on the window sill, or in a sunny spot in the yard, enough can be raised for general use. Gather and dry them as follows: parsley and tarragon should be dried in June and July, just before flowering; mint in June and July; thyme, marjoram and savory in July and August; basil and sage in August and September; all herbs should be gathered in the sunshine and dried by artificial heat; their flavor is best preserved by keeping them in air-tight tin cans, or in tightly corked glass bottles.

Dried Celery and Parsley.—In using celery, wash the leaves, stalks, roots and trimmings, and put them in a cool oven to dry thoroughly; then grate the root, and rub the leaves and stalks through a sieve, and put all into a tightly corked bottle, or tin can with close cover; this makes a most delicious seasoning for soups, stews and stuffing. In using parsley, save every bit of leaf, stalk or root, and treat them in the same way as the celery. Remember, in using parsley, that the root has even a stronger flavor than the leaves, and do not waste a bit.

Tarragon Vinegar.—Use a bunch of fresh tarragon in summer, or the dried herb in winter; put it in an earthen bowl, and pour on it one pint of scalding hot vinegar; cover it and let it stand until the next day; then strain it and put it into a bottle tightly corked. Either put more hot vinegar on the tarragon, or dry it, and save it until wanted to make more; a gallon or more can be made from one bunch; only every time it is used it must stand a day longer.

Celery Salt.—Mix celery root, which has been dried and grated as above, with one fourth its quantity of salt; it makes a nice seasoning, and keeps a long time.

Spice Salt.—This can be made nicely by drying, powdering and mixing by repeated siftings the following ingredients: one quarter of an ounce each of powdered thyme, bay-leaf and pepper; one eighth of an ounce each of marjoram and cayenne pepper; one half of an ounce each of powdered clove and nutmeg; to every four ounces of this powder add one ounce of salt, and keep the mixture in an air-tight vessel. One ounce of it added to three pounds of stuffing, or force meat of any kind, makes a delicious seasoning.

How to Clean the Kitchen.—(1.) Dust down the ceiling and side walls with a feather duster, or a clean cloth tied over a broom. (2.) Sweep the floor, setting the broom evenly upon the floor, and moving it with long, regular strokes, being careful not to fling the refuse about the room, or to raise much dust. (3.) Wash the paint with a piece of clean flannel dipped in hot water, in which borax has been dissolved in the proportion of one tablespoonful to a gallon of water; if the spots are not easily rubbed off, use a little soap, rinsing it off thoroughly, and wiping the paint with the flannel wrung out of clean water. (4.) Wash the window-glass with a soft cloth which does not shed lint, dipped in clean water and wrung out; polish the glass with a clean, dry cloth, or with newspaper. (5.) Scrub the tables with hot water, in which a little washing soda and soap have been dissolved, using a stiff brush; then rinse them with a cloth wrung out of clean, hot water, and wipe them as dry as possible. (6.) Scrub the floor in the same manner, and wipe it quite dry. (7.) Wash all the scrubbing brushes and cloths in hot water containing a little soda and soap. (8.) Wash all the dish cloths and kitchen towels in hot water, with soap and soda, or borax, every time they are used, and keep a clean, dry stock of them on hand.

How to Clean the Stove.—(1.) Let down the grate and take up the cinders and ashes carefully to avoid all unnecessary dirt; put them at once into an ash-sifter fitted into the top of a pail or keg with handles, and closed with a tight fitting cover; take the pail out of doors, sift the cinders, put the ashes into the ash-can, and bring the cinders back to the kitchen. (2.) Brush the soot and ashes out of all the flues and draught-holes of the stove, and then put the covers on, and brush all the dust off the outside. A careful cook will save all the wings of game and poultry to use for this purpose. If the stove is greasy wash it off with a piece of flannel dipped in hot water containing a little soda. (3.) Mix a little black-lead or stove polish with enough water to form a thin paste; apply this to the stove with a soft rag or brush; let it dry a little and then polish it with a stiff brush. (4.) If there are any steel fittings about the stove, polish them with emery paper; if they have rusted from neglect, rub some oil on them at night, and polish them with emery paper in the morning. A "burnisher," composed of a net-work of fine steel rings, if used with strong hands, will make them look as if newly finished. (5.) If the fittings are brass, they should be cleaned with emery or finely powdered and sifted bath brick dust rubbed on with a piece of damp flannel, and then polished with dry dust and chamois skin. (6.) Brush up the hearthstone, wash it with a piece of flannel dipped in hot water containing a little soda, rinse, and wipe it dry with the flannel wrung out of clean hot water.

How to Light the Fire.—Put a double handful of cinders in the bottom of the grate, separating them so that

the air can pass freely between them; put on them a layer
of dry paper, loosely squeezed between the hands; on the
paper lay some small sticks of wood cross-wise, so as to permit a draught from the bottom; place a double handful of
small cinders and bits of coal on top of the wood; close the
covers of the stove; open all the draughts, and light the
paper from the bottom of the grate. As the fire burns up
gradually add mixed coal and cinders until there is a clear,
bright body of fire; then partly close the draughts, and
keep the fire bright by occasionally putting on a little coal.
The condition of the draught closely affects the degree of
heat yielded by a given amount of fuel; just enough air
should be supplied to promote combustion; but if a strong
current blows through the mass of fire, or over its surface,
it carries off a great portion of the heat which should be
utilized for cooking purposes, and gradually deadens the
fire.

How to Keep up the Fire.—As soon as the heat of the
fire shows signs of diminishing, add a little fuel at a time,
and often enough to prevent any sensible decrease of the
degree of heat required for cooking. Keep the bottom of
the fire raked clear, and never let the ash-pan get choked
up near the grate with ashes, cinders, or refuse of any kind.
There is no economy in allowing a fire to fail for want of
fuel; if the fire is not replenished until the heat falls below
the temperature necessary for cooking purposes, there is
a direct waste of all the heat which is supplied by fresh
fuel until the surface and ovens of the stove are again
heated to the proper degree; whereas, if, when that heat
has once been reached, it is sustained by the gradual addition of a little fuel at a time, this waste is avoided, and
much of the cook's time is saved. In kitchens where this
fact is not understood there is a continual waste of time and
fuel, to say nothing of the trial of patience which is the
too apt response to a request for the services of the cook

when "she has just mended the fire, and nothing can be cooked until it burns up."

Degrees of Heat from Fuel.—The advantage which one kind of fuel possesses over another depends upon its local abundance and cheapness. We append the average temperature of a clear fire made of different combustibles, and a table of the degree of heat necessary for various operations in cookery, so that some definite idea of the relative values of fuel can be reached:

Willow Charcoal	600° Fahr.
Ordinary "	700 "
Hard Wood	800 to 900 "
Coal	1,000 "

Shell-bark Hickory has the greatest heating value among woods; that is, the coals it produces are hotter and retain the heat longer than the coals from soft woods. Soft woods burn with a quicker flame and more intense heat than hard woods, and produce more flame and smoke; they are therefore best to make a quick, fierce fire. Hard woods burn more slowly, with less heat, flame, and smoke, but produce harder coals, which retain the heat, and are consequently the best for long continued cooking operations.

Charcoal is the residue of wood, the gaseous elements of which have slowly been burned away in covered pits or furnaces, with a limited supply of air. Newly-made charcoal burns without flame, but after it has gathered moisture from exposure to the air it makes a slight blaze; it burns easily and rapidly, and produces a greater heat in proportion to its weight than any other fuel.

Anthracite coal is the mineral remains of ancient vegetation which has lost all its elements except a little sulphur, an excess of carbon and the incombustible ash. It kindles slowly, but burns with an intense and steady volume of heat which is exceedingly valuable for cooking purposes.

Coke, the residue of any kind of coal from which illuminating gas has been manufactured, is an inexpensive fuel, yielding an intense but transient heat, and is very well adapted for boiling and for cooking operations which do not require long sustained heat.

Prof. Youmans quotes the following figures as representing the comparative heating values of the above named fuels, but remarks that the actual degree of heat derived from them, under ordinary circumstances, will fall below this estimate: 1 lb. of dry, hard wood will raise 35 lbs. of water from the freezing to the boiling point; 1 lb. of coal will similarly heat 60 lbs. of water; and 1 lb. of wood charcoal, 73 lbs. of water.

Cooking Temperatures.—The following table represents the degrees of heat to which food is subjected during its preparation for the table:

Glucose, or grape sugar, melts	80° Fahr.
Beef tallow "	100 "
Mutton tallow "	106 "
Stearin "	111 "
Butter "	135 "
Albumen coagulates	145 "
Scalding water	150 "
Starch is transformed to sugar	160 "
Water simmers (after boiling)	180 "
Milk boils	199 "
Water boils	212 "
Moderate oven for sponge cake	220 "
" rice pudding	220 "
Baking heat for ordinary cakes	240 "
" biscuits	240 "
" macaroni	240 "
" meat	240 "
First baking heat for bread	280 "
After five minutes moderate to	240 "
Baking heat for pies	280 "

Baking heat for puff paste	300° Fahr.
Frying temperature, ranging up . .	345 "
Smoking hot fat	345 "
Thick fish *Filets*, fry at . . .	380 "
Croquettes " . . .	385 "
Saratoga potatoes "	385 "
Fritters " . . .	385 "
Rissoles "	385 "
Kromeskies " . . .	385 "
Whitebait "	400 "
Lard boils	565 "
Oil "	600 "
Heat of open roasting fire	1000 "
" broiling fire	1000 "

Best Material for Cooking Utensils.—There can be no question of the superiority of copper cooking utensils over those composed of any other metal, providing they are used with care. Their first cost is about double that of those made of iron, and considerably greater than that of tin, but they endure exposure to heat much better, retain it longer, and wear a greater length of time; even when they are worn quite thin, which would not happen in a lifetime with ordinary care, they can be sold as old copper. Copper is a better conductor of heat than either iron or tin, and consequently cooking in copper utensils can be done with less fire than when other metal vessels are used. The inside of all copper vessels used over the fire should be coated with tin, in order to prevent the formation of the oxide of copper, which, combining with carbonic acid, forms the poisonous carbonate of copper, indicated by the appearance of a greenish color on the surface of the metal. Acids, oils and salt, all tend to produce injurious compounds when copper is long exposed to their action; therefore, articles of food should never be allowed to stand in them, and they should be thoroughly cleaned every time they are used. Copper melts at about 1996° Fahr.

Tin vessels are liable to be affected by any of these substances, although to a less extent; and for that reason food should not be kept in them for any length of time. On the other hand, the quantity of tin collected by food during its general preparation is not sufficient to produce any very injurious effect upon the health. The danger in using tin vessels is to be apprehended from the possible contamination of the metal by the presence of such foreign substances as copper, lead, and arsenic, which may form deleterious compounds, with some vegetable salts and acids. However, if they are kept clean and free from rust they answer ordinary kitchen requirements. Tin melts at about 442° Fahr.

Iron is employed in the manufacture of kitchen utensils to a greater extent than any other metal; it is cheap and readily obtained, and seems to meet the approbation of many housekeepers. When the inside of iron cooking utensils is coated with tin, or with a layer of enamel, there is no inconvenience to be feared from rust, and they are easily cleaned. Brightly polished tin or metal saucepans take longer to heat than tarnished ones, but they retain the heat better. Except in the case of steam, color affects the heating qualities of a cooking utensil; the temperature of a black one, which absorbs the rays of luminous heat, will be raised more quickly than that of a bright one.

The housekeeper must be guided in the selection of her kitchen outfit by convenience and expediency; we have given the above facts as explanatory of the merits of the different metals; but we have used all kinds successfully in the New York School of Cookery. We append our own methods of cleaning the different kinds.

How to Clean Coppers.—(1.) If the utensils are very much tarnished, let them stand fifteen minutes in scalding hot water with a tablespoonful of soda dissolved in each gallon of water; then scour the inside with fine sand and soap well rubbed on with the hand, or with a soft rag, until perfectly clean and bright; wash, and dry with a soft, dry cloth; clean the outside in the same way, and wash and dry with a clean cloth. (2.) Never use vinegar or lemon-juice unless to remove spots which can not be scoured off as directed above; if acid is used, mix it with salt, apply it quickly, and thoroughly wash it off at once; this care will serve to prevent the possible collection of verdigris upon the copper, but the utensils tarnish much more quickly when they are cleaned with acid than when any other method is employed. Salt is sometimes substituted for sand in the above named process. (3.) One of the best *chefs* belonging to the N. Y. School of Cookery always had the coppers cleaned with the following mixture, rubbed on with the hand, and then washed off with clean, cold water, and employed a soft towel to dry them thoroughly; the mixture consisted of equal parts of salt, fine sand, and flour, made into a thick paste with milk or butter-milk.

How to Clean Iron Ware.—(1.) Wash thoroughly inside and out with hot water, soap, and soda; rinse and wipe thoroughly with a clean towel, and finish drying near the fire. If the inside is coated with the remains of food, put the pot over the fire, fill it with hot water, dissolve a tablespoonful of soda in it, and let the water boil for fifteen minutes; this will soften the dirt so that it can be scoured off with sand and soap. (2.) When about to use a fish kettle, set it over the fire empty to heat; if it is not perfectly clean, an odor will be perceptible; in that case clean it as directed above before using it. (3.) If you are obliged to use the same gridiron for broiling steak that has been used for fish, wash it thoroughly with hot water, soap, and soda, rinse it in clean, hot water, heat it over the fire, rub it thoroughly with clean brown paper, and then with an onion cut in two pieces.

How to Clean Enamelled Ware.—Put it over the fire, filled with hot water containing a tablespoonful of soda to every gallon of water, and let it boil fifteen minutes; then if it is not perfectly clean, scour it with a little soap and fine sand, wash it well, and dry it with a clean cloth.

How to Clean Tin Ware.—(1.) Scour till bright with fine sand or powdered and sifted brickdust, moistened with water and rubbed on with chamois skin; polish with dry whiting and chamois skin. (2.) If the tin is very much tarnished, boil it in hot water with soda before scouring. If no whiting is at hand dry flour may be substituted for it.

How to Clean Japanned Ware.—Wash it with a sponge dipped in clean, cold water, wipe it dry and polish it with dry flour well rubbed on with a soft cloth.

How to Clean Plated Ware.—(1.) Put it in hot soda water for five minutes, then wipe it on a clean, dry cloth, and polish it with chamois skin. (2.) If it is much tarnished use a little very fine whiting or silver powder in polishing it, taking care to brush it all out of the crevices and chased work on the plate.

How to Clean Steel Knives.—Rub them on a leather-covered board with a little finely-powdered brickdust, and wipe them thoroughly on a clean, dry towel. Bear the fact in mind that knives are hardened at a temperature of from 380° Fahr. to 550° Fahr.; and consequently will lose their temper if exposed to a greater degree of heat; the temperature of hot fat ranges from 340° Fahr. to 600° Fahr., so if you put a knife into hot fat it will be ruined.

How to Clean Sieves and Jelly-bags.—(1.) Put the sieves into hot water containing a little soda or borax, but no soap; scrub them well with a clean brush, rinse them thoroughly in plenty of boiling water, and shake them dry. (2.) Never use soap for washing jelly-bags; wash them in as hot, clean water as the hands can endure, rinse them in boiling water, and wring them as dry as possible; then dry them where no dust will reach them, and keep them in a clean place.

General Kitchen Cleanliness.—(1.) Never cease to exercise the greatest care in keeping the kitchen clean; it is the best place in the house to recall to mind the proverb that " *Cleanliness is next to Godliness.*" (2.) After attention has been given to all the directions enumerated in this chapter, remember to *watch the sinks and drains;* flush them several times a day with boiling water. (3.) Take care that no scraps of meat or parings of vegetables accumulate in them to attract vermin, or choke the traps. (4.) Never throw soapsuds into the sink without afterwards flushing it with clean hot water. (5.) Run hot water containing a little chloride of lime into the drains at least once a day in summer, and once in every two or three days in winter, to counteract all unpleasant and unhealthy odors.

Remember that the best cook always has the cleanest kitchen.

CHAPTER II.

FIRST LESSON OF THE FIRST ARTISAN COURSE.

THIS course of lessons is designed for the instruction of the young daughters of working people in the preparation of those simple dishes which add variety to their daily fare without increasing its cost. The system of teaching in the New York Cooking School includes marketing with the pupils for the materials to be used during the lesson, or allowing them to purchase the articles themselves, and then returning them the price when they bring the ingredients to the school. This gives them a practical knowledge of the prices and qualities of different articles of food which they could not acquire in any other way.

Two or three girls are chosen for their attention and quickness, and allowed to assist the demonstrator in preparing the dishes to be cooked during the lesson; the choice is so fixed during the series of lessons as to enable every deserving scholar to engage in the actual work of making the dishes; this serves not only to excite an excellent spirit of emulation among the members of the class, but also to develop the faculty of expression to such an extent as to enable the young assistants to gradually take rank as pupil teachers, and to instruct their comrades during practice hours in the kitchen, or at their own homes.

This course of instruction includes the setting of the table, bringing in the dinner, waiting upon the table, clearing away the soiled dishes after the conclusion of the meal, washing the dishes and regulating the dining-room. After the dishes composing the first lesson are prepared and placed upon the stove to cook, the scholars are shown by the teacher how to go through these various operations, the oldest girl working with the teacher. At the second lesson another girl is selected to perform the entire routine, without assistance from the teacher; and when her work is done it is criticised by the other pupils, and corrected to correspond with instructions imparted during the first lesson. A different girl is chosen at every lesson, until all the pupils have participated in the dining-room practice in turn; but after the first lesson the task of instruction is vested in the criticism of the class, the teacher acting only as an umpire in case of any disputed question. The result of these lessons is highly satisfactory, and the pupils practice them at home to the great improvement of their tables and table manners.

How to Choose Soup Materials.—The reasons why soup

is an economical and healthy article of food will be found in the appendix. The materials for soup should be fresh vegetables and untainted meat; but they may both be the cheapest of their kind; a very little meat, or a few bones, will serve as the basis of excellent soup, and it is often made of vegetables alone.

In the previous chapter we have spoken of making a collection of seasonings; if the herbs cannot be raised at home, they may be bought, a few cents' worth at a time, until a good variety is accumulated.

Economical soup may be made from the remains of cooked food instead of newly-bought materials, care being taken to compound and season the soup properly.

VEGETABLE PORRIDGE.

INGREDIENTS.

1 carrot - - - - - - - -	1 cent.
1 turnip - - - - - - - -	1 "
1 oz. celery stalks - - - - -	1 "
½ oz. parsley - - - - - - -	1 "
Seasonings - - - - - - -	1 "
1 qt. tomatoes - - - - - -	5 cents.
¼ lb. rice - - - - - - -	2 "
Total - - - - -	12 cents.

(1.) Pare the carrot, turnip and tomatoes. (2.) Cut them into dice a quarter of an inch square. (3.) Cut the celery stalks in the same way. (4.) Chop the parsley fine. (5.) Pick over the rice, and wash it by putting it in a colander, and running water through it. (6.) Put all these ingredients into the soup kettle with four quarts of cold water, one tablespoonful of salt, half a level saltspoonful of pepper, and one sprig each of thyme and marjoram tied up with three bay leaves, and six whole cloves. (7.) Put the kettle over the fire, bring it slowly up to a boil, and then simmer it gently about two hours, until the vegetables are quite tender. (8.) After adding enough boiling water to increase the quantity to four quarts, see if the seasoning suits the taste; if it does not, alter it, and the soup will be ready to serve.

PEA SOUP WITH CROÛTONS.

INGREDIENTS.

1 carrot - - - - - - - -	1 cent.
1 onion - - - - - - - -	1 "
Bread - - - - - - - -	1 "
1 oz. suet and seasonings - - - -	1 "
1 pt. dried peas - - - - - - -	5 cents.
Drippings - - - - - - - -	2 "
Total - - - - - -	11 cents.

(1.) Peel and slice the onion, fry it brown in the soup-kettle with the suet chopped fine. (2.) Pick over the peas, put them into the colander and wash them by running cold water through them. (3.) Add them to the onion with four quarts of cold water, a tablespoonful of salt, half a level saltspoonful of pepper, and the carrot peeled and sliced. (4.) Set the kettle over the fire, and let the soup simmer slowly for about two hours, or until the peas are soft. (5.) A wineglassful of cold water should be added every twenty minutes to check the boiling and help soften the peas. (6.) Cut two slices of stale bread in half inch dice, fry them in the two ounces of dripping, which must be smoking hot before the bread is put into them; as soon as the bread is brown take it up with a skimmer, lay it on brown paper for a minute to absorb all the grease from it, and then put it into the bottom of the soup tureen. (7.) When the peas are tender pass the soup through the sieve with the potato masher and return it with the pot to heat, adding enough boiling water to make four quarts. (8.) If the soup shows any sign of settling, mix together a tablespoonful each of butter and flour by rubbing them together dry until they form a smooth paste, and then stir this into the soup; it will hold the peas in suspension. (9.) See if the seasoning is right, and then serve the soup.

SCOTCH BROTH WITHOUT MEAT.

INGREDIENTS.

1 carrot - - - - - - - -	1 cent
1 turnip - - - - - - - -	1 "
1 onion and seasonings - - - - -	1 "
1 oz. celery stalks - - - - - -	1 "
Bread - - - - - - - - -	1 "
Drippings - - - - - - -	2 cents
4 oz. oatmeal - - - - - - -	2 "
4 oz. pearl barley - - - - - -	3 "
Total - - - - -	12 cents

(1.) Steep the barley over night in cold water, and rinse it well in clean water before using it. (2.) Pare the turnip, carrot and onion, and cut them in quarter inch dice. (3.) Cut the celery in small bits. (4.) Put all these ingredients into the soup kettle with four quarts of boiling water, a level tablespoonful of salt, quarter of a saltspoonful of pepper, and as much cayenne as can be taken up on the point of a small penknife blade. (5.) Set the kettle over the fire, and let it simmer slowly for one hour. (6.) Mix the oatmeal to a smooth batter with cold water; add it to the soup and let it simmer another hour. (7.) Cut the bread in quarter inch dice, and fry them brown in the drippings, which must be made smoking hot before the bread is put into them; when they are brown, take them up with the skimmer, lay them for a minute on brown paper to free them from grease, and then put them into the soup tureen. (8.) When the soup is done, add boiling water enough to make two quarts, see that it is properly seasoned, pour it into the soup tureen, and serve it.

BEEF AND VEGETABLE SOUP.

INGREDIENTS.

1 carrot - - - - - - - -	1 cent.
1 turnip - - - - - - - -	1 "
1 onion and seasonings - - - - -	1 "
1 oz. celery stalks - - - - - -	1 "
1 lb. soup meat - - - - - -	6 cents.

½ lb. rice   -   -   -   -   -   -   -   4 cents.
1 qt. tomatoes -   -   -   -   -   -   -   5 "

          Total   -   -   -   -   19 cents.

(1.) Break any bones on hand, either raw or cooked, and put them into the bottom of the soup kettle; cut the meat in half-inch dice, put it on the bones, add four quarts of cold water, set the kettle over the fire, and let it come slowly to a boil. (2.) Skim it carefully and constantly until clear. (3.) Meantime wash the rice by putting it into a colander, and running plenty of cold water through it; (4.) pare the vegetables, and cut them in quarter inch dice; cut the celery in small bits. (5.) When the soup is skimmed clear, add these ingredients to it, season it with a level tablespoonful of salt, quarter of a saltspoonful of pepper, and a *bouquet* made as directed in Chapter I. (6.) Let it simmer steadily for two hours; add enough boiling water to make four quarts, see that the seasoning is proper, and serve it in the soup tureen, being careful to remove all the bones as the soup is taken up.

NOTE.—(1.) In preparing meat for soup do not wash it, because that process will carry off more or less of its nutriment; if it is soiled in any way, wipe it with a clean, damp cloth, or cut away the injured portion. (2.) Pare the vegetables very thin, cut them in even-sized pieces, and let them lay in cold water if they are prepared before wanted for use. (3.) Season lightly; it is very easy to add more seasoning, but impossible to remove it; (4.) it may, however, be overpowered by stronger flavors; for instance, a little Worcestershire sauce, or a tablespoonful of vinegar and a lump of sugar, will generally modify the flavor of a dish too highly salted.

CHAPTER III.

SECOND LESSON OF THE FIRST ARTISAN COURSE.

How to Choose Fish.—The nutritive and economic value of fish is given in the appendix; it is, therefore, sufficient to state here that all fish should be chosen by their firm flesh, rigid fins, clear, full eyes, and ruddy gills; if the flesh is soft and flabby, the fins limp, the eyes dull and sunken and the gills pale, the fish is stale and unfit for food.

Oysters, clams, scollops and mussels should be used as soon as they are taken from the shell, because their flavor is impaired by exposure to the air; when they are fresh and good their shells are tightly closed.

Lobsters, crabs and cray-fish should always be bought alive; they should be chosen for their heaviness in proportion to their size, the bright colors of their shells, and their lively movements; dull-looking, half-dead shell-fish are not fit to eat; shell-fish are cooked by putting them head first into a large pot full of boiling water, containing a handful of salt; this contact with the boiling water kills them instantly; they are done in from ten to twenty minutes, as soon as their shells turn a bright red color.

BOILED HADDOCK WITH PARSLEY SAUCE.

INGREDIENTS.

A 3 lb. haddock - - - - - - -	15 cents
1 oz. butter - - - - - - - - -	2 "
½ " parsley - - - - - - - -	1 cent
Flour and seasonings - - - - - -	1 "
Total - - - -	19 cents

(1.) As soon as the fish comes from market wash it thoroughly, and lay it in a large pan containing plenty of cold water and a handful of salt. (2.) When it is time to cook it, put it into the fish kettle with cold water enough to cover it, a gill of vinegar, a tablespoonful of salt, the root of the parsley, six cloves, and one sprig each of thyme and marjoram. (3.) Set the kettle over the fire and bring it to a boil. (4.) By the time the kettle boils the fish is usually done, but it may be tested by pulling out a fin; if the fin comes out easily, and the flesh of the fish looks clear white, it is done. (5.) Lift the kettle off the fire, and let the fish stand in the water until wanted for use. (6.) Make the sauce by stirring together over the fire one ounce, or one tablespoonful each of butter and flour until they bubble. (7.) Then slowly stir in half a pint of boiling water, or a little more if the flour thickens the sauce too much, and stir it constantly until it boils up all over, and clings to the spoon a little when it is lifted from the sauce. (8.) Move the sauce to the side of the fire, chop the parsley fine, and add it to the sauce with a salt-spoonful of salt, and quarter of a saltspoonful each of pepper and grated nutmeg; the sauce will then be ready to use. (9.) To serve the fish, take it up carefully without breaking, remove the skin by scraping it gently, so as to avoid tearing the fish, pour the sauce over it, and it will be ready for the table.

FRIED *FILETS* OF FLOUNDER.

INGREDIENTS.

1 egg	1 cent.
A 2 lb. flounder	12 cents.
Bread, fat for frying and seasonings	7 "
Total	20 cents.

Cut the *filets* as follows. (1.) Wash the flounder, wipe it on a clean cloth, and lay it flat on the table; with a sharp, thin-bladed knife, cut down to the bone in the center of the fish, following the course of the back bone from the head to the tail. (2.) Turn the edge of the knife towards the outer fin, insert the point in the cut already made, lay the blade flat against the bone, and cut outwards towards the fin, keeping the knife pressed close against the bone, being careful not to mangle the fish, and taking off the whole side-piece, or *filet*, entire. (3.) Cut off all the four side pieces of the fish in the same way, and lay them, skin down flat upon the table, with the ends towards the demonstrator; (4.) place the tips of the fingers of the left hand firmly upon the end of one of the *filets*, lay the point of the knife on the *filet* with the back against the fingers, press the blade down flat, cutting between the skin and the *filet*, and away from the end held down by the fingers; if the end is held firmly, the knife laid flat, and the cut made with a steady hand, the whole *filet* can be cut from the skin without mangling it; skin all the *filets* in this way, lay them on a dish, and wash and dry the table. (5.) Bread each *filet* as follows: spread upon the table some bread crumbs, which have been dried in the oven, rolled fine, and sifted; beat up one egg with a tablespoonful of cold water; lay the *filet* upon the crumbs, press it gently, turn it over, press it again, dip it into the beaten egg and quickly remove it, so that the crumbs will not be washed off; lay it again in the crumbs, pressing it into a neat shape with a knife; bread all the *filets* in this way, and lay them on a clean dish. (6.) Heat enough fat to cover three or four *filets*, until it begins to smoke; drop the *filets* into it, one at a time, fry them light brown, take them up with a skimmer, and lay them for one minute on brown paper, to free them from grease. (7.) Arrange them neatly on a dish with a few parsley leaves around them, and serve them.

BROILED *FILETS* WITH *MAÎTRE D' HOTEL* BUTTER.

INGREDIENTS.

A 2 lb. flounder	12 cents.
1 oz. butter	2 "
1 egg	1 cent.

Lemon juice - - - - - - - -	1 cent.
Seasonings, parsley and bread crumbs - -	1 "
Total - - - - -	17 cents.

(1.) Prepare the *filets* as directed in the previous receipt, but do not fry them: (2.) Make the *maître d' hotel* butter by chopping fine a tablespoonful of parsley, and mixing it thoroughly with the butter, a teaspoonful of lemon juice, and a very little salt and pepper. (3.) Broil the *filets* on an oiled gridiron, over a moderate fire; lay them on a hot dish, spread the butter over them, and serve them at once. The dish may be garnished with a few slices of lemon.

GRILLED FISH BONES.

INGREDIENTS.

1 tablespoonful salad oil - - - - -	1 cent.
1 " vinegar - - - - -	1 "
1 " mustard, pepper and salt -	1 "
Total - - - - -	3 cents.

(1.) Trim the ragged edges from the bones of the flounders used in making the *filets*. (2.) Mix the oil, vinegar and mustard together, seasoning them well with pepper and salt; and spread this paste over the bones with a knife. (3.) Broil the bones on an oiled gridiron, and serve them on a hot dish, with a few sprigs of parsley, or slices of lemon laid around them.

CHAPTER IV.

THIRD LESSON OF THE FIRST ARTISAN COURSE.

How to Choose Eggs.—Eggs are so nutritious, and at some seasons of the year so abundant and cheap, that directions for choosing and keeping them, and a variety of methods for cooking them are always welcome. New laid eggs have a pearly, semi-transparent shell, a little rough to the touch, and are heavy in proportion to their size; as they grow stale they decrease in weight, because some of their moisture evaporates from exposure to the air; the shells wear smooth by rubbing against each other, and their color clouds a little.

How to Keep Eggs.—(1.) Pack them in salt or sawdust while they are quite fresh, and close the vessel in which they are packed to keep out the air and prevent evaporation. (2.) Or dip them in melted suet or a thick solution of gum arabic, taking care that the shells are entirely covered with it; dry them, and then dip them in it the second time; then pack them as above, and keep them in a dry place.

BOILED EGGS.

6 eggs - - - - - - - - - 6 cents.

(1.) Place a saucepan half full of water over the fire; as soon as it boils, put the eggs into it, using a large spoon to drop them gently into the water; if they are wanted soft, take them up in three minutes, by the clock; if wanted medium hard, let them cook four minutes; if wanted hard, let them cook ten minutes. (2.) Place the eggs in a bowl, pour some warm water over them, and let them stand one minute; then drain them, cover them with boiling water, and let them stand ten minutes; they will then be cooked medium rare, evenly all the way through, and can be easily digested. Ducks' eggs cook in less time than hens' eggs.

POACHED EGGS.

INGREDIENTS.

6 eggs - - - - - - - - -	6 cents.
Bread and butter - - - - - - -	2 "
Salt and vinegar - - - - - -	1 "
Total - - - - -	9 cents.

(1.) Break the eggs, each one in a saucer by itself, so that a chance stale one may not spoil the rest. (2.) Put a shallow pan over the fire, half fill it with water, add to it a teaspoonful of salt and two tablespoonfuls of vinegar, and let it get scalding hot. (3.) Drop the eggs into the water, and let them stand five minutes without boiling. (4.) Meantime make six small slices of buttered toast and lay them on a dish. (5.) Take up the eggs one by one on a skimmer, trim each one evenly and slip it off upon a slice of toast; put a few grains of salt and pepper in the center of each egg and serve them hot.

FRIED EGGS.

INGREDIENTS.

6 eggs - - - - - - - -	6 cents.
Fat and seasonings - - - - - - -	4 "
Total - - - - -	10 cents.

(1.) Put some fat in a frying-pan over the fire to get smoking hot. (2.) Break the eggs, each one in a separate saucer; as soon as the fat begins to smoke, slip the eggs into it without breaking, and fry them brown; take them up with a skimmer, lay them for one minute on some brown paper to free them from grease, and then arrange them neatly on a dish for serving.

OMELETTE.

INGREDIENTS.

3 eggs - - - - - - - -	3 cents.
Butter, pepper and salt - - - - -	1 "
Total - - - - - -	4 cents.

(1.) Break the eggs, putting the whites in one dish and the yolks in another. (2.) Add quarter of a saltspoonful of salt and a dash of pepper to the yolks, and beat them half a minute. (3.) Put a bit of butter as large as a chestnut into a clean omelette pan, and set it over the fire to heat. (4.) Beat the whites to a stiff froth, mix the yolks gently into it, and put the omelette into the pan. (5.) Stir the omelette with a fork, running it close to the bottom of the pan, and piling the omelette in a heap in the center. (6.) When it is done enough, pile it on one side of the pan, hold a hot dish close to it, and toss the omelette out on it. Serve it immediately.

An omelette of three eggs is large enough for two persons; if more are to be served, a second omelette of three eggs may be made; a larger one can not be made so light, or cooked so well.

PARSLEY OMELETTE.

INGREDIENTS.

3 eggs - . - - - - - - - -	3 cents.
Parsley, butter, pepper and salt - - - -	2 "
Total - - - - - -	5 cents.

Prepare the omelette as directed in the last receipt, mixing with it one tablespoonful of chopped parsley; cook, and serve it in the same way.

SWEET OMELETTE.

INGREDIENTS.

3 eggs - - - - - - - - -	3 cents.
Butter and sugar - - - - - - - -	1 cent.
Total - - - - - -	4 cents.

(1.) Prepare the eggs as directed for plain omelette, substituting one teaspoonful of powdered sugar for the salt and pepper, and cooking in the same way. (2.) While the omelette is being cooked, rub the poker clean and heat it red hot. (3.) After the omelette has been turned out on the dish dust it thickly with powdered sugar, and score the top in diamonds with the red hot poker, taking care only to brown, and not to burn the sugar black. Serve it hot.

CHAPTER V.

FOURTH LESSON OF THE FIRST ARTISAN COURSE.

Baker's and Homemade Bread.—Good homemade bread is healthier and cheaper than baker's bread, and the task of making it is not beyond the skill of a bright, strong girl; the greatest difficulty is in learning how to bake it properly. If the pupils are too young to understand this, the lesson may begin with the making of biscuit; and the practice in bread may be deferred until later in the course of instruction.

YEAST.

INGREDIENTS.

2 oz. hops	5 cents.
½ lb. brown sugar	5 "
1 " flour	4 "
3 " potatoes	5 "
Salt	1 cent.
Total	20 cents.

(1.) Boil the hops in four quarts of water for half an hour, strain the liquor, and let it stand until it is only lukewarm. (2.) Dissolve in it the sugar and two table-spoonfuls of salt. (3.) Add this mixture by degrees to the flour, beating it quite smooth. (4.) Put it in an earthen jar or bowl, and let it stand in a warm place four days to ferment. (5.) On the third day, boil, peel and mash the potatoes, stir them into the yeast, and let it stand another day. (6.) The next day strain and bottle it, and keep it in a cool place.

HOMEMADE BREAD, (About 8 lbs.)

INGREDIENTS.

7 lbs. flour	28 cents.
Salt, sugar, yeast	1 cent.
	29 cents.

(1.) Put seven pounds of flour into a deep pan, and make a hollow in the center; into this put one quart of lukewarm water, one tablespoonful of salt, one teaspoonful of sugar, and half a gill of yeast; have ready three pints more of warm water, and use as much of it as is necessary to make a rather soft dough, mixing and kneading it well with both hands. (2.) When it is smooth and shining, strew a little flour upon it, lay a large towel over it folded, and set it in a warm place by the fire for four or five hours to rise.

The remainder of the process must be deferred until the next lesson.

BISCUIT.

INGREDIENTS.

1 lb. flour - - - - - - -	4 cents.
¼ " lard - - - - - - - -	3 "
1 pint milk, (or cold water) - - - -	4 "
Baking powder and salt - - - - -	1 cent.
Total - - - - -	12 cents.

(1.) Sift the flour with one tablespoonful of baking powder, and one teaspoonful of salt. (2.) Rub the lard quickly into the flour in small flakes. (3.) Dust a little flour over the baking pan and pastry-board. (4.) Pour the milk into the flour and lard, mix them rapidly together, turn the dough out on the pastry board, roll it out an inch thick, cut out the biscuit as fast as possible, put them on the baking pan, and set the pan in a quick oven. (5.) All this must be done very quickly, in order to get the biscuit into the oven before the carbonic acid gas, which results from the mixture of the baking powder and milk, has time to escape; the dough is made light by this gas forcing its way up through it, and if the biscuit are not baked until it has escaped they will be heavy. (6.) When the biscuit are half done—in about ten minutes—open the oven door, brush the tops with a little milk, and then finish baking them. (7.) Water may be substituted for milk in making biscuit.

MILK ROLLS.

INGREDIENTS.

1 lb. flour - - - - - - - -	4 cents.
¼ " lard - - - - - - - -	3 "
1 pt. milk - - - - - - - -	4 "
Baking powder and salt - - - -	1 cent.
Total - - - - -	12 cents.

(1.) Proceed as directed for biscuit until the dough is cut out. (2.) Brush the top of each round of dough with melted lard. (3.) Take hold of each round by the sides, stretch it out, then fold one half the way over, and press it gently in place; finish and bake according to the directions for biscuit.

BREAKFAST TWIST.

INGREDIENTS.

1 lb. flour - - - - - - - - -	4 cents.
¼ lb. lard - - - - - - - - -	3 "
1 pt. milk - - - - - - - - -	4 "
Baking-powder and salt - - - - -	1 cent.
Total - - - - - -	12 cents.

(1.) Proceed as directed for biscuit until the dough is rolled out half an inch thick. (2.) Cut it in strips half an inch wide and three inches long. (3.) Roll them gently under the palm of the hand to smooth them. (4.) Lay the ends of three strips one over the other, pinch them together and braid them, closing the end of the braid with a pinch. (4.) Finish and bake them according to the directions for biscuit.

CHAPTER VI.

FIFTH LESSON OF THE FIRST ARTISAN COURSE.

How to Choose Macaroni.—Good macaroni is of a yellowish color; it does not break in cooking, and if properly cooked, yields nearly four times its bulk. The imported Italian macaroni can be bought in the Italian stores in New York for fifteen cents a pound. It should never be soaked or wet before boiling, or put to cook in cold or lukewarm water. If it appears soiled or dusty, it should be wiped with a clean dry cloth.

How to Boil Macaroni.—Put it into boiling water, to every quart of which a teaspoonful of salt has been added;

sometimes an onion is boiled with it, being peeled and put whole into the boiling water. Macaroni will boil tender in about twenty minutes; test it by pressing it between the fingers; if it is done it will yield easily, but should not be boiled too soft; as soon as it is done, drain it in a colander and rinse and lay it in cold water; it will keep good for several days if the water has a little salt added to it, and is changed every day.

MACARONI, FARMER'S STYLE.

INGREDIENTS.

½ lb. macaroni - - - - - - -	8 cents.
1 oz. butter - - - - - - - -	2 "
Onion, flour, and seasonings - - - -	2 "
Total - - - - - -	12 cents.

(1.) Boil half a pound of macaroni as directed in the previous receipt. (2.) Meantime, stir together over the fire one ounce each of butter and flour until they begin to bubble; gradually add to them half a pint of boiling water, stirring the sauce with an egg-whip until it is smooth, and then season it with one teaspoonful of salt, and quarter of a saltspoonful each of white pepper and grated nutmeg. (3.) Drain the macaroni, and put it into this sauce to heat. (4.) Peel and slice the onion, and fry it in a very little drippings. (5.) Put the macaroni on a hot dish, pour the onion on it, and serve it.

MACARONI WITH *BÉCHAMEL* SAUCE.

INGREDIENTS.

½ lb. macaroni - - - - - -	8 cents.
1 oz. butter - - - - - - - -	2 "
½ pt. milk - - - - - - - -	2 "
Flour and seasonings - - - - -	1 cent.
Total - - - - -	13 cents.

(1.) Boil half a pound of macaroni as already directed. (2.) Make a sauce of one ounce each of butter and flour as directed in the previous receipt, substituting half a pint of boiling milk for the boiling water. (3.) Drain the macaroni, heat it in the sauce, and serve in a hot dish.

BAKED MACARONI.

INGREDIENTS.

½ lb. macaroni - - - - - - -	8 cents.
¼ " cheese - - - - - - - -	4 "
1 oz. butter - - - - - - - -	2 "
Bread crumbs and seasonings - - -	1 cent.
Total - - - - -	15 cents.

(1.) Boil the macaroni as already directed. (2.) Grate the cheese. (3.) Put the macaroni on a *gratin* pan, or any kind of baking dish suitable to send to the table, adding the sauce and cheese to it; dust over the top a few bread crumbs, which have been dried in the oven and sifted, put a few bits of butter on the top, and brown it quickly in a very hot oven. If the macaroni can be browned with a salamander, the sauce will not be dried away so much as when it is browned in the oven. A salamander is à round plate of iron attached to a long handle, the plate being heated red hot before using it.

How to Mould, Prove, and Bake Bread.—(1.) After the bread sponge has risen over night, or sufficiently long in the day time, turn it out on a floured bread-board, and knead it for fifteen minutes, using enough flour to keep it from sticking to the board or hands. (2.) Put it again into the bread pan, and let it rise plump and full. (3.) Then divide it into four loaves, knead it two or three minutes, put it into the baking pan, and bake it in a quick oven. In cold weather, the dough should be mixed in a warm room, and not allowed to cool while rising; if it does not rise well, set the pan containing it over a large vessel of boiling water; it is best to mix the bread at night, and let it rise till morning in a warm and even temperature. The above receipt will make about eight pounds of bread, and divided into four loaves, will bake in a little over an hour's time. (4.) To test the bread while baking, run a larding or knitting needle into the loaf; if it comes out bright the bread is done; if it is tarnished, the bread is not sufficiently baked.

CHAPTER VII.

SIXTH LESSON OF THE FIRST ARTISAN COURSE.

Leguminous Vegetables.—The valuable qualities of these vegetables entitle them to careful culinary treatment, while their cheapness recommends them to every economical person. The best known are peas and beans; but these two, excellent as they are, rank lower as nutriments than the less familiar lentils. A more extended reference to their value will be found in the appendix.

PEAS AND BACON.
INGREDIENTS.

1 lb. bacon - - - - - - -	12 cents.
1 pt. dried peas - - - - - -	5 "
Total - - - - -	17 cents.

(1.) Scrape and wash the bacon, and put it into three quarts of cold water, over the fire. (2.) Pick over the peas, and put them into the pot with the bacon. (3.) Let them boil gently for about two hours, throwing in, every fifteen minutes, a wineglassful of cold water, to check the boiling and soften the peas. (4.) As soon as they are soft, which will be in about two hours, drain them, lay them in a baking-dish, season them with salt and pepper, put the bacon on them, and brown them in a rather quick oven.

WHITE HARICOT BEANS, *BORDELAISE* STYLE.
INGREDIENTS.

1 pt. White Haricot beans - - - -	6 cents.
1 oz. butter - - - - - - -	2 "
1 " drippings - - - - - -	1 cent.
Parsley, onion, and seasonings - - -	1 cent.
Total - - - - -	10 cents.

(1.) Pick over the beans, put them in a colander, run plenty of cold water over them from the faucet, put them into a saucepan with two quarts of cold water and the drippings, and set them over the fire to cook. (2.) Let them boil gently for about two hours, throwing in every fifteen minutes a wineglassful of cold water, for the reason given in the previous receipt. (3.) At the end of one hour add a level tablespoonful of salt, and quarter of a teaspoonful of pepper. (4.) When they are soft, but not broken, drain them, and put them into a frying pan with the butter, and a tablespoonful of chopped parsley and onion. (5.) Let them get thoroughly hot, shaking them about to prevent burning, and serve them hot.

BOILED LENTILS.

INGREDIENTS.

1 pt. lentils - - - - - - -	10 cents.
1 onion - - - - - - - - -	1 cent.
½ oz. butter - - - - - - -	1 "
1 oz. drippings - - - - - - -	1 "
Parsley and seasonings - - - - -	1 "
Total - - . - -	14 cents.

(1.) Pick over the lentils and wash them as directed in the previous receipt. (2.) Put them over the fire in a saucepan with two quarts of cold water, one onion peeled, but not cut, and the drippings. (3.) Let them boil gently until soft, about three hours, adding a wineglassful of cold water every fifteen minutes. (4.) At the end of one hour season them with a level tablespoonful of salt, and a quarter of a teaspoonful of pepper. (5.) When the lentils are soft drain off the water, take out the onion, if desired, add the butter, a teaspoonful of sugar, and a tablespoonful of chopped parsley; see if the seasoning is palatable and then

FRIED LENTILS.
INGREDIENTS.

1 pt. lentils - - - - - - -	10 cents.
2 oz. drippings - - - - - - -	2 "
Onion, parsley, and seasonings - - -	1 cent.
Total - - - - - -	13 cents.

(1.) Boil the lentils as directed above. (2.) Chop one ounce of onion fine. (3.) Fry it light yellow in two ounces of dripping. (4.) Put the lentils into the onion and drippings, with one tablespoonful of chopped parsley and see if the seasoning is palatable. (5.) Shake them until they brown a little, and then serve them hot.

RED KIDNEY BEANS, STEWED.
INGREDIENTS.

1 pt. red beans - - - - - - -	6 cents.
1 oz. butter - - - - - - -	2 "
Seasonings - - - - - - - -	1 cent.
Total - - - - - -	9 cents.

(1.) Pick over the beans, wash them in cold water, as directed in the receipt for White Haricots, and boil them in a similar manner. (2.) When they are nearly done, drain off the water, add the butter, season them with a level tablespoonful of salt and a quarter of a level teaspoonful of pepper, let them finish cooking, and serve them hot.

CHAPTER VIII.

SEVENTH LESSON OF THE FIRST ARTISAN COURSE.

How to Choose Potatoes.—Smooth, even, medium-sized potatoes are the most economical; those which are heavy in proportion to size will be the mealiest when cooked. They should be perfectly ripe before gathering, otherwise they will dry and shrivel, because their skins are so porous as to permit the evaporation of their moisture. The earliest varieties of potatoes to be found in the New York market are the Alpha and Early Rose; the former is an excellent vegetable, of medium size, with a clear skin tinged with red, and when cooked is white, fine-grained, and mealy; the Early Rose is a kidney-shaped potato, with a reddish skin, and white, mealy flesh. The white Peach-blow is one of the best winter sorts, but frequently the Chili White is sold instead of it; when cooked it is poor and soggy, while the Peach-blow is dry and mealy. The yellow Peach-blow is inferior to either the white or red variety. The Prince Albert potato is a winter variety of inferior quality. The red Peach-blow is one of the best late varieties. The Snow-flake is an excellent winter potato; it is rather large, of uniform size, of firm, white flesh, and agreeable flavor; it will keep till the late spring in a cool, dry cellar.

How to Keep Potatoes.—Potatoes keep best in bins or heaps in a dry cellar of even temperature; they should be selected for the winter's use with reference to the points cited in the previous paragraph, and examined occasionally to see that they are in good condition. In the spring, when they begin to sprout, they should be spread a little, and the sprouts removed as soon as they show, if it is necessary to use them for cooking. They are not really fit for food after germination begins, because the sprouts draw their substance from the starch cells which make the healthy tuber mealy.

Potatoes lose some of their weight in cooking; peeling and boiling being the most extravagant way of cooking; baking in the skins the next most wasteful method, and boiling them in their jackets the most economical.

BOILED POTATOES.

INGREDIENTS.

1 qt. potatoes	3 cents.
Salt	1 cent.
Total	4 cents.

A boiled potato is mealy in proportion to the amount of

starch it contains, for, in proper cooking, the starch absorbs the moisture of the potato; the amount of starch depends, first upon the ripeness of the potato, and second, upon its preservation. (1.) New potatoes contain an excess of water and but little starch, and are consequently watery; they should be prepared for boiling by washing them well with plenty of water, and laying them in cold water well salted for an hour before cooking. Then put them over the fire in plenty of well-salted boiling water, boil them until just tender enough to pierce easily with a fork, drain them, shake them in the sauce-pan for one minute with a teaspoonful of salt, and serve them in their jackets. (2.) Pare some potatoes very thinly, put them into boiling water well salted, and boil and finish them as directed above. (3.) Potatoes which have been stored should be prepared for boiling by carefully washing them, removing the defective parts and paring off one ring around each; they should then be cooked quickly in plenty of boiling water, well salted, until tender enough to pierce with a fork; the water should then be drained off, the potatoes covered with a clean towel, and the sauce-pan shaken and set on a brick at the back of the stove. Treated in this way potatoes can be kept hot and mealy for hours.

LYONNAISE POTATOES.

INGREDIENTS.

Cold boiled potatoes - - - - - -	3 cents.
1 oz. butter - - - - - - - -	2 "
Parsley, onion and seasonings - - - -	1 cent.
Total - - - - -	6 cents.

(1.) Pare and slice the potatoes. (2.) Chop one tablespoonful of parsley. (3.) Slice half an onion, put it into the frying pan with the butter, and shake it about over the fire until it is of a pale yellow color. (4.) Put in the potatoes, shake the pan to prevent burning, and toss the potatoes about to brown them slightly and equally, for five minutes. (5.) Sprinkle them with the chopped parsley. (6.) Season them with pepper and salt, and **serve them hot.**

GERMAN POTATOES.

INGREDIENTS.

1 qt. potatoes	3 cents.
¼ lb. sausages	3 "
Seasonings	1 cent.
Total	7 cents.

(1.) Wash the potatoes thoroughly, put them in the oven, and cook them half an hour. (2.) Take them up, cut a slice from the top of each one, scoop out the center of the potato with the bowl of a teaspoon; chop this part of the potato very fine, mix it with the sausage meat and season it rather highly. (3.) Fill the potatoes with this forcemeat, fit on each the slice cut from it and return them to the oven to finish baking. When quite tender, take them up on a clean napkin, arranged neatly on a dish, and serve them hot. With a good, brisk oven, they will cook in about forty minutes; if a longer time is required on account of a poor oven, the potatoes will not be so good. Never cover baked potatoes, or they will absorb their own steam and become soggy.

POTATO SALAD.

INGREDIENTS.

Cold potatoes	3 cents.
Oil, vinegar and seasonings	6 "
1 onion	1 cent.
Total	10 cents.

(1.) Pare and slice some cold boiled potatoes. (2.) Peel and slice thin one onion. (3.) Mix them together on a salad dish, pour over them the following dressing. (4.) Stir together in a cup, one saltspoonful of salt, quarter of a saltspoonful of pepper, one tablespoonful of vinegar, and

iree of oil. (5.) Dress the salad with this dress
ecorate it with a few leaves of parsley, and serve.

CHAPTER IX.

EIGHTH LESSON OF THE FIRST ARTISAN COURS

How to Choose Vegetables.—All green vegetable
e very crisp, fresh, and juicy; they are best jus
owering, and are in prime condition for use if gathe
i the morning, and not afterwards exposed to the
ie sun; green vegetables which have laid in the
alls for any time should not be bought if fresh o
e obtained; but if their use is unavoidable they ca
ored by sprinkling them with cold water, and layi
i a cool, dark place.

Roots and tubers, such as carrots, turnips, and p
re good from the time of ripening until they l
rout; after that their elements are disarranged
red by the process of germination, and they do
ly the same kind or amount of nutriment. The
e plump and even sized, with fresh, unshrivelle
id should form the principal part of the day's pr
cause they are both cheap and wholesome.

How to Keep Vegetables.—In summer we hav
iat the best way to keep salads of all kinds fr
isp is to cleanse them thoroughly, and then lay
ie ice in the refrigerator; they will keep for a da
i this way. Other green vegetables should be k
ol, dark place; but they should never be laid in
rge quantities, because many of their wholesom
ies are lost with the evaporation of their moistur
Roots of all kinds should be kept in dark, *dr*
here the temperature does not vary, and where
ght, warmth, nor moisture are present to inv

without danger of loss, if care and discrimination are taken in its selection. In the previous lesson special directions are given for the selection and care of potatoes.

How to Boil Green Vegetables.—(1.) Put a large pot two-thirds full of water over the fire with a heaping table-spoonful of salt to every gallon of water, and let it come to a boil. (2.) Thoroughly cleanse the vegetables, trim off any decayed parts, and lay them in plenty of cold water. (3.) When the pot is boiling, drain the vegetables from the cold water, throw them into the boiling water, press them down under it with a wooden spoon, let them come quickly to a boil, and boil them rapidly *without covering the pot*, only until they are tender. (4.) Drain them in a colander, run plenty of cold water through them, and lay them in cold water and salt until wanted for use.

HOT SLAW.

INGREDIENTS.

1 cabbage	5 cents.
1 oz. butter	2 "
Sugar, seasonings, vinegar and spice	5 "
Total	12 cents.

(1.) Cleanse the cabbage thoroughly, and cut it in slivers. (2.) Put the butter into the bottom of the sauce-pan with two tablespoonfuls of sugar, one gill of vinegar, a level teaspoonful of mixed spice, a teaspoonful of salt, and half a saltspoonful of pepper. (3.) Put the cabbage on these ingredients, set the saucepan over a moderate fire, and simmer slowly for about two hours, until the cabbage is tender, stirring occasionally to prevent burning.

BAKED TURNIPS.

INGREDIENTS.

1 qt. turnips	3 cents.
1 oz. butter	2 "
Flour, bread-crumbs and seasonings	1 cent.
Total	6 cents.

(1.) Pare and slice the turnips, and boil them as directed for green vegetables, until tender; then drain them and finish as follows. (2.) Meantime make a white sauce by stirring together over the fire one ounce each of butter and flour, until they bubble, then gradually stirring in half a pint of boiling water, and seasoning with one level saltspoonful of salt, and quarter of a saltspoonful each of pepper and grated nutmeg. (3.) When the turnips are tender, lay them on a baking dish suitable to send to the table, pour the sauce over them, dust them over thickly with bread crumbs, and brown them in a quick oven. Put the baking dish on a clean dish and serve them.

PARSNIP FRITTERS.

INGREDIENTS.

2 parsnips - - - - - - - -	2 cents.
Oil, flour and seasonings - - - - -	3 "
2 eggs - - - - - - - -	2 "
4 oz. lard for frying - - - - - -	3 "
Total - - - - - -	10 cents.

(1.) Pare the parsnips, cut them in strips about two inches long and quarter of an inch thick, and boil them as directed for green vegetables until tender; then drain them, dry them on a clean cloth, and dip them in the following batter.

Plain Frying Batter.—Mix quarter of a pound of flour with the yolks of two raw eggs, a level saltspoonful of salt, half a saltspoonful of pepper, quarter of a saltspoonful of grated nutmeg, one tablespoonful of salad oil, (which is used to make the batter crisp,) and one cup of water, more or less, as the flour will take it up; the batter should be stiff enough to hold the drops from the spoon in shape when they are let fall upon it; now beat the whites of the two eggs to a stiff froth, beginning slowly, and increasing the speed until you are beating as fast as you can; the froth will surely come; then stir it lightly into the batter. Dip the parsnips into it, lift them out with a fork, and drop them into plenty of smoking hot fat; fry them golden brown in smoking hot fat. Serve them on a neatly folded napkin with a few sprigs of parsley around them. The fat that is used in frying will not cost over four cents, for you must strain the fat and save it after you fry your fritters, to use for other purposes.

CHAPTER X.

NINTH LESSON OF THE FIRST ARTISAN COURSE.

Cheapest Cuts of Meat.—Joints of meat for roasting and baking, and chops and steaks for broiling, are always high-priced, and seldom economical, although they are preferred by many persons on account of their intense flavor. Where the cost of a meal materially affects the enjoyment with which it is eaten, the choice of the dishes composing it becomes an important question. Meat is desired by the majority of people at least once a day, and there are several of the cheaper cuts which can be made into very palatable dishes, such as Potato-pot, and the *À la mode* beef given in this chapter.

Combination Dishes.—Since vegetables are cheap and plentiful at all seasons, and meat always comparatively dear, it is necessary for the economical housewife to know how to combine these two articles of food with reference to the appetite of her family as well as to their physical needs. Every one of our little pupils will grow up to be a house-wife some day, and meantime they can do a great deal to make father and mother comfortable at home. They ought to know that a little meat, especially if it is salted or smoked, will make a large dish of vegetables taste nicely; and that enough nourishment can be found in such com-

have chosen Pork and Beans, and Bacon and Cabbage as examples of this kind of dishes.

POTATO POT.

INGREDIENTS.

1 qt. potatoes - - - - - - -	3 cents.
2 lbs. neck of beef - - - - - -	12 "
¼ lb. bacon - - - - - - - -	3 "
Onions, flour, and seasonings - - - -	2 "
Total - - . - -	20 cents.

(1.) Slice the bacon, cut the beef in small pieces, and put them over the fire in a frying pan to brown. (2.) Peel and slice two onions and brown them with the meat. (3.) Peel and quarter the potatoes and lay them in cold water. (4.) When the meat and onions are brown put them into a deep baking dish, in layers with the potatoes. (5.) Make a pint of gravy by adding boiling water and seasonings to the drippings in the frying-pan, and thickening it with an ounce of flour dissolved in a little cold water; pour the gravy over the meat and potatoes, and put them into a quick oven to bake. The dish will cook in about an hour, and should be served hot; if it is sent to the table in the same dish it is baked in, a clean dish must be placed under it.

BEEF À *LA MODE*, VICTORIA STYLE.

INGREDIENTS.

2 lbs. rump steak - - - - - -	20 cents.
½ lb salt pork - - - - - - -	6 "
Carrots and turnips - - - - - -	3 "
Flour and seasonings - - - - - -	1 cent.
Total - - - - -	30 cents.

(1.) Cut the steak in pieces, one inch thick, two inches wide, and four inches long; lay the pieces flat on the table and season them with pepper, salt and powdered thyme. (2.) Slice the pork thin and lay a slice on each piece of meat. (3.) Roll up each piece compactly, and tie it with a cord. (4.) Put the trimmings of meat and scraps of pork in the bottom of a saucepan, lay the rolls on them, and put them over the fire to brown. (5.) When the meat is brown, stir in a tablespoonful of flour and let it brown. (6.) Then add enough hot water to cover the meat, and let it simmer until tender, about one hour. (7.) Meantime, pare the vegetables, cut them in small, even dice, or olives; wash them, boil them until tender in boiling water and salt; drain them and lay them in cold water to retain their color. (8.) When the meat is done, lay it on a hot dish in an even pile, and keep it hot while the vegetables can be drained out of the cold water and warmed in the gravy. (9.) Then arrange them neatly around the meat, pour the gravy over the meat without slopping it around the dish, and serve it hot.

PORK AND BEANS.

INGREDIENTS.

1 pt. white beans - - - - - -	6 cents.
½ lb. salt pork - - - - - -	6 "
Molasses, salt and pepper - - - - -	2 "
Total - - - - -	14 cents.

(1.) Pick over the beans, put them on the fire in cold water enough to cover them, with the pork; boil them slowly for two hours, or until tender, but not broken, adding a wineglassful of cold water every fifteen minutes, to check the boiling and soften the beans. (2.) Drain them, put them into a deep bean-pot, season them with a teaspoonful of salt and quarter of a saltspoonful of pepper; pour over them two tablespoonfuls of molasses, and four of the water in which the beans were boiled; lay the pork on them, cover them tight and bake an hour in a moderate oven.

BACON AND CABBAGE.

INGREDIENTS.

1 head of cabbage - - - - -	5 cents.
1 lb. bacon and seasonings - - -	12 cents.
Total - - - -	17 cents.

(1.) Put the bacon over the fire in a pot half full of cold water, and bring it slowly to a boil. (2.) Meantime, thoroughly cleanse a head of cabbage, cut it in thin slices, and when the bacon has boiled an hour put the cabbage with it to boil, taking care that the water is boiling when the cabbage is put into it. (3.) When the bacon is done, and the cabbage is tender, take up the cabbage in a colander, press the water out of it, lay it on a dish, and put the bacon on it, and serve it hot.

CHAPTER XI.

TENTH LESSON OF THE FIRST ARTISAN COURSE.

The Entrails of Animals.—Those parts of the carcass called the entrails, such as the haslet, kidneys, and tripe, and the cheap cuts, such as the head, feet, and tail, are much more commonly used for food in Europe than in this country. The tongue, brains, and sweetbreads are well known here, but they are generally considered delicacies, and are not often served at ordinary meals in the city; in the country the brains and sweetbreads are often thrown away. Tripe and feet are very digestible, but not very nourishing; the heart and lights, or lungs, are full of flesh-forming elements, and on account of their density of fiber, should be thoroughly cooked; the kidneys should be cooked quickly, or they will become hard and indigestible. All these articles, except beef-tongues and veal-sweetbreads, are cheap and plentiful in the vicinity of *abattoirs* and packing houses. In New York, at many retail markets and butcher's stores, these articles are now being kept in answer to the increasing demand for them.

HASLET *RAGOÛT*
INGREDIENTS.

1 Sheep's haslet - - - - - - -	6 cents.
1 qt. potatoes - - - - - - - -	3 "

½ " onions - - - - - - -	2 cents.	
2 oz. drippings - - - - - -	2 "	
Seasonings, bacon and flour - - - -	2 "	

Total - - - - -	15 cents.

(1.) Peel and slice the onions, put them into a saucepan with the drippings, and one ounce of bacon cut in small dice, and fry them brown. (2.) Meantime scald the haslet and cut it in pieces two inches square, and let it lay in scalding hot water until wanted. (3.) When the onions are brown, mix one ounce of flour among them, drain the haslet, and add it to them with one gill of vinegar and boiling water enough to cover it. Season it with two teaspoonfuls of salt, quarter of a level teaspoonful of pepper, and a *bouquet* made by tying together two sprigs each of parsley and thyme, two bay leaves, and six whole cloves. Simmer it slowly two hours, sprinkle in a little chopped parsley and serve it hot.

STEWED TRIPE.

INGREDIENTS.

2 lbs. tripe - - - - - - -	15 cents.	
2 oz. drippings - - - - - - -	2 "	
2 onions and vinegar - - - - -	2 "	
Parsley and seasonings - - - - -	1 "	

Total - - - - -	20 cents.

Tripe is usually dressed before it is sold, but it is well to cleanse it by scalding and scraping before using it; it should be white, thick, and fat; some persons prefer the honeycomb, and others the double tripe. (1.) Peel and slice the onions and fry them light brown in the drippings. (2.) Cut the tripe in strips half an inch wide and two inches long, and add it to the onions. (3.) Chop one tablespoonful of parsley, add it to the tripe with a level tablespoonful of salt, a saltspoonful of pepper, a tablespoonful of vinegar, and just water enough to cover the tripe; stew it gently for one hour. Serve it hot.

STUFFED HEART.

INGREDIENTS.

1 beef's heart - - - - - - - -	10 cents.
1 oz. butter - - - - - - - -	2 "
1 qt. potatoes - - - - - - - -	3 "
Bread, onion and seasonings - - - - -	2 "
Total - - - - - - -	17 cents.

(1.) Soak two slices of stale bread in cold water until they are soft, and wring them dry in a clean towel. (2.) Peel and chop one onion and fry it light yellow with the butter. (3.) Add the soaked bread to it with a teaspoonful of salt, half a level saltspoonful of pepper, and a saltspoonful of powdered herbs, and stir this forcemeat over the fire in the frying-pan until it is scalding hot. Wash the heart in cold water, stuff it with the forcemeat, sew it up and lay it on a baking pan with the potatoes, pared and washed; put it in a quick oven and bake it one hour.

BROILED KIDNEYS.

INGREDIENTS.

1 lb. kidneys - - - - - - -	10 cents.
1 oz. butter - - - - - - - -	2 "
Onion, herbs and seasonings - - - -	2 "
Total - - - - - -	14 cents.

(1.) Chop fine one teaspoonful each of onions, parsley and any green herb in season. (2.) Mix them with one level teaspoonful of salt, half a level saltspoonful of pepper, as much cayenne as can be taken up on the point of a small pen knife blade, and the butter; put them on a dish and set it where it will get hot. (3.) Wash the kidneys in cold water and salt, split them, take out the white centres, broil them quickly, and put them on the hot dish, turning them over to cover them equally with the seasonings. Serve them hot, with a few sprigs of parsley or slices of lemon on the dish.

CHAPTER XII.

ELEVENTH LESSON OF THE FIRST ARTISAN COURSE.

How to Cook for Invalids.—Sickness is, unhappily, such an every day occurrence in all families that we should not do our duty by even our youngest pupils if we failed to show them how to prepare a few delicate dishes for invalids. There are five points which we wish to impress upon our pupils' minds in regard to diet in sickness.

(1.) Sick persons do not require such hearty food as healthy people. (2.) Food for sick persons must be of such good quality as to afford all the nourishment they need from a very small quantity. (3.) Food for sick persons must be cooked so as to enable weak digestive organs to assimilate, or make use of all its nourishing qualities without being over taxed, and, therefore, very digestible articles should be chosen. (4.) Sick persons should always be reminded that if they hold their food in their mouths for a few minutes before swallowing it, and allow the saliva to mingle with it, it will be more easily digested than if it is eaten hastily; it would be wise for well people also to remember this fact. (5.) The doctor should always prescribe the diet of a very sick person, and no additions or alterations should be made without his knowledge.

TOAST.

INGREDIENTS.

Stale bread - - - - - - - -	1 cent.
Butter (the best kind) - - - - - -	2 cents.
Total - - - -	3 cents.

The reason why we need stale bread to make good toast, is because we want it dry; after the moisture has evaporated from bread it is less tough and solid, and consequently more easily digested, and the heat of the fire more readily changes the bread into pure wheat farina, which is not as likely to sour in the stomach as fresh, moist bread.

(1.) Cut two even slices of stale bread about half an inch thick, taking care to have them smooth and of even size, because a sick person's appetite is very capricious, and the looks of a dish has a great influence upon it. (2.) Put the bread on a toasting-fork and expose it to the heat of a moderate fire, holding it so that it will turn golden brown all over, and being careful not to burn it; turn the slice and toast the other side in the same way. This makes dry toast, which should be eaten at once. (3.) Buttered toast is prepared in the same way; spread very thinly and evenly with a little nice butter, and set it in the oven for five minutes to make it crisp, and to mingle the butter thoroughly with it, so that it will digest equally, and then serve hot.

TOAST-WATER.

INGREDIENTS.

Stale bread - - - - - - - 1 cent.

(1.) Make a slice of toast as directed in the previous receipt, toasting it to a deep brown color, but taking care not to burn it. (2.) Drop it into a small pitcher containing a pint of boiling water, cover the pitcher and let the toast-water cool; then strain it through a piece of fine muslin or flannel, and use it. (3.) If toast-water is wanted for immediate use, put the toast, made as above, into only boiling water enough to cover it; let it stand two minutes, strain it, and add a little cold water to it. It will then be ready for use.

TEA.

INGREDIENTS.

½ oz. tea - - - - - - - -	2 cents.
1 gill milk - - - - - - -	1 cent.
1 oz. sugar - - - - - - -	1 "
Total - - - - - -	4 cents.

(1.) Rinse out the teapot with boiling water, put the

tea into it, pour half a pint of boiling water on it, and set
the pot where it will keep hot without boiling, for five minutes.   (2.) Pour one pint and a half of boiling water into
the pot at the end of five minutes, and use the tea at once.   If
tea is boiled, tannic acid is developed in it, and it tastes
strong and bitter, and is very unhealthy.

BEEF TEA.
INGREDIENTS.
1 lb. lean beef - - - - - - - 12 cents.

(1.) Chop one pound of lean beef fine, lay it in one pint
of cold water for one hour, then put it over the fire in the
same water, and bring it slowly to a boil; boil from fifteen
to thirty minutes, as time will permit, and then strain it;
season it with a very little salt and pepper, if the doctor allows it, and use it. If there is not time to let it stand an hour,
less time will answer, but not so well, because the longer
the meat lays in cold water, the more of its nutriment will
be extracted.   (2.) Chop one pound of lean beef fine, put
it in a covered earthen jar *without water*, and set it in a
moderate oven for four hours; then strain off the liquid,
season it slightly, if the doctor allows it, and serve it. This
preparation contains every nutritious element of the beef.

CHICKEN JELLY.
INGREDIENTS.
A 2 lb. fowl - - - - - - - 24 cents.

(1.) Skin a fowl, remove all the fat, draw it carefully,
so as to avoid breaking the gall or intestines, cut up the
meat, and break the bones by pounding.   (2.) Put it into
a saucepan with two quarts of cold water, bring it slowly
to a boil, skimming it until clear; cover the saucepan tightly,
and simmer it slowly until the chicken is reduced to a
pulp, that is from two to four hours.   (3.) Strain the
liquid through fine cloth or flannel until clear, and return it to the fire to simmer until it becomes a jelly.   This
point can be decided by putting a teaspoonful of the jelly

on a saucer and cooling it; if it is firm the jelly is done. Season it very slightly, as directed by the doctor, and cool it in cups. It may be eaten cold, or warmed a little.

PANADA.

INGREDIENTS.

Bread - - - - - - - - -	2 cents.
1 oz. sugar - - - - - - -	1 cent.
Seasonings - - - - - - - -	1 "
Total - - - - -	4 cents.

(1.) Put a pint of water over the fire to boil, with an ounce of loaf sugar, and an inch of stick cinnamon, or the yellow rind of half a lemon, if the doctor allows the use of either. (2.) Crumb two slices of stale bread, put it into the water when it boils, and let it boil as fast as possible until it begins to thicken; then take it up, and use it either hot or cold.

BARLEY WATER.

INGREDIENTS.

2 oz. pearl barley - - - - - -	2 cents.

Thoroughly wash two ounces of pearl barley, to remove any musty or bad flavor, put it over the fire in two quarts of cold water, and boil it until it is reduced to one quart; then strain and cool it; a little sugar may be used with it, if the doctor allows it.

APPLE WATER.

INGREDIENTS.

3 apples - - - - - - - -	3 cents.
1 oz. sugar and lemon rind - - - -	1 cent.
Total - - - - -	4 cents.

Pare, core, and slice thin three spicy, juicy apples, put them in a pitcher with the sugar, and the yellow rind of half a lemon; pour one pint of boiling water over them, cover the pitcher and let the water cool; then strain and use it as a beverage, when allowed by the doctor.

CHAPTER XIII.

TWELFTH LESSON OF THE FIRST ARTISAN COURSE.

Nutritive Value of Pies and Puddings.—All little girls are very fond of pies and puddings, and they sometimes persuade their mothers to make such dishes when they cannot well be afforded. Because they do like such things we will show them how to make some very nice and cheap dishes of this kind, but they must not forget that greasy pies and rich cakes are very unhealthy, while good, substantial puddings are both wholesome and economical.

SWISS PUDDING WITH CREAM SAUCE.

INGREDIENTS.

½ lb. flour - - - - - - -	2 cents.
6 oz. granulated sugar - - - - - -	4 "
3 " butter - - - - - - -	6 "
1 pt. milk - - - - - - - -	4 "
1 egg, baking powder, and flavoring - -	4 cents.
Total - - - - -	20 cents.

Sift together half a pound of flour, one heaping teaspoonful of baking powder, and one of salt; rub together four ounces of granulated sugar and two ounces of butter, and when they are well mixed, so as to be granular but not creamy, add the flour gradually until all is used; make a hollow in the middle of the flour, put into it one egg, half a teaspoonful of lemon flavoring, and half a pint of milk; mix to a smooth paste, put into a well buttered and floured mould, and set this into a large pot with boiling water enough to come two-thirds up the side of the mould; steam the pudding three-quarters of an hour, or until a broom splint can be run into it without finding the pudding sticking to the splint. Turn the pudding out of the mould, and send it to the table with the following sauce.

Cream Sauce.—Stir together over the fire one ounce each

of flour and butter; as soon as they are smooth, pour into them half a pint of boiling milk, add two ounces of sugar and half a teaspoonful of lemon flavoring, and use with the pudding as soon as it boils up. This makes a very nice pudding for the Sunday dinner.

CREAM RICE PUDDING.

INGREDIENTS.

4 oz. rice - - - - - - - -	3 cents.
3 " sugar - - - - - - - -	2 "
1¼ qts. milk - - - - - - -	12 "
Flavoring - - - - - - - -	1 cent.
Total - - - - - -	18 cents.

Wash four ounces of rice through two waters, put it into a baking dish with three ounces of sugar and a teaspoonful of flavoring; pour in one quart and a pint of milk, and put it into a moderate oven to bake an hour and a half, or until it is of a creamy consistency. This pudding is very delicate and wholesome.

APPLE TARTS.

INGREDIENTS.

½ lb. flour - - - - - - - -	2 cents.
4 oz. butter - - - - - - - -	8 "
4 " sugar - - - - - - - -	3 "
2 qts. apples - - - - - - -	10 "
1 egg - - - - - - - -	1 cent.
Total - - - - - -	24 cents.

(1.) Pare and slice the apples, and stew them tender with the sugar and one gill of water. (2.) Make the pastry as follows. Put the flour in a heap in the middle of the pastry-board and make a hollow in its center; into this put a saltspoonful of salt, the yolk of the egg, and a piece of the butter as large as a walnut. (3.) Mix these ingredients with the fingers of the right hand, and when they are well mixed gradually add enough cold water to make a stiff paste, about half a pint. (4.) Roll this about on the pastry-board, working it well with the right hand, and dusting the board with flour until the paste ceases to stick to it. (5.) Work the butter a minute with the hand to press out the buttermilk, and dry it in a clean napkin. (6.) Roll out the paste in a round as large as a dinner plate, dust it with flour, lay the butter in the center of it, fold the edges up over the butter so as to cover it completely, press the folded edges down slightly and turn the lump of paste over on the board; flatten it with the roller and roll out evenly, taking care not to break the butter through it; fold one side half over, and then bring the other side up over the first, roll it out and fold it twice more and set it in a cool place, on the ice if possible. (7.) Let it stand five minutes to cool, roll it out again, line the pie plates with it, and fill them with the stewed apple. (8.) Cover them with paste, ornament the cover a little, brush it with beaten egg, or dust it with powdered sugar, and bake it in a rather quick oven.

GOLD CAKE.

INGREDIENTS.

½ lb. granulated sugar - - - - -	6 cents.
½ lb. flour - - - - - - - -	2 "
2 oz. butter - - - - - - -	4 "
½ pt. milk, (½ scant) - - - - - -	2 "
6 eggs - - - - - - - -	6 "
Flavoring and baking powder - - - -	1 cent.
Total - - - - -	21 cents.

(1.) Line the cake pans with buttered paper. (2.) Sift one teaspoonful of baking powder and one saltspoonful of salt with one cup of flour. (3.) Beat the butter and sugar to a cream. (4.) Add to them by degrees two-thirds of a cup of milk, and one cup of flour, and beat the mixture smooth with an egg whip. (5.) Beat the yolks of six eggs to a cream, and stir them into the above ingredients. (6.) Stir in the cup of flour which has been sifted with the salt and baking powder, flavor the batter with Vanilla extract, put it quickly into the baking pan, and bake the cake in a rather moderate oven. (7.) To test the cake run a clean broom splint into its center; if it is done the splint will come out clean. (8.) When it is done, turn it quickly out of the pan and let it cool.

SILVER CAKE.

INGREDIENTS.

½ lb. granulated sugar - - - - -	6 cents.
½ " flour - - - - - - - -	2 "
2 oz. butter - - - - - - -	4 "
½ pt. milk (⅛ scant) - - - -	2 "
Flavoring and baking powder - - -	1 cent.
6 whites of egg (cost counted in last receipt)	
Total - - - - -	15 cents.

Proceed according to the receipt for Gold Cake, substituting the whites of the eggs for the yolks, and flavoring with Bitter Almond instead of Vanilla.

PART II.

CHAPTER I.

FIRST LESSON OF THE SECOND ARTISAN COURSE.

THIS course of lessons is intended for the instruction of the grown daughters and wives of workingmen, who can afford to vary their daily fare at a moderate expense. The lessons are arranged in the form of bills of fare, any one of which, used entire, is suitable for a holiday dinner; or which may be separated to suit the taste and convenience of the family using it; the different dishes composing the bills of fare may be employed at discretion for either breakfast, dinner, or supper. Their preparation calls for a little more care and judgment than the previous course, and leads up to the succeeding one. The meats given are all in the form of side-dishes, and afford a good example of the importance of such preparations for economy and excellence.

As pupils are expected to study the whole of this book, introductory paragraphs will be dispensed with throughout this course of lessons, being replaced by the necessary explanatory notes affixed to the receipts which call for them; and the scholars are referred to the preceding course, and to the appendix, for any questionable points which may suggest themselves.

Oxtail Soup.
Baked Herrings.—Liver Rolls.
Cassel Puddings.

OXTAIL SOUP.

INGREDIENTS.

2 oxtails	10 cents.
1 oz. butter	2 "
Onion, flour, herbs and seasonings	3 "
1 carrot	1 cent.
1 turnip	1 "
Total	17 cents.

(1.) Cut the oxtails in joints, and put them over the fire in three quarts of cold water to blanch, *i. e.*, to come to a boil. (2.) Meantime make a *bouquet* of one sprig each of parsley, thyme, marjoram and two bay leaves, tied up compactly. (3.) Peel the onion and stick six whole cloves in it; peel the carrot and turnip and cut them in half inch dice. (4.) When the oxtails have come to a boil, drain them, rinse them by running cold water over them, dry them in a clean towel; put them again into the sauce-pan with one ounce of butter, and fry them brown; stir in one ounce of flour and let it brown. (5.) Pour over them three quarts of cold water, put in the carrot, turnip, onion and *bouquet;* season the soup with a level tablespoonful of salt, and half a saltspoonful of pepper, cover the sauce-pan and let the soup simmer gently for two hours. (6.) Then take out the onion and *bouquet*, and serve the soup.

The soup should be of á rich brown color; if it is not of the proper hue, darken it with caramel.

CARAMEL.

INGREDIENTS.

1 oz. sugar	1 cent.

Put one ounce of brown sugar over the fire in a frying-pan, and stir it until it turns very dark brown, but do not let it burn; when it is the proper color, pour into the pan half a pint of boiling water, and stir it until the sugar is thoroughly dissolved. Let the caramel cool, and then strain and bottle it; it is a good and harmless coloring for soups, sauces and stews of various kinds.

BAKED HERRINGS.

INGREDIENTS.

2 lbs. herrings - - - - - - -	12 cents.
Vinegar and seasonings - - - - -	5 "
Total - - - - -	17 cents.

(1.) Scale and clean the fish carefully without washing them, unless it is absolutely necessary; split them down the back and remove the backbones; sprinkle them inside with a little pepper, salt and powdered mace mixed together; if there are any roes enclose them in the fish; put the fish in layers in a deep baking dish with half a dozen whole cloves, the same number of pepper corns, and two bay-leaves between them; cover them with vinegar and water equally mixed, salt plentifully, tie a sheet of oiled or buttered paper over the top of the dish, and bake them in a moderate oven for one hour. (2.) Proceed exactly as above except that the backbone should not be removed; no water should be added to the vinegar, and the fish should bake four hours instead of one; the action of the salt and vinegar, and the long continued heat, will completely dissolve the bones. The fish may be used either hot or cold.

LIVER ROLLS.

INGREDIENTS.

1 lb. liver - - - - - - - - -	10 cents.
¼ lb. bacon - - - - - - - -,	3 "
Vegetables, herbs and seasonings - - -	2 "
Total - - - - - -	15 cents.

(1.) Cut the bacon in thin slices. (2.) Scald the liver with boiling water, cut it in pieces two inches wide and three inches long, season it with salt and pepper, lay a slice of bacon on each piece, roll each up and tie it firmly. (3.) Put any remaining scraps of bacon, some trimmings from soup vegetables, and a few herbs in the bottom of the saucepan, lay the liver rolls on them, season them with pepper and salt, cover them with boiling water, and simmer them over a slow fire for about one hour. (4.) Take up the liver rolls, remove the strings and lay them on a hot dish to keep warm; strain the gravy, if it is not thick add a little flour to it, color it dark brown with caramel, pour it over the rolls, put a few sprigs of parsley about the dish and serve it hot.

CASSEL PUDDINGS WITH HARD SAUCE.

INGREDIENTS.

2 eggs - - - - - - - -	2 cents.
8 oz. granulated sugar - - - - -	6 "
6 " butter - - - - - - -	12 "
4 " flour - - - - - - - -	1 cent.
Peel and juice of half a lemon - - -	1 "
Total - - - - - -	22 cents.

(1.) Mix four ounces each of butter and sugar to a cream. (2.) Grate the rind of the lemon into them. (3.) Beat the whites of the eggs to a stiff froth, and the yolks to a cream. (4.) Add the yolks to the butter and sugar, and stir in the flour; then stir the whites in lightly, put the puddings into six buttered cups or tins, making them two-thirds full, and bake them in a moderate oven about thirty minutes, testing them with a broom splint at the end of twenty minutes. When they are done turn them out of the cups and serve them with hard sauce.

Hard Sauce.—Rub together two ounces of butter, four ounces of sugar, and the juice of half a lemon, until the ingredients are thoroughly mixed; shape the sauce in some pretty form, and keep it cold until wanted for use.

CHAPTER II.

SECOND LESSON OF THE SECOND ARTISAN COURSE.

Crécy Soup.
Filets of Fish with Spanish Sauce.
Ragoût of Spareribs and Peas.
Caramel Custards.

CRÉCY SOUP.
INGREDIENTS.

Soup bones - - - - - - - -	5 cents.
Carrots - - - - - - - - -	5 "
Bread and drippings - - - - -	2 "
2 onions, celery, and seasonings - - - -	3 "
Total - - - - -	15 cents.

(1.) Break the bones in small pieces, lay them in the bottom of a pot, add to them four quarts of cold water, bring slowly to a boil, and skim carefully. (2.) Peel two onions and slice them thin. (3.) Scrape half a dozen carrots, and slice them. (4.) Cut three stalks of celery in small pieces. (5.) Make a *bouquet* of herbs. (6.) When the soup is quite free from scum put all these ingredients into it, season it with a level tablespoonful of salt, and simmer it slowly for about two hours, or until the vegetables are tender. (7.) Take out the bones and the *bouquet*, rub the rest of the ingredients through a sieve with a potato masher, and return them to the fire to heat. (8.) Cut two slices of stale bread in dice, fry them in smoking hot drippings, place them in the soup tureen, pour the soup over them and serve it hot.

If the soup shows any sign of settling when it is returned to the fire to heat, rub one tablespoonful each of flour and butter to a paste, and stir them into it.

FILETS OF FISH WITH SPANISH SAUCE.

INGREDIENTS.

3 lb. blue fish	24 cents.
Materials for sauce	10 "
Total	84 cents.

(1.) Cut one ounce of fat bacon in dice, and fry it in the bottom of a sauce-pan with one ounce of drippings and two ounces each of carrot, onion, and tomato, cut small; stir in two ounces of flour when the other ingredients are brown, and let it brown too; then add one quart of hot water, or water and the remains of any brown gravy; season with a teaspoonful of salt and half a saltspoonful of pepper, and let the sauce simmer for nearly an hour, skimming it clear. (2.) Prepare the *filets* of fish as directed on page 32, bake them about twenty minutes, and keep them hot while the sauce is finished. (3.) When the vegetables are soft, rub the sauce through a sieve, see if the seasoning is palatable, pour a little of it on the dish with the fish, and serve the rest in a sauce-boat. Garnish the fish with a few sprigs of parsley.

RAGOÛT OF SPARE RIBS AND PEAS.

INGREDIENTS.

1 can peas	20 cents.
5 lbs. spareribs	15 "
1 oz. butter	2 "
Meat or herbs and seasonings	1 cent.
Total	38 cents.

(1.) Cut the spareribs in small pieces, leaving two or three ribs in each piece. (2.) Put the butter in a sauce-pan, heat it, put in the spareribs, two sprigs of mint, or sweet herbs, a teaspoonful of salt, half a saltspoonful of pepper, and enough boiling water to cover the spareribs, and stew them for half an hour. (3.) Then add the peas, heat them thoroughly, and serve the *ragoût* with the spareribs in the center of the dish, and the peas arranged neatly around them.

When green peas are in season this dish is less expensive than when prepared with canned peas.

CARAMEL CUSTARDS.

INGREDIENTS.

1 pint of milk - - - - - - - -	4 cents.
4 eggs - - - - - - - -	4 "
2 oz. sugar and half lemon rind - - -	2 "
Total - - - - -	10

(1.) Put three drops of caramel, made as directed on page 67, into the bottoms of six cups. (2.) Boil a pint of milk with two ounces of sugar and half the yellow rind of a lemon; meantime beat four eggs, and strain the milk into them; mix thoroughly, strain again, and pour into the cups; set these in a baking pan containing hot water enough to reach half way up the sides of the cups, and either set the pan over the fire until the custards are firm, or bake them in the oven; they will set in twelve or fifteen minutes. Cool the custards, and turn them out on saucers; serve them cold.

CHAPTER III.

THIRD LESSON OF THE SECOND ARTISAN COURSE.

Mulligatawny Soup.
Persillade of Fish.—Fried Brains.
Lemon Dumplings with Lemon Sauce.

MULLIGATAWNY SOUP.

INGREDIENTS.

1 rabbit - - - - - - - - -	20 cents

Carrot, turnip, parsley and seasonings - - 3 cents.
Curry powder, flour and drippings - - 4 "

Total - - - - - 32 cents.

Mulligatawny soup may be made either of chicken or rabbit. (1.) Choose a tender rabbit or hare, which will cost at the market about twenty cents, and which if young will be plump, and have a short neck, thick knees, and fore paws whose joints break easily; hang it by the hind legs and skin it, beginning at the tail and ending at the head; wipe it carefully with a damp cloth to remove the hairs; take out the entrails, saving the brains, heart and liver, and cut it in joints. (2.) Lay the rabbit in a saucepan with two ounces of drippings, the onions peeled and sliced, a teaspoonful of salt, ten whole cloves, and a quarter of a level teaspoonful of pepper, and fry it gently for twenty minutes. (3.) Pare the carrot and turnip, and cut them in small dice. (4.) Make a *bouquet* of one sprig each of parsley, thyme, marjoram and two bay leaves. (5.) When the rabbit is brown, stir a tablespoonful of flour into it, add the vegetables, *bouquet*, and three quarts of boiling water, and simmer until the vegetables are tender enough to rub through a sieve with a wooden spoon. (6.) Meantime, boil the rice as follows: throw it into one quart of boiling water containing two teaspoonfuls of salt, and boil it fast ten minutes; drain it in a colander. Meantime, just grease the pot with sweet drippings, put the rice back in it, cover it, and set it on a brick on the top of the stove, or in a cool oven, and let it stand ten minutes to swell; be careful not to burn it. (7.) Strain the soup, rub the vegetables through a sieve; put the vegetable *purée* thus made into a clean pot with the soup and the rabbit; ascertain if it is salt enough, add a heaping tablespoonful of curry powder, set the pot over the fire, bring the soup just to a boil and serve it hot. (8.) The rice is sent to the table with the soup. Mulligatawny is made from chicken in the same way.

PERSILLADE OF FISH.
INGREDIENTS.

3 lbs. codfish - - - - - - -	16 cents.
2 oz. butter - - - - - - - -	4 "
Onions and parsley - - - - - -	1 "
Flour, bread crumbs and seasonings - -	1 "
Total - - - - -	22 cents.

(1.) Make a White Sauce by stirring together over the fire one ounce each of butter and flour, until they bubble; add half a pint of boiling water gradually, stirring until the sauce is smooth, and then season it with a teaspoonful of salt and quarter of a saltspoonful each of pepper and nutmeg. Set the saucepan containing the sauce in a pan half full of boiling water, to keep it from drying up, while the fish is prepared. (2.) Chop one tablespoonful each of onion and parsley. (3.) Remove the skin and bones from two pounds of cold boiled codfish, lay it on a buttered baking dish which can be sent to the table, moisten it with the white sauce, sprinkle it with the chopped onion and parsley, dust it thickly with dried and sifted bread crumbs, dot it over with a very little butter, and brown it quickly in a hot oven, or with a salamander.

FRIED BRAINS WITH TOMATO SAUCE.
INGREDIENTS.

Brains - - - - - - - - -	10 cents.
1 egg, vinegar, herbs and vegetables - -	3 "
1 qt. tomatoes - - - - - - -	5 "
1 oz. butter - - - - - - -	2 "
¼ lb. lard - - - - - - - -	3 "
Flour, bread crumbs and seasonings - -	2 "
Total - - - - -	25 cents.

(1.) Lay the brains in salt and water for at least one hour. (2.) Make the Tomato Sauce as follows: peel and slice one quart of tomatoes, half a carrot, half a turnip, and one onion, and after reserving two slices of each put them into a saucepan over the fire with one pint of boiling water, or broth, one sprig each of thyme and parsley, three cloves, three peppercorns, and a bayleaf; boil these ingredients gently until they are tender enough to rub through a sieve with a wooden spoon; mix together over the fire one tablespoonful each of butter and flour until they begin to bubble, stir gradually into them half a pint of boiling water, then mix smoothly with the strained tomato sauce; keep the sauce hot as directed in the previous receipt. (3.) While the sauce is being made take the brains from the water, carefully remove the membrane which covers them, and put them over the fire to blanch in cold water enough to cover them, with the slices of vegetables reserved from the tomato sauce, a bayleaf, three cloves, one sprig each of parsley and thyme, a tablespoonful of salt, and half a cup of vinegar; boil them gently fifteen minutes, then take them up, dry them and bread them as follows. (4.) Sift a thick layer of dried bread crumbs on the table, beat up the egg with a tablespoonful of cold water; roll the brains in the crumbs, dip them in the egg quickly enough to avoid washing off the crumbs, and fry them in smoking hot fat. Take them up when brown, lay them for a moment on brown paper to free them from fat, put them on a hot dish with a little tomato sauce under them, garnish the dish with some bits of parsley, and serve hot. The remainder of the sauce must be saved for garnishing fried chops.

LEMON DUMPLINGS WITH LEMON SAUCE.

INGREDIENTS.

¼ lb. suet	2 cents.
½ " bread crumbs	2 "
2 lemons	4 "
3 oz. sugar	2 "
2 eggs	2 "
½ pt. milk	2 "
1 oz. butter	2 "
Flour, sugar, and nutmeg for sauce	2 "
Total	18 cents.

(1.) Shred the suet and chop it very fine. (2.) Grate the yellow rind and squeeze the juice of one lemon. (3.) Mix together the suet, bread crumbs, three ounces of sugar, the eggs, the rind and juice of one lemon, and enough milk to moisten these ingredients; divide them into six equal parts; dip six small pudding cloths in boiling water, dust them with flour, tie up a dumpling in each, and drop them into a pot full of boiling water; boil steadily for an hour, keeping the pot covered all the time or the dumplings may be heavy. When they are done, take them up, turn them out of the cloths, arrange them on a dish, dust them with powdered sugar, and serve them with lemon sauce.

Lemon Sauce.—Grate the yellow rind, and squeeze the juice of one lemon; mix together over the fire one ounce each of butter and sugar, until they bubble; stir in half a pint of boiling water, one ounce of sugar, the rind and juice of the lemon, and serve in a sauce boat with the pudding. Do not let the sauce boil after adding the lemon, or it will be bitter.

CHAPTER IV.

FOURTH LESSON OF THE SECOND ARTISAN COURSE.

Tripe Soup.
Fried Halibut Neck.—Kolcannon.—Bubble and Squeak.
Apple Fritters.

TRIPE SOUP.
INGREDIENTS.

2 lbs. tripe	15 cents.
1 pt. milk	4 "
½ qt. onions	3 "
Flour, parsley, and seasonings	2 "

(1.) Scald the tripe, scrape it with a dull knife, rinse it in hot water, cut it in strips two inches long and half an inch wide, and put it over the fire in three quarts of cold water. (2.) Pare and slice the onions and add them to the soup. (3.) Peel the carrot and turnip, cut them in small dice and add them to the soup and boil it slowly for one hour. (4.) Mix three ounces of flour with the milk, add it to the soup, season it with a level tablespoonful of salt, half a level saltspoonful of pepper, and a tablespoonful of chopped parsley, and serve it hot.

FRIED HALIBUT NECK.

INGREDIENTS.

2 lbs. halibut neck - - - - - -	12 cents.
¼ lb. lard - - - - - - - -	3 "
1 egg, bread crumbs, seasonings - - -	5 "
Total - - - - - -	20 cents.

The neck of halibut is extremely fat and gelatinous, much cheaper than the more solid parts of the fish, and when well seasoned, makes a delicious dish. (1.) Wash the fish in well salted cold water, cut it in pieces three inches square, bread and fry it as directed in the receipt for Fried Brains on page 74. (2.) Garnish it with lemon or parsley, or serve it with *maître d' hotel* butter.

KOLCANNON.

INGREDIENTS.

1 qt. potatoes - - - - - - -	3 cents.
1 cabbage - - - - - - - -	5 "
Butter and seasonings - - - - -	2 "
Total - - - - - -	10 cents.

(1.) Cleanse and boil a cabbage, and chop it very fine. (2.) Boil and peel a quart of potatoes and mash through a colander. (3.) Put the cabbage and potatoes over the fire in a frying-pan, with half a tablespoonful of butter, a teaspoonful of salt, half a level saltspoonful of pepper, and a tablespoonful of chopped parsley, and heat them thoroughly. (4.) Heat a tin mould, butter it, put the Kolcannon into it, press it down well, and set the mould in a moderate oven for half an hour to brown. (5.) Turn it from the mould and serve it hot. Cold vegetables can be rewarmed in the same way.

BUBBLE AND SQUEAK.

INGREDIENTS.

2 lbs. cold meat - - - - - -	20 cents.
Remains of cold cabbage - - - - -	3 "
Onion, drippings and seasoning - - -	2 "
Total - - - - - -	25 cents.

(1.) Put an ounce of drippings in the frying-pan to heat. (2.) Peel half an onion, and chop with it any cold vegetables on hand. (3.) Slice the cold meat rather thick, fry it in one ounce of drippings, lay it in the middle of a hot dish, and keep it hot. (4.) Put the onion into the pan in which the meat was fried, and fry it pale yellow. (5.) Add the cold vegetables to the onion, and fry them until they are a little brown, seasoning them with a teaspoonful of salt, and half a saltspoonful of pepper. (6.) Put them around the meat on the hot dish, and serve it hot.

APPLE FRITTERS.

INGREDIENTS.

3 apples - - - - - - - -	3 cent.
Sugar and spice - - - - - -	2 "
4 oz. lard - - - - - - - -	3 "
2 eggs - - - - - - - -	2 "
Oil and flour - - - - - - -	2 "
Total - - - - -	12 cents.

(1.) Peel and slice the apples, and lay them in a bowl, sprinkling them with sugar, any ground spice preferred, and a little wine if it is convenient; turn them over frequently, and let them lay in the sugar and spice, which is called a sweet *marinade*, for about an hour. (2.) Make a batter as directed for Parsnip Fritters, on page 51. (3.)

Dip the slices of apple into the batter, lift them out on a fork, drop them into smoking hot fat, fry them golden brown, and lay them on brown paper a moment, to free them from grease; arrange them on a dish, dust them with powdered sugar, and serve them hot. If they are allowed to get cold they will be less crisp then when used warm.

CHAPTER V.

FIFTH LESSON OF THE SECOND ARTISAN COURSE.

Gravy Soup.
Boiled Pike with Egg Sauce.—Curry of Pork.
Orange Omelette.

GRAVY SOUP.
INGREDIENTS.

1 lb. soup meat with marrow bone - -	10 cents.
4 oz. ham trimmings - - - - - -	3 "
Veal bones - - - - - - -	2 "
Onions, carrots, turnips, celery and seasonings	5 "
Total - - - - - -	20 cents.

(1.) Cut all the meat from the bones, chop it fine, and put it into the bottom of a saucepan, with the bones and a tablespoonful of drippings, and set it over the fire to get brown. (2.) Meantime peel the vegetables, stick the onion with ten whole cloves, and make a *bouquet* as already directed. (3.) As soon as the meat is brown, add three quarts of boiling water, and let it boil gently until it is clear, adding two teaspoonfuls of salt, and removing the scum as fast as it rises. (4.) When it is clear, add the vegetables whole, and the *bouquet*, and simmer the soup gently two hours, or longer if there is time. (5.) Strain the soup through a jelly-bag without pressing either the meat or vegetables; the meat will have but little nutriment in it, but may be used minced with some potatoes, well seasoned and warmed; the vegetables may be saved for Bubble and Squeak. (6.) Let the soup cool, if there is time, so as to remove the fat in a solid cake, which will rise to the top as it cools; if there is not time, carefully skim off the fat, see if the soup is properly seasoned, and heat and serve it. If it is allowed to cool *do not cover it, or it may sour,* and when it is wanted for use, heat and season it.

BOILED PIKE WITH EGG SAUCE.

INGREDIENTS.

1½ lb. pike - - - - - -	20 cents.
Vinegar, herbs and seasonings - - -	3 "
1 oz. butter - - - - - -	2 "
Egg, flour and parsley - - - -	2 "
Total - - - - -	27 cents.

(1.) Cleanse the fish in cold water and salt, dry it on a clean towel, truss it in the shape of the letter ∞, by turning the head to one side and the tail to the other, and securing them in place with a cord carried by a trussing needle. (2.) Boil it as directed in the receipt for Boiled Haddock, on page 31. (3.) Boil one egg hard and let it get quite cold. (4.) Meantime, make the Egg Sauce as follows: stir one ounce each of butter and flour together over the fire until they bubble; gradually add half a pint of boiling water, stirring the sauce with an egg-whip until it is quite smooth; season it with a level teaspoonful of salt, half a level saltspoonful of pepper, and as much cayenne as can be taken up on the point of a small pen-knife blade; set the sauce-pan containing it in a basin half full of boiling water, to keep it hot until wanted for use. (5.) Remove the shell from the hard boiled egg, chop it fine or cut it in small dice, as preferred, and put it in the sauce just before using it. (6.) When the fish is done it may be served laid in a dish, with the sauce poured over it, or on a neatly folded napkin, garnished with parsley, and the sauce sent to the table, in a sauce-boat, with it.

CURRY OF PORK.
INGREDIENTS.

2 lbs. fresh pork - - - - - -	20 cents.
1 oz. butter - - - - - - - -	2 "
Curry, onion, flour and seasonings - -	3 "
½ lb. rice - - - - - - - -	5 "
2 apples - - - - - - - -	2 "
Total - - - - -	32 cents.

(1.) Cut the pork in pieces two inches square; put it over the fire to brown in the butter, with half an onion, peeled and chopped. When it is brown stir into it one ounce of flour, and let it brown. (2.) Wipe the apples with a damp cloth, slice them quarter of an inch thick, remove the cores, and put them with the pork. (3.) When the pork is brown cover it with boiling water, with any cold gravy on hand mixed with it, season it with two teaspoonfuls of salt, and simmer it for one hour. (4.) Meantime, boil half a pound of rice as directed in the receipt for Mulligatawny Soup, on page 72. (5.) When the pork is nearly done, stir into it one ounce of curry powder, cover it closely, and let it finish cooking. If the curry is added in the early stages of preparation, or if the saucepan is left uncovered, much of its flavor and aroma will escape with the steam.

When the curry is done, shake the rice out on a platter, push it towards the edges of the dish with a fork, to make a sort of rampart, pour the curry inside this, and serve it hot.

Veal may be prepared in the same way, except that the apples may be omitted; and it will resemble chicken curry.

ORANGE OMELETTE.
INGREDIENTS.

1 orange - - - - - - - -	2 cents.
3 eggs - - - - - - - -	3 "
Butter and powdered sugar - - -	1 cent.
Total - - - - -	6 cents.

(1.) Grate the yellow rind and squeeze the juice of one orange. (2.) Beat the yolks of the eggs to a cream, and add the orange rind and juice to them, with two teaspoonfuls of powdered sugar. (3.) Beat the whites to a stiff froth. (4.) Meantime have a clean, smooth frying pan on the fire heating, with a piece of butter as large as a chestnut. (5.) When the pan is hot, put the omelette into it, lift it constantly from the bottom of the pan with a fork, piling it in the middle; when it seems nearly done pile it at one side of the pan, hold a hot dish close to it, and turn it out lightly and quickly. Dust it with powdered sugar, and serve it at once.

CHAPTER VI.

SIXTH LESSON OF THE SECOND ARTISAN COURSE.

Turtle Bean Soup.
Fish Chowder—Chicken Pie.
Corn Starch Puddings.

TURTLE BEAN SOUP.

INGREDIENTS.

1 pt. turtle beans	7 cents.
1 lemon	2 "
2 eggs	2 "
1 lb. soup meat	6 "
Onion and seasonings	1 cent.
Total	18 cents.

Turtle beans are small, black Haricot beans, plentiful and cheap, and it is claimed by the lovers of this soup that it is very much like mock turtle soup. (1.) Pick over the beans, wash them, and put them over the fire in three quarts of cold water, with the meat; bring the water slowly to a boil, skimming it carefully until it is clear. (2.) Peel one onion, stick it with ten cloves, add it to the soup with a *bouquet* of herbs, made as already directed, and let the soup boil gently for about two hours, adding a wine-glassful of cold water every fifteen minutes, to check the boiling and soften the beans. (3.) Boil two eggs hard, remove the shells and whites, chop the yolks fine or cut them in small dice, and put them into the soup tureen. (4.) When the beans are soft, remove the meat, saving it for some little dish, and rub the beans and onion through a sieve with a wooden spoon; pour the soup through with them. (5.) Put it over the fire, season it with two tea-spoonfuls of salt, half a level saltspoonful of pepper, and as much cayenne as can be taken up on the point of a small penknife blade; when it is hot, pour it into the tureen upon the egg, slice the lemon thin and throw it into the soup and serve it.

FISH CHOWDER.

INGREDIENTS.

3 lb. cod fish	- - - - - - -	16 cents.
½ " salt pork	- - - - - - -	6 "
1 " sea biscuit	- - - - - -	10 "
1 qt. potatoes	- - - - - - -	3 "
½ " onions	- - - - - - -	3 "
Seasonings	- - - - - - -	1 cent.
Total	- - - - -	39 cents.

(1.) Pare and slice the potatoes and lay them in cold water; peel and slice the onions. (2.) Wash the fish in well-salted cold water, and cut it in slices an inch thick. (3.) Cut the salt pork in half inch dice, put it in the bottom of a saucepan and fry it brown. (4.) Put the fish, potatoes drained from the water, and the onions into the pot in alternate layers, seasoning each layer from a saucer containing a tablespoonful of salt, and a level teaspoonful each of pepper and powdered thyme. Cover all these ingredients with cold water, bring the chowder gradually to a boil, and simmer it slowly for thirty minutes. Then lay a pound of sea biscuit in warm water, or milk, for five minutes to soften them, put them into the chowder, boil it five minutes longer and serve it hot. A tablespoonful of chopped parsley is sometimes added to it.

A bottle of champagne and half a bottle of port wine transforms the above receipt into that for the famous New York St. James Chowder.

CHICKEN PIE.
INGREDIENTS.

2 lbs. chicken - - - - - - -	30 cents.
½ lb. flour - - - - : - - -	2 "
2 oz. salt pork - - - - - -	2 "
5 " butter - - - - - - - -	10 "
Onion, parsley, and seasonings - - -	1 cent.
Total - - - - - -	45 cents.

(1.) Choose a rather tender fowl, pluck all the pin feathers, singe off the hairs with a piece of burning paper, or a little alcohol poured on a plate and lighted with a match; then wipe the fowl with a clean, damp cloth, draw it carefully by slitting the skin at the back of the neck, and taking out the crop without tearing the skin of the breast; loosen the heart, liver, and lungs by introducing the forefinger at the neck; and then draw them, with the entrails, from the vent. Unless you have broken the gall, or the entrails, in drawing the bird, *do not wash it*, for this greatly impairs the flavor, and partly destroys the nourishing qualities of the flesh. (2.) Cut it in joints and put it into a hot frying pan with an ounce of butter, and the salt pork cut in dice, and fry it brown. (3.) When it is brown stir an ounce of flour with it, and let the flour brown; season it with a teaspoonful of salt, a level teaspoonful of pepper, and a tablespoonful of chopped parsley; cover it with boiling water and let it simmer gently for an hour, or until the chicken is tender. Meantime make the pastry for the pie as follows.

Pastry for Meat and Game Pies.—(1.) Put half a pound of flour in a heap on the pastry-board, make a hollow in the center into which put a teaspoonful of salt and four ounces of butter. (2.) Mix with the finger tips, using cold water enough to make a stiff paste. (3.) Roll the paste out, line the edges of a baking dish half way down with a strip of the paste. (4.) Put the chicken into the dish, pour over it the gravy, fit on it a cover of the paste, ornamenting it a little, and leaving some holes in the top for the steam to escape; bake it about an hour in a moderate oven until the crust is nicely browned. Then serve it.

CORN-STARCH PUDDINGS.

INGREDIENTS.

3 oz. corn-starch	3 cents.
2 eggs	2 "
4 oz. sugar	4 "
1 qt. milk	8 "
Flavoring	1 cent.
Total	18 cents.

(1.) Make a custard by mixing together two eggs, four ounces of sugar, three ounces of cornstarch, and a teaspoonful of flavoring; gradually add one quart of sweet milk, and stir the custard over the fire until it is just ready to boil. (2.) Then put it into cups, and set them in a dripping pan half full of water; set the pan in a moderate oven and bake the little puddings about half an hour, until they are firm, and nicely browned. (3.) Either serve them hot in the cups, or cool them and turn them out on saucers.

CHAPTER VII.

SEVENTH LESSON OF THE SECOND ARTISAN COURSE.

Wrexham Soup.
Fish Croquettes.—Créole Sausages.
Apple Croûtes.

WREXHAM SOUP.

INGREDIENTS.

1 lb. lean soup beef - - - - - -	10 cents.
½ qt. of tomatoes - - - - - - - -	2 "
2 turnips - - - - - - - - -	2 "
2 carrots - - - - - - - - -	2 "
½ qt. onions - - - - - - - -	3 "
Celery and parsley - - - - - -	2 "
Seasonings and herbs - - - - -	2 "
Total - - - - -	23 cents.

(1.) Pare the vegetables and cut them in thick slices. (2.) Cut the meat in thin slices. (3.) Make the usual *bouquet* of parsley and herbs, adding to it an ounce of celery. (4.) Mix together in a saucer a tablespoonful of salt, a teaspoonful of sugar, and a saltspoonful of pepper. (5.) Put these ingredients in alternate layers in an earthen crock or jar, pour in cold water enough to fill the jar, put on the cover, cement it with a thick paste made of flour and water, so that no steam can escape, and bake it in a moderate oven five hours.

Remove the *bouquet* before serving the soup, which contains all the nutriment of the articles composing it.

FISH *CROQUETTES.*

INGREDIENTS.

1 lb. cold boiled fish - - - - -	8 cents.
¼ lb. lard - - - - - - -	3 "
1 oz. butter - - - - - - -	2 "
1 egg - - - - - - - - -	1 "
Bread crumbs, flour and seasonings - -	2 "
Total - - - - -	16 cents.

(1.) Free one pound of cold boiled fish from skin and bones, and chop it in small dice. (2.) Mix together over the fire one ounce each of butter and flour until they bubble; then stir in a pint of boiling water, season with a teaspoonful of salt, and quarter of a saltspoonful each of pepper and nutmeg. (3.) Put the fish into this sauce, stir it over the fire until it begins to thicken, and then pour it out about an inch and a half thick on an oiled dish. Set it away from the heat to cool and stiffen. (4.) Dust the table thickly with sifted bread crumbs, and beat up an egg with a tablespoonful of cold water. (5.) Cut the *croquette* paste in strips an inch and a quarter wide and two inches long. (6.) Wet the hands with cold water, and form the *croquettes* in little rolls like corks; toss them upon the sifted crumbs, roll them over, and pat them lightly into shape. (7.) Dip them into the beaten egg quickly, so as not to wash off the crumbs, roll them again in the crumbs and lay them on a clean dish. (8.) When all the *croquettes* are shaped, drop them into smoking hot fat, fry them golden brown, lay them on brown paper a moment to free them from grease, and serve them hot.

CRÉOLE SAUSAGES.
INGREDIENTS.

1 lb. sausages	12 cents.
1 qt. tomatoes	5 "
Seasonings	1 cent.
Total	18 cents.

(1.) Wipe a pound of sausages on a damp cloth, prick them with a fork and put them into a deep saucepan. (2.) Peel and slice a quart of fresh tomatoes, or use half a can of that vegetable; put them into the saucepan with the sausage. (3.) Break up a bulb of garlic, select a small clove, or division of it, bruise it and add it to the sausages. (4.) Season them with a teaspoonful of salt, and quarter of a saltspoonful of pepper; cover the saucepan closely, and simmer the sausages gently for half an hour; they will then be ready to serve.

APPLE CROÛTES.
INGREDIENTS.

1 qt. apples	5 cents.
Stale bread	2 "
Sugar and spice	3 "
Total	10 cents.

(1.) Pare, cut in halves and core a quart of apples. (2.) Cut as many small pieces of stale bread as there are pieces of apple. (3.) Lay a piece of apple on each piece of bread, arrange them on a dripping pan, dust them thickly with powdered sugar, put a little spice on each, and bake them in a moderate oven. When they are done, which will be in about half an hour, arrange them neatly on a dish, dust them with powdered sugar, and serve them either hot or cold.

CHAPTER VIII.

EIGHTH LESSON OF THE SECOND ARTISAN COURSE.

Brunoise Soup.
Clam Fritters.—Mutton Rechauffé.
Cabinet Pudding.

BRUNOISE SOUP.

INGREDIENTS.

1 lb. soup meat and bone - - - - -	6 cents.
1 oz. butter - - - - - - - -	2 "
Carrot, turnip, onion, leek, celery - - -	5 "
Seasonings - - - - - - - -	1 cent.
Total - - - - -	14 cents.

(1.) Put the soup meat over the fire in two quarts of cold water and bring it slowly to a boil, skimming it clear. (2.) Peel the vegetables, cut them in dice half an inch square, put them over the fire to brown with the ounce of butter, a teaspoonful of powdered sugar, and a quarter of a saltspoonful of pepper. (3.) Make the usual *bouquet*, and add it to the vegetables. (4.) Take the meat from the soup, put it with the vegetables, strain the broth into them, season with a level desertspoonful of salt, simmer until the meat and vegetables are tender; remove the meat and *bouquet,* and then serve the soup hot.

CLAM FRITTERS.
INGREDIENTS.

1 bunch of clams - - - - - -	10 cents.
Materials for batter - - - - - -	5 "
Lard for frying - - - - - -	3 "
Total - - - - -	18 cents.

(1.) Chop the clams fine. (2.) Make a batter as directed for Parsnip Fritters on page 51. Put the clams into it, mix, and fry them in smoking hot fat, dropping them into the fat by the tablespoonful; fry them golden brown, drain them a moment on brown paper, to free them from grease, and serve them hot.

MUTTON *RECHAUFFÉ.*
INGREDIENTS.

1 lb. cold mutton - - - - - -	10 cents.
1 oz. butter - - - - - - -	2 "
4 " lard - - - - - - - -	3 "
Bread crumbs, flour, onion, seasonings -	2 "
1 egg - - - - - - - - -	1 cent.
Total - - - - -	18 cents.

(1.) Slice the cold meat. (2.) Make a sauce as follows: fry one ounce of chopped onion pale yellow in one ounce of butter; stir into it one ounce of flour, and one gill of boiling water, and stir until the sauce begins to cleave away from the sides of the saucepan. Add a saltspoonful of salt, and quarter of a saltspoonful of pepper; beat in the yolk of a raw egg, and pour out the sauce on a dish. (3.) Oil the bottom of a shallow dish. (4.) Spread the slices of cold mutton with this sauce, first on one side, and then on the other, laying the side first spread on the dish, and then covering the other with the sauce. (5.) When all the slices of mutton have been covered with the sauce, beat up an egg with a tablespoonful of cold water. (6.)

Dust the table thickly with sifted bread crumbs. (7.) Lightly bread the slices by dipping them first in the bread crumbs, then in the beaten egg, and, finally, in the crumbs. (8.) When all the slices are breaded, fry them in smoking hot fat until they are golden brown. Lay them for a moment on brown paper to free them from fat, and serve them with a few sprigs of parsley to garnish the dish.

CABINET PUDDING WITH JELLY SAUCE.

INGREDIENTS.

Stale bread	3 cents.
¼ lb. dried currants	3 "
1 pt. milk	4 "
Currant jelly	3 "
4 eggs	4 "
3 oz. sugar	3 "
Total	20 cents.

(1.) Pick over the currants very carefully, wash them in the colander with plenty of cold water, and dry them on a clean towel. (2.) Slice the bread. (3.) Butter a plain pudding mould, put the bread and currants into it in alternate layers, and pour over them a custard made as directed on page 72. (4.) Set the mould containing the pudding in a saucepan half full of boiling water; cover the saucepan and let the pudding steam an hour. Meantime make the sauce as follows.

Jelly Sauce.—Melt one ounce of sugar, and a couple of tablespoonfuls of currant jelly over the fire in half a pint of boiling water, and stir into the sauce half a teaspoonful of corn starch dissolved in half a cup of cold water. Let it come to a boil, and then it will be ready for use.

CHAPTER IX.

NINTH LESSON OF THE SECOND ARTISAN COURSE.

Pot-au-Feu.
Devilled Crabs.—Beef and Vegetables.
French Pancakes.

POT-AU-FEU.

INGREDIENTS.

3 lbs. rump beef	30 cents.
4 carrots	4 "
1 qt. small white turnips	3 "
1 " onions	5 "
Celery and parsley	5 "
Leek, herbs, and seasonings	2 "
1 oz. drippings	1 cent.
Total	50 cents.

Pot-au-Feu is the popular dish of France, which combines the soup and the *bouilli*, or boiled beef, and vegetables, that constitute the ordinary dinner of the French people. Its excellence cannot be too highly esteemed, for when it is carefully prepared it yields a larger amount of nutriment, and satisfies the appetite better than almost any other dish of equal cost. It should be made of perfectly fresh meat and vegetables, and the greatest care should be given to its cooking. When it is finished and served it gives a clear, amber-colored soup of delicious flavor, and an inviting dish of brown *bouilli* garnished with fresh-colored vegetables.

(1.) Choose a tender piece of the round of beef, bind it well together with tape or narrow strips of cloth, to keep it in a compact shape; put the drippings into the bottom of a saucepan to heat, and then put in the beef and turn it about until it is of a uniform brown color. (2.) Add four quarts of boiling water, and a teaspoonful of salt, and set the saucepan where it will simmer gently; remove the scum as fast as it rises, throwing in a wineglassful of cold water every fifteen minutes until it is clear. Then simmer it gently for three hours. (3.) Meantime, scrape and quarter the carrots, peel the onions and the turnips, which should not be larger than the onions, stick ten whole cloves in one onion, and make a *bouquet* of the celery, leek, parsley, three bay-leaves, and one sprig each of thyme and marjoram; lay all these ingredients in cold water until wanted. (4.) At the end of three hours, add the vegetables to the soup, a handful at a time, so as to avoid cooling the broth too rapidly; season it with a tablespoonful of salt, ten pepper corns, and a lump of loaf-sugar, and boil it gently until the vegetables are tender. (5.) If crusts, or *croûtons*, are desired for the soup, make them as follows; slice some stale bread, cut it in small dice, or stamp it in rounds with an apple-corer, and fry them golden brown in smoking hot fat. Take them up with a skimmer, lay them on brown paper for a moment to free them from grease, and put them in the soup tureen. (6.) When the vegetables are tender, put the meat on a platter, take out the *bouquet*, and arrange the vegetables around it; strain the soup into the tureen, and serve both dishes hot.

DEVILLED CRABS.

INGREDIENTS.

6 crabs - - - - - - - -	15 cents.
Butter, bread crumbs, and seasonings - -	5 "
Total - - - - -	20 cents.

(1.) Choose live crabs, heavy in proportion to their size, plunge them head first into a large pot two thirds full of well salted boiling water, and boil them rapidly until they are red, about fifteen minutes; then take them out and cool them a little. (2.) Take off the back shells whole, and wash them thoroughly; pick out all the meat and mix it over the fire in a saucepan, with an ounce of butter, two slices of bread soaked in cold water and wrung dry in a clean towel, a level teaspoonful each of dry mustard and salt, a tablespoonful of chopped parsley, a level saltspoonful of pepper, and as much cayenne as can be taken up on the point of a small penknife blade. (3.) As soon as this forcemeat is hot fill the shells with it, dust them with bread crumbs, dot them over with bits of butter, arrange them on a pan, and brown them quickly in a hot oven. Serve them on a napkin with a few sprigs of parsley or slices of lemon as a garnish.

BEEF AND VEGETABLES.

The directions for this dish are included in the receipt for *Pot-au-Feu.*

FRENCH PANCAKES.

INGREDIENTS.

2 eggs	2 cents.
½ pt. milk	2 "
2 oz. granulated sugar	2 "
2 " butter	4 "
Flour and jelly	5 "
Total	15 cents.

(1.) Beat the butter and sugar to a cream. (2.) Beat the eggs separately, the yolks to a cream and the whites to a froth, and add the yolks to the butter and sugar. (3.) Stir the milk into these ingredients. (4.) Butter six tin pie-plates. (5.) Sift two ounces of flour with a teaspoonful of baking powder, and stir it quickly into the above named mixture, with the whites of the eggs; put the batter quickly upon the buttered plates, and bake the pancakes brown in a quick oven. (6.) Dust them with powdered sugar, lay them one over the other, with a little jelly between, dust the top with sugar and serve them hot.

CHAPTER X.

TENTH LESSON OF THE SECOND ARTISAN COURSE.

Créole Soup.
Boiled Ray with Piquante Sauce.
Salmi of Duck.
Baroness Pudding.

CRÉOLE SOUP.

INGREDIENTS.

1 qt. tomatoes - - - - - - - -	5 cents.
1 oz. butter - - - - - - - - -	2 "
2 " rice - - - - - - - - -	2 "
1 carrot - - - - - - - - - -	1 cent.
1 turnip - - - - - - - - -	1 "
Onion, parsley and seasonings - - - -	1 "
Total - - - - - -	12 cents.

(1.) Slice one onion, put it in a saucepan, and fry it brown in one ounce of butter. (2.) Wash one quart of tomatoes, break them in the hand, and add them to the onion. (3.) Peel and slice one carrot and one turnip and add them to the tomatoes, with a *bouquet* made of one sprig each of parsley, thyme and marjoram, two bay-leaves, one blade of mace and six whole cloves. (4.) Add two quarts of boiling water and simmer slowly for two hours. (5.) Meantime, boil two ounces of well-washed rice in boiling water and salt, until the grains are soft but not broken, drain it and keep it a little warm until wanted. (6.) When the vegetables are tender, rub them through a sieve with a wooden spoon, season them with a level tablespoonful of salt and half a level saltspoonful of pepper. If the soup is quite thick add to it a little boiling water or broth, put the rice into it, simmer it for fifteen minutes, and serve

If canned tomatoes and broth are used for this soup it will be more expensive than when made as above.

BOILED RAY WITH *PIQUANTE* SAUCE.

INGREDIENTS.

3 lb. Ray	24 cents.
1 oz. butter	2 "
Herbs and seasonings	2 "
Onion, pickle, capers and vinegar	5 "
Total	33 cents.

The Ray and Skate, which are used in the same way, are similar fish, and in the late winter, may often be found at large fish markets at a very reasonable price, because the real merits of the fish are comparatively unknown. Both skate and ray are very wholesome, and the young fish are delicate and tender. In cool weather the fish improves by being hung a day after it is caught. The fins and liver are the best parts; the skin should be removed either before or after cooking, and the fish served with a sharp sauce. The fish should be broad and thick, with firm flesh, and creamy under side; the upper side is rather dark. (1.) Wash the fish after cleaning it, put it into enough cold water to cover it, with two tablespoonfuls of salt, one lemon sliced, one onion peeled and stuck with ten cloves, a *bouquet* of herbs, and a gill of vinegar; bring slowly to a boil, and boil gently for fifteen minutes. (2.) Make the sauce as directed in the next paragraph, while the fish is cooking. (3.) Then take it carefully out of the water in which it was boiled, remove the skin without breaking the fish, pour the sauce over it and serve it hot.

Piquante Sauce.—Chop fine a tablespoonful each of pickle, capers, and onion; put them over the fire with a gill of vinegar, and stir them until the vinegar evaporates; then add one ounce each of butter and flour, a teaspoonful of salt, quarter of a saltspoonful of pepper, as much cayenne as can be taken up on the point of a small penknife-blade, and half a pint of boiling water; let the sauce come to a boil and pour it over the fish.

SALMI OF DUCK.

INGREDIENTS,

1 wild duck - - - - - - -	25 cents.
1 pint button onions - - - - - -	5 "
1 oz. butter - - - - - - -	2 "
Stale bread - - - - - - - -	2 "
Flour, and seasonings - - - - -	1 cent.
Total - - - - - -	35 cents.

(1.) Pluck the duck, cut it in joints, as for *fricassée,* put it into a saucepan with the butter, and fry it brown quickly. (2.) Meantime, peel a pint of button onions and lay them in cold water. (3.) When the duck is brown, add the onions to it, with enough boiling water to cover, season with a level tablespoonful of salt, half a level salt-spoonful of pepper, and a *bouquet* of herbs, and let it simmer for one hour. (4.) Cut the bread in heart-shaped pieces; lay them on a baking pan, and brown them in a quick oven. (5.) When the duck is done, remove the *bouquet,* pour the *salmi* upon a dish, garnish it with the *croûtons,* or browned bread, and serve it hot.

BARONESS PUDDING.

INGREDIENTS.

½ lb. stale bread crumbs - - - -	2 cents.
½ " raisins - - - - - - -	6 "
½ " suet - - - - - - - -	4 "
6 oz. granulated sugar - - - - -	4 "
½ pint of milk - - - - - - -	2 "
Total - - - - -	18 cents.

(1.) Shred the suet and chop it fine. (2.) Seed and chop the raisins. (3.) Mix together the suet, raisins, bread crumbs, four ounces of sugar, and the milk. (4.)

of boiling water, and boil it steadily for four hours. (5.) Turn it out of the cloth, dust it thickly with powdered sugar and serve it hot.

Any pudding sauce may be served with it if desired.

CHAPTER XI.

ELEVENTH LESSON OF THE SECOND ARTISAN COURSE.

Mutton Broth.
Fish Pie.—Kromeskies.—Fricadels.
Apple Charlotte, plain.

MUTTON BROTH.
INGREDIENTS.

3 lbs. neck of mutton	18 cents.
¼ lb. pearl barley	3 "
1 carrot	1 cent.
1 turnip	1 "
1 onion and seasonings	1 "
Total	24 cents.

(1.) Cut the meat from a neck of mutton into two-inch dice; break the bones, put both into a sauce-pan with three quarts of cold water, and bring it slowly to a boil, skimming it carefully until clear. (2.) Meantime pick over and wash the barley and lay it in hot water. (3.) Peel the carrot and turnip, and cut them into half inch dice; peel the onion and stick it with ten cloves, and make the usual *bouquet*. (4.) When the soup is quite clear, season it with a tablespoonful of salt, and quarter of a saltspoonful of pepper; add the barley and vegetables, and boil it slowly and steadily for three hours, or until the barley is soft. (5.) Take out the bones and *bouquet*, and serve the

FISH PIE.

INGREDIENTS.

2 lbs. codfish	15 cents.
1 " stale bread	3 "
1 qt. potatoes	3 "
Seasonings	1 cent.
Total	22 cents.

(1.) Boil the potatoes in boiling water and salt. (2.) Soak the bread in cold water, and wring it dry in a clean towel; season it well with pepper, salt and a tablespoonful of chopped parsley. (3.) Cut the fish in small slices and lay it in cold salted water. (4.) When the potatoes are done, peel them, mash them through a colander, and season them with salt and pepper. (5.) Put the fish and bread in alternate layers in a pudding dish, make a top crust of the potatoes, and bake the pie an hour in a moderate oven.

KROMESKIES.

INGREDIENTS.

1 lb. cold meat	10 cents.
1 oz. butter	2 "
Onion, flour and seasoning	2 "
¼ lb. lard	3 "
Materials for batter	5 "
1 egg	1 cent.
Total	23 cents.

(1.) Chop one onion and fry it pale yellow in one ounce of butter. (2.) Cut the cold meat in small dice. (3.) When the onion is yellow, add to it an ounce of flour; stir until smooth, then add half a pint of boiling water, or cold gravy, and stir until the sauce is ready to boil. (4.) Put in the cold meat, a tablespoonful of chopped parsley, a teaspoonful of salt, and the yolk of one raw egg, and stir until the mixture is scalding hot. (5.) Turn it out on an oiled platter, spreading it an inch thick, and let it cool. (6.) When it is cold, cut it in strips an inch wide and two inches long; pat them into even shapes with a knife blade dipped in cold water; drop them into the Plain Frying Batter, given on page 51, lift them out with a fork and drop them into smoking hot fat to fry golden brown. (7.) When they are done, lay them on brown paper for a moment to free them from grease, pile them nicely on a clean napkin, garnish them with sprigs of parsley, and serve them hot.

FRICADELS.

INGREDIENTS.

4 oz. sausage meat - - - - - -	3 cents.
4 " stale bread - - - - - - -	2 "
2 eggs - - - - - - - - -	2 "
4 oz. lard - - - - - - - -	3 "
Bread crumbs and seasonings - - - -	2 "
Total - - - - - -	- 12 cents.

(1.) Soak the bread in cold water, and wring it dry in a towel. (2.) Mix it with the sausage meat, and one egg, and season it with one teaspoonful of salt, and quarter of a saltspoonful each of pepper and nutmeg. (3.) Dip the hands in cold water, shape the fricadels in the form of little corks, and roll them in sifted bread crumbs; dip them in beaten egg, without washing off the crumbs, roll them again in cracker dust, and serve them as directed in the last receipt.

APPLE CHARLOTTE, PLAIN.

INGREDIENTS.

1 qt. apples - - - - - - -	5 cents.
1 lb. bread - - - - - - - -	3 "
1 lemon - - - - - - -	2 "
2 oz. butter - - - - - - - -	4 "
4 " sugar - - - - - - - -	3 "
Total - - - - - -	- 17 cents.

(1.) Butter a plain pudding-mould rather thickly. (2.) Cut to fit the mould enough slices of bread to half fill it, and spread them with butter. (3.) Pare, core, and slice the apples. (4.) Grate the yellow rind and squeeze the juice of the lemon. (5.) Fill the mould with alternate layers of bread and butter and apple, sprinkling plenty of sugar and lemon between. (6.) Cover the top of the mould to prevent burning, bake it three quarters of an hour, turn it out on a dish, sprinkle it well with powdered sugar and serve it hot.

CHAPTER XII.

TWELFTH LESSON OF THE SECOND ARTISAN COURSE.

Purée of Fish.
Baked Cod with Cream Sauce.
Curried Tripe.
Sago Pudding.

PURÉE OF FISH.

INGREDIENTS.

1 lb. fish	10 cents.
2 qts. milk	16 "
2 oz. butter	4 "
Flour and seasonings	1 "
Total	31 cents.

(1.) Boil a pound of any fish in season in plenty of boiling water and salt; when it is done so that it flakes, take it up, cool it, remove the skin and bones, and rub it through a sieve with a wooden spoon. (2.) While it is cooling, mix together over the fire two ounces each of butter and flour until they bubble, and gradually add to them two quarts of boiling milk; add the fish, season the soup with a level tablespoonful of salt, and quarter of a saltspoonful each of pepper and nutmeg, and serve it at once.

BAKED COD WITH CREAM SAUCE.

INGREDIENTS.

3 lbs. cold boiled cod - - - - -	16 cents.
1 oz. butter - - - - - - -	2 "
Bread crumbs and seasonings - - - -	2 "
½ pt. milk - - - - - - -	2 "
Total - - - - -	22 cents.

(1.) Make a Cream Sauce by stirring together over the fire one ounce each of butter and flour until they bubble; then stir in gradually half a pint of boiling milk, and season the sauce with a teaspoonful of salt and half a saltspoonful each of white pepper and grated nutmeg. (2.) Remove the skin and bones from the fish, tear it in flakes with two forks, lay it on a baking dish which can be sent to the table, season it with a little salt and pepper, pour the sauce over it, dust it thickly with bread crumbs, dot it over with some small bits of butter, and brown it in a quick oven. (3.) Set the dish containing it on a clean dish, and serve it hot.

CURRIED TRIPE.

INGREDIENTS.

2 lbs. tripe - - - - - - -	16 cents.
½ lb. rice - - - - - - - -	5 "
Onions, drippings, curry, and seasonings -	5 "
Total - - - - - - -	26 cents.

(1.) Thoroughly wash two pounds of tripe, parboil it in well salted water, put it into boiling water and boil it until tender, about one hour; then lay it on a clean, dry cloth to drain. (2.) Then put half a pound of rice into the same water, and boil it fast for twenty minutes. (3.) Cut the tripe in pieces two inches square. (4.) Slice two onions, frying them in two ounces of drippings, season with one teaspoonful of salt, quarter of a level teaspoonful of pepper, and one tablespoonful of vinegar; add the tripe and cook all together for fifteen minutes, stirring occasionally to prevent burning.   (5.) When the tripe is done add a table-spoonful of curry and stir it well.   (6.) Drain the rice into a colander, shake it out into a dish, and serve it with the tripe.

SAGO PUDDING.

INGREDIENTS.

¼ lb. sago - - - - - - -	3 cents.
6 oz. sugar - - - - - - - -	4 "
6 eggs - - - - - - - -	6 "
1 pt. milk - - - - - - - -	4 "
Butter and flavoring - - - - -	1 cent.
Total - - - - - -	18 cents.

(1.) Soak the sago in water or milk over night; or, if that is impossible, put it over the fire in enough water or milk to cover it, until it is soft, which will be in about an hour.   (2.) Beat together in the pudding-dish the sugar and eggs.   (3.) Stir in the sago, milk, and a teaspoonful of Vanilla or Lemon flavoring; dot the pudding over with bits of butter, and bake it one hour in a moderate oven.   It may be used either hot or cold.

PART III.

CHAPTER I.

FIRST LESSON OF THE PLAIN COOKS' COURSE.

THIS course of lessons is designed to serve a double requirement. In the New York Cooking School it has been found to meet the wants of young housewives beginning married life in comfortable or moderate circumstances, and to serve for domestics wishing to take service in families where the table is nice without being too expensive.

The lessons are so arranged that the entire course can be taken by pupils needing the full instruction, or certain lessons can be chosen to cover specific points, for it is sometimes inconvenient for girls at service to attend the entire course in successive lessons, even though they wish to master it all. In the New York Cooking School this course of lessons is repeated throughout the entire season, extra lessons being given to girls needing any training which it does not include; by pursuing this plan they are enabled to attend all the lessons, replacing in the successive courses those which they have missed in the preceding ones.

The kind of instruction given in this course is a combination of plain and middle class cookery, which affords a fair variety for the use of persons who appreciate nice dishes, but do not wish to increase their expenses to any great extent. In this, as in the Second Artisan Course, introductory matter will be dispensed with, points not covered by the receipts proper being explained in notes appended to them.

STOCK.

INGREDIENTS.

4 lbs. soup meat and bones - - - -	24 cents.
Soup vegetables - - - - - - -	5 "
Seasonings - - - - - - - -	1 cent.
Total - - - - - - -	- 30 cents.

Good soup can be made from the scraps of meat, providing it is fresh, and from any fresh vegetables, or cereals. Pot liquor in which meat has been boiled makes good soup stock if it has been skimmed clear at its first boiling; it needs to have all the fat removed, to be seasoned and finished by the addition of cereals, dumplings, rice, or macaroni.

Experiments made by European chemists show that the flavor and nutriment of soup can be heightened by chopping the meat fine, soaking it for one hour in cold or luke-warm water, and then boiling it in the same water. This method is admirable where all the nutritive elements of the meat are desired for the use of invalids or convalescents; but under ordinary circumstances it is far better to cut the meat from the bones in a solid piece, and make the soup according to the directions given below; under such treatment enough of the nourishment contained in the meat passes into the broth, while that which it retains makes it available for highly seasoned meat *croquettes, vinaigrettes* and similar *entrées.*

If pupils will closely follow the directions here given, they cannot fail to understand the principles of soup-making to a sufficient extent to enable them to prepare a good variety at any season of the year.

(1.) Where there is a family of any size it is well to keep a clean pot or saucepan on the back of the stove to receive all the clean scraps of meat, bones and remains of poultry and game, which are found in every kitchen; but vegetables should not be put into it, as they are apt to sour. The proper proportions for soup are one pound of meat and bone to one and a half quarts of cold water; the meat to be left whole, and the bones to be well chopped and broken up, and put over the fire in cold water, being brought slowly to a boil, carefully skimmed as often as any scum rises, and being maintained at a steady boiling point from two to six hours, as time permits; one hour before the stock is done, add to it one carrot and one turnip pared, one onion stuck with three cloves, and a *bouquet* of sweet herbs. (2.) When the soup is to be boiled six hours, two quarts of cold water must be allowed to every pound of meat; this will be reduced to one quart in boiling. Two gills of soup are usually allowed for each person at table when it is served as the first part of the dinner, and meats are to follow it. Care should be taken that the stock-pot boils slowly and constantly, from one side; for rapid and irregular boiling clouds and darkens the stock as much as imperfect skimming. Stock should never be allowed to cool in the stock-pot, but should be strained into an earthen jar, and left standing to cool uncovered, and all the fat removed and saved to clarify for drippings; the stock is then ready to heat and use for soup or gravy. (3.) When stock has been darkened and clouded by careless skimming and fast boiling, it can be clarified by adding to it one egg and the shell, mixing first with a gill of cold water, then with a gill of boiling soup, and stirring it briskly into the soup until it boils; then remove it to the back of the fire where it will not boil, and let it stand until the white and shell of the egg have collected the small particles clouding the soup; then strain it once or twice, until it looks clear.

Flavoring, Thickening and Coloring Soup.—The flavor of soup stock may be varied by using in it a little ham, anchovy, sausage, sugar or a calf's foot. Herbs in the sprig, and whole spices should be used in seasoning, as they can be easily be strained out. All delicate flavors and wine should be added to soup just before serving it, unless

5

10

the contrary is expressly directed in the receipt, because boiling would almost entirely evaporate them; one gill of wine is usually allowed to every three pints of soup.

Soups which precede a full dinner should be less rich than those which form the bulk of the meal. Corn starch, arrow root and potato flour are better than wheat flour for thickening soup. The meal of peas and beans can be held in suspension by mixing together dry a tablespoonful of butter and flour, and stirring it into the soup; a quarter of a pint of peas, beans or lentils, is sufficient to make a quart of thick soup. Two ounces of macaroni, vermicelli, pearl barley, sago, tapioca, rice or oatmeal are usually allowed for each quart of stock.

If you wish to darken soup, use a teaspoonful of caramel; but avoid burnt flour, carrot, and onion, as all these give a bad flavor. Caramel can be made as directed on page 67, of the Second Artisan Course.

CLEAR SOUP, OR *CONSOMMÉ*.

INGREDIENTS.

4 lbs. soup meat	24 cents.
Soup vegetables	5 "
7 eggs	7 "
Seasonings	1 cent.
Total	37 cents.

This is made by straining two quarts of stock, which has been cooled and freed from fat, through a piece of flannel or a napkin until it is bright and clear; if this does not entirely clear it, use an egg, as directed for clarifying soup in paragraph 3 of the preceding receipt; then season it to taste with salt, using at first a teaspoonful, and a very little fine white pepper, say a quarter of a saltspoonful; and color it to a bright straw color with caramel, of which a scant teaspoonful will be about the proper quantity. *Consommé* is sent to the table clear, but sometimes a deep dish containing poached eggs, one for each person, with enough *consommé* to cover them, accompanies it.

Poached Eggs for *Consommé.*—Break the eggs, which should be very fresh, into a deep saucepan half full of boiling water, seasoned with a teaspoonful of salt, and half a gill of vinegar; cover the saucepan, and set it on the back part of the fire until the whites of the eggs are firm; then lift them separately on a skimmer, carefully trim off the rough edges, making each egg a regular oval shape, and slip them off the skimmer into a bowl of hot, but not boiling water, where they must stand for ten minutes before serving.

SCOTCH BROTH.

INGREDIENTS.

4 lbs. neck of mutton	24 cents.
¼ " pearl barley	3 "
2 oz. butter	4 "
Carrot and turnip	2 "
Soup greens	1 cent.
Onion, flour and seasonings	1 "
Total	35 cents.

(1.) Put four ounces of barley to soak in cold water over night. (2.) From four pounds of the neck of mutton, cut the lean meat in dice half an inch square; cut up the rest in small pieces, and make a stock as directed in the receipt for stock on page 104, adding two and a half quarts of water and the barley, and boiling and skimming for two hours. (3.) At the end of an hour and a half put the dice of meat into a saucepan with two ounces of butter, and fry them brown, and then stir in one ounce of flour. (4.) Cut in dice a yellow turnip and a carrot, chop four ounces of onion, and put these with the meat; add the barley and the stock strained; season the broth with a teaspoonful of salt and quarter of a saltspoonful of pepper, and simmer it one hour. Then sprinkle into it a tablespoonful of chopped parsley, and serve it.

VERMICELLI SOUP.

INGREDIENTS.

4 lbs. soup meat - - - - - -	24 cents.
Soup vegetables and seasonings - - -	5 "
Egg and Vermicelli - - - - - -	5 "
Total - - - - -	34 cents.

(1.) The stock for this soup is made as for *consommé.* (2.) To every quart of stock is added one ounce of Vermicelli, blanched as follows: put the paste into plenty of boiling water, with one tablespoonful of salt to each quart of water, and boil until tender; then drain it, and put it in cold water until required for use. (3.) It should be placed in the hot soup long enough to heat thoroughly before serving.

JULIENNE SOUP.

INGREDIENTS.

4 lbs. soup meat - - - - - -	24 cents.
Soup, vegetables and seasonings - - -	10 "
1 egg - - - - - - - - -	1 cent.
Total - - - - -	35 cents.

(1.) The stock for *Julienne* Soup is made as for *consommé.* (2.) When the stock is clear, free from fat, and of the proper color, the following vegetables, finely shredded, are added to it; half an ounce of onion, quarter of an ounce of celery leaves, and three ounces each of carrot, white and yellow turnips, cabbage, and string-beans; below we give plain directions for shredding the vegetables. Sometimes the vegetables are slightly browned in an ounce of butter before being put into the soup. (3.) The soup is gently simmered until the vegetables are tender, the seasoning is tested, and then it is served.

How to Shred Vegetables.—This process is not really a

about half an inch high. (2.) They should be pressed firmly down on the table with the tips of the fingers of the left hand, the tips being bent in toward the palm of the hand, and the knuckles nearest the ends of the fingers projecting outward. (3.) The knife should then be taken in the right hand, the blade laid flat against the lower knuckles of the left, the point of the knife resting upon the table, and the broadest part of the blade being held over the vegetables. (4.) The blade should then be brought down upon the vegetables, cutting off thin slivers at each stroke. The fingers should be moved back gradually, so as to afford a surface for the knife to cut into the vegetables, and the knuckles being always kept bent outward to protect the tips of the fingers.

SPINACH SOUP.
INGREDIENTS.

1 qt. spinach	5 cents.
2 qts. milk	16 "
1 oz. butter	2 "
Flour and seasonings	1 cent.
Total	24 cents.

(1.) Wash and trim one quart of green spinach, put it into a saucepan holding at least three quarts of boiling water, and three tablespoonfuls of salt, and boil it rapidly with the cover off, until it is tender, which will be in from three to seven minutes, according to the age of the spinach; while it is boiling press it under the water with a wooden spoon. As soon as it is tender drain it in a colander, run plenty of cold water over it from the faucet, chop it fine, and rub it through a sieve with a wooden spoon. (2.) While the spinach is boiling prepare the soup as follows: put the milk over the fire to boil, first putting into the kettle a gill of cold water, to prevent burning. Mix together over the fire an ounce of butter and an ounce and a half of flour until they bubble; then gradually add the boiling milk, season it with a level tablespoonful of salt, half a saltspoonful of white pepper and quarter of a saltspoonful of grated nutmeg. (3.) When this broth is done stir into it enough of the spinach to color it a delicate green, and serve it hot. (4.) If it is prepared before it is needed at the table, set the saucepan containing it in another half full of boiling water to keep it hot without boiling.

PEA SOUP.

INGREDIENTS.

1 pt. dried peas	- - - - -	5 cents.
Soup vegetables and seasonings	- - -	5 "
Bones and stale bread	- - - - -	5 "
Total	- - - - -	15 cents.

(1.) Use a pint of dried peas for every four quarts of soup. Put them in six quarts of cold water, after washing them well; bring them slowly to a boil; add a bone, or bit of ham, one turnip, and one carrot peeled, one onion stuck with ten cloves, and simmer three hours, stirring occasionally to prevent burning. (2.) Then take out the bone, pass the soup through a sieve with the aid of a potato-masher, return it to the fire, and if it shows any sign of settling stir into it one tablespoonful each of butter and flour mixed together dry; this will prevent settling; meantime cut some dice of stale bread, about two slices, half an inch square, brown them in the oven or fry them, and put them in the bottom of the soup tureen in which the pea

CHAPTER II.

SECOND LESSON OF THE PLAIN COOKS' COURSE.

FISH is an important article of diet; and in this country, where it is so excellent and so abundant, it is worth all the trouble that can be taken in preparing it for the table. Care should be taken to have the utensils used in cooking it perfectly clean, in order to preserve the flavors of the different varieties, some of which are exceedingly delicate.

BOILED COD WITH *HOLLANDAISE* SAUCE.

INGREDIENTS.

5 lbs. codfish	24 cents.
3 eggs	3 "
1 oz. butter	2 "
Flour and seasonings	5 "
Total	34 cents.

Fish boiled *à la Hollandaise* is properly cooked in sea water; but as sea water is not always obtainable, well salted water is generally used. (1.) After thoroughly washing the fish, put it over the fire in cold water, well salted, and bring it slowly to a boil; it will be done when the fins can easily be pulled out. (2.) Set the pot off the fire, and let the fish stand in the water in which it was boiled until it is wanted for use. (3.) While the fish is boiling, make the sauce according to the receipt given below. (4.) After the sauce is made, take the fish up on a napkin, garnish it with some sprigs of parsley, and send it to the table with the sauce in a sauce boat.

Hollandaise Sauce.—Put one ounce of butter and one ounce of flour in a saucepan over the fire, and stir constantly until it bubbles; then add gradually two gills of boiling water, remove the sauce from the fire, stir in the yolks of three eggs, one at a time, add one saltspoonful of dry mustard, one tablespoonful of vinegar and three of oil, gradually, drop by drop, stirring constantly till smooth. Serve it with the fish.

FILET OF SOLE WITH CAPER BUTTER.

INGREDIENTS.

A 2 lb. flounder - - - - - -	12 cents.
Egg, bread, seasoning and lard - - - -	8 "
Materials for sauce - - - - - -	5 "
Total - - - - -	25 cents.

Prepare and cook the *filets* as directed on pp. 32 and 33; lay them on a dish on a little Caper Butter, made as directed below, garnish them with a few whole capers, and serve them either hot or cold.

Caper Butter.—Chop one tablespoonful of capers very fine, rub them through a sieve with a wooden spoon, and mix them with a saltspoonful of salt, quarter of a saltspoonful of pepper, and an ounce of cold butter. Put a layer of this butter on a dish and serve the fish on it.

BAKED BASS.

INGREDIENTS.

3 lbs. bass - - - - - - -	45 cents.
Vegetables, bread and seasonings - - -	5 "
Materials for sauce - - - - - -	5 "
4 oz. salt pork - - - - - - -	3 "
Total - - - - -	58 cents.

(1.) Choose a fresh bass, wash it well, and wipe it with a clean, dry cloth; stuff it with the following forcemeat. (2.) Put four ounces of stale bread to soak in sufficient cold water to cover it. (3.) Chop the following ingredients. (4.) Fry one ounce of chopped onion in one ounce of butter until it is light brown; then wring the bread dry in a clean towel, put it into the onion with two tablespoonfuls of chopped parsley, one ounce of salt pork chopped fine, one teaspoonful of chopped capers or pickles, one teaspoonful of salt, quarter of a saltspoonful of white pepper, and one gill of broth or hot water; stir this forcemeat until it is scalding hot, when it will cleave from the bottom and sides of the saucepan. (5.) Then stuff the fish with it, and lay it in a dripping pan on one ounce of carrot and one ounce of onion sliced, one bay leaf and two sprigs of parsley. (6.) Cover the fish with slices of salt pork, season it with a saltspoonful of salt, and one fourth that quantity of pepper, and bake it in a moderate oven for half an hour, basting it occasionally with a little butter, or stock. (7.) When it is done, put it on a dish to keep hot while you prepare a sauce by straining the drippings in the pan, and adding to them one tablespoonful each of Walnut catsup, Worcestershire sauce, chopped capers, and chopped parsley. Pour a little of this sauce in the bottom of the dish under the fish, and serve the rest with it in a bowl.

BROILED SHAD WITH *MAÎTRE D'HOTEL* BUTTER.

INGREDIENTS.

1 shad	25 cents.
1 oz. butter	2 "
Lemon and seasonings	3 "
Total	30 cents.

(1.) Choose a medium-sized shad, weighing about three pounds, have it cleaned and split down the back. (2.) Turn it occasionally for an hour or more, in a marinade made of one tablespoonful of salad oil, or melted butter, one of vinegar, a saltspoonful of salt, and quarter of a saltspoonful of pepper. (3.) Lay it on a gridiron, rubbed with a little butter to prevent sticking, broil it slowly, doing the inside first; and, after laying it on a hot dish, spread over it some *maître d'hotel* butter.

Maître d'Hotel Butter.—Mix together cold, one ounce of butter, a tablespoonful of chopped parsley, a teaspoonful of lemon juice, and quarter of a saltspoonful of pepper; and spread it over the broiled shad. This butter is excellent for any kind of broiled fish.

CHAPTER III.

THIRD LESSON OF THE PLAIN COOKS' COURSE.

THIS lesson is devoted to such *entrées,* or side-dishes, as represent certain methods that may be applied to other ingredients, and may be considered typical dishes indicating the proper preparation of an extended range of stews, curries, *ragoûts, sautés,* and broils. The pupils should pay special attention to the two last dishes of the lesson, for they are seldom well done, even by professed cooks.

BLANQUETTE OF VEAL.

INGREDIENTS.

3 lbs. breast of veal - - - - - -	24 cents.
2 eggs - - - - - - - -	2 "
1 oz. butter - - - - - - -	2 "
Flour, vegetables and seasonings - -	5 "
Total - - - - -	33 cents.

(1.) Cut three pounds of the breast of veal in pieces two inches square, put them in enough cold water to cover them, with one saltspoonful of white pepper, one teaspoonful of salt, a *bouquet* of sweet herbs, half a carrot scraped, a turnip peeled, and an onion stuck with three cloves; bring slowly to a boil, skim carefully until no more scum rises, and cook gently for thirty or forty minutes until the veal is tender; then drain it, returning the broth to the fire, and washing the meat in cold water. (2.) Meantime make a white sauce by stirring together over the fire one ounce of butter and one ounce of flour, until they are smooth, then adding a pint and a half of the broth gradually; season with a little more salt and pepper if they are required, and quarter of a saltspoonful of grated nutmeg; when the sauce has boiled up well, stir into it with an egg-whip the yolks of two raw eggs, put in the meat and cook for five minutes, stirring occasionally; a few mushrooms are a great improvement to the *blanquette*; or it may be served with two tablespoonfuls of chopped parsley sprinkled over it after it is put on a hot platter.

CHICKEN CURRY.

INGREDIENTS.

3 lbs. chicken - - - - - -	36 cents.
½ " rice - - - - - - - -	5 "
Curry, butter, onion, flour and seasonings -	5 "
Total - - - - -	46 cents.

(1.) Choose a tender fowl, pluck it, carefully remove the pin-feathers, singe the bird over the flame of an alcohol lamp, or a few drops of alcohol poured on a plate and lighted; wipe it with a damp towel and see that it is properly drawn by slitting the skin at the back of the neck, and taking out the crop without tearing the skin of the breast; loosen the heart, liver and lungs by introducing the forefinger at the neck, and then draw them, with the entrails, from the vent. Unless you have broken the gall, or the entrails in drawing the bird, *do not wash it,* for this greatly impairs the flavor, and partly destroys the nourishing qualities of the flesh. Cut up the fowl as for a *fricassée,* in joints. (2.) Peel and slice an onion, and brown it slightly in the bottom of the saucepan with an ounce of butter; put in the chicken, and brown it completely. (3.) Then stir in an ounce of flour and brown that. (4.) Pour enough boiling water on the chicken to cover it, season it with a level teaspoonful of salt, and quarter of a saltspoonful of pepper; add a *bouquet* of herbs, and simmer it for an hour, or until the chicken is tender. (5.) Meantime boil the rice as directed in the receipt for Mulligatawny Soup, on page 72. (6.) When the chicken is nearly done add half an ounce of curry powder to it, cover it closely, and let it finish cooking. (7.) Serve the curry on a platter and the rice on a separate dish, or enclose the curry in a border of rice.

RAGOÛT OF BEEF.

INGREDIENTS.

2 lbs. round of beef - - - - - - -	24 cents.
2 oz. butter - - - - - - - -	4 "
Onions, carrot, flour and seasonings - -	5 "
Total - - - - - -	33 cents.

(1.) Cut the beef in pieces two inches square, and fry it brown in the butter. (2.) Stir in two ounces of flour, and let that brown. (3.) Cut a carrot in pieces an inch square; peel three medium-sized onions and make a *bouquet.* (4.) Add these ingredients to the beef, with a level tablespoonful of salt, quarter of a saltspoonful of pepper, and enough boiling water to cover them, and simmer till the beef is quite tender. (5.) Then take out the *bouquet,* see if the seasoning is high enough, and serve the *ragoût.* A tablespoonful of chopped parsley may be sprinkled over it, or some heart-shaped *croutons,* or slices of bread fried or browned in the oven, may be placed around it.

All *ragoûts* are brown stews, rather highly seasoned; the addition of a little nice table sauce often hightens their flavor agreeably.

MUTTON CHOPS, SAUTÉ.

INGREDIENTS.

1 lb. mutton chops - - - - - -	12 cents.
1 oz. butter - - - - - - -	2 "
Seasonings - - - - - - -	1 "
Total - - - - -	15 cents.

To be able to *sauter,* or "jump," a mutton chop is usually the mark of a good cook, because the meat requires to be very quickly and delicately cooked, to be rare without being raw, and to have all its juices preserved. The *sauté-*pan has two handles, which the cook grasps, and giving the pan a quick toss, turns the pieces of meat over. In the absence of such a utensil an ordinary frying-pan may be used, but it must be smooth and clean, and the meat must be turned over without piercing it with a fork.

Put an ounce of butter into a clean pan, heat it over the fire, put the chops into it, toss them quickly over the fire for about ten minutes, season them with salt and pepper, and serve them hot, garnished with parsley or cresses.

BROILED STEAK.

INGREDIENTS.

2 lbs. sirloin steak - - - - - - 30 cents.

How Meat should be Broiled.—In broiling all meats remember that the surface should not be cut or broken any more than is absolutely necessary; that the meat should be exposed to a clear, quick fire, close enough to sear the surface without burning, in order to confine all its juices; if it is approached slowly to a poor fire, or seasoned before it is cooked, it will be comparatively dry and tasteless, as both of these processes are useful only to extract and waste those precious juices which contain nearly all the nourishing properties of the meat.

To broil a beefsteak nicely, rub the bars of the gridiron smooth, and then grease them slightly; lay on a sirloin steak weighing about two pounds; put the gridiron over a hot fire; if the fire is not clear throw a handful of salt into it to clear it; broil the steak, turning it frequently so that it cannot burn, until it is done to the required degree. Do not cut into it to ascertain this, but test it by pressing the tips of the fingers upon it; if it springs up again after the pressure is removed it is done rare; if it remains heavy and solid it is well done; while it is being broiled prepare some *maître d'hotel* butter according to the receipt given on page 33; spread it over the steak after you have laid it on a hot dish, and garnish it with sliced lemon, parsley, or water cresses; or season it with pepper and salt, and spread it with

CHAPTER IV.

FOURTH LESSON OF THE PLAIN COOKS' COURSE.

THE large meat dishes which compose this lesson are intended to replace the too frequent roast-beef and boiled leg of mutton of ordinary family dinners, of which we all grow woefully tired, and which many mistresses would be glad to vary with new and equally substantial joints.

À *LA MODE* BEEF.

INGREDIENTS.

4 lbs. round of beef	48 cents.
¼ " fat pork	3 "
1 pt. button onions	5 "
1 " string beans	5 "
Carrots and turnips	5 "
Lemon, herbs, spice, seasonings	5 "
Oil and vinegar	5 "
Total	76 cents.

(1.) Prepare a *marinade*, or pickle, for the beef, as follows: cut in slices four ounces each of carrot and onion, two ounces of turnip and one ounce of leek; chop a quarter of an ounce each of parsley and celery, if in season; slice one lemon; add to these one level tablespoonful of salt, one saltspoonful of pepper, six cloves, four allspice, one inch of stick cinnamon, two blades of mace, one gill of oil, a pint of vinegar and one pint of water. Mix all these ingredients thoroughly, and use the *marinade* for beef, game or poultry, always keeping it in a cool place. (2.) *Daube* a piece of round of beef, by inserting, with the grain, pieces of larding pork, cut as long as the meat is thick, and about half an inch square, setting the strips of pork about two inches apart; this can be done either with a large larding needle, called a *sonde*, or by first making a hole with the carving-knife steel, and then thrusting the pork in with the fingers. (3.) Lay the beef in a deep bowl containing the *marinade*, or pickle, given in the previous paragraph, and let it stand from two to ten days in a cool place, turning it over every day. (4.) Then put it into a deep pot just large enough to hold it, together with the *marinade*, and turn it occasionally over the fire until it is nicely browned; cover it with hot stock or water, and simmer it gently four hours. (5.) When it has been cooking three hours, cut about four ounces each of carrots and turnips in the shape of olives; pare two dozen button onions, and cut one pint of string beans in pieces one inch long; put all these vegetables on the fire in boiling water, in separate vessels, each containing a teaspoonful of salt and half a saltspoonful of sugar, and let them boil till tender; then lay them in cold water to keep their color until ready to use them. (6.) When the meat is tender, take it up and keep it warm; strain the sauce in which it has been cooked, and stir it over the fire until it is thick enough to coat the spoon; drain the vegetables and let them scald up in the sauce, and pour all over the beef.

BREAST OF VEAL, STUFFED.

INGREDIENTS.

3 lbs. breast of veal - - - - - - -	24 cents.
¼ lb. salt pork - - - - - - - -	3 "
Bread, onion, and seasonings - - - - -	3 "
1 oz. butter - - - - - - - -	2 "
1 egg - - - - - - - - -	1 cent.
Total - - - - - -	33 cents.

(1.) Make what is called a pocket in a three-pound breast of veal, by cutting the flesh of the upper side free from the breast bones, taking care to leave three outer sides of the meat whole, so as to hold the stuffing. (2.) Prepare a bed of scraps of vegetables, herbs, and pork in the dripping pan. (3.) Stuff the veal with forcemeat made as below, sew it up, lay it on the vegetables, put four ounces of salt pork cut in thin slices on the top, season it with a teaspoonful of salt, and a quarter of a saltspoonful of pepper, and bake it in a moderate oven about one hour, till thoroughly done; serve it with a brown gravy made by rubbing the dripping in the pan, together with the vegetables, through a sieve, adding a little boiling water, and seasoning properly.

Forcemeat for Roast Veal.—(1.) Steep four ounces of bread in cold water. (2.) Chop one ounce of onion, and fry it yellow in one ounce of butter. (3.) Wring the bread dry in a towel, and add it to the butter and onion; season with one saltspoonful of salt, quarter of a saltspoonful each of pepper and powdered thyme, or mixed spices, and stir till scalding hot; then remove from the fire, stir in the yolk of one raw egg, and stuff the breast of veal with it. This is a very good stuffing for poultry or lamb.

CANTON OF LAMB.

INGREDIENTS.

4 lbs. shoulder of mutton	24 cents.
Carrots and turnips	3 "
Bread, onion, and seasonings	4 "
1 oz. butter	2 "
2 eggs	2 "
Total	35 cents.

(1.) Lay the shoulder, which should come from the market uncut, on the table with the inner part up; cut out the shoulder blade, and boil it to clean it thoroughly; then with a sharp, thin-bladed knife, cut out the first length of the fore leg bone and half the second, breaking it off midway between the first and second joints, and being careful not to mangle the meat, or cut through the skin. (2.) Trim off the end of the bone to look like a duck's bill. (3.) Stuff the shoulder with the following

oven about twenty minutes to each pound. (5.) Meantime prepare the garnish by paring the carrots and turnips, cutting them in little balls, boiling them only till tender in well-salted boiling water, and laying them in cold water to keep their color. (6.) When the *Canton* is done take it up on a hot dish, and keep it hot without drying, while the sauce is made. (7.) Make the sauce as directed in the preceding receipt for Breast of Veal. (8.) When ready to serve the *Canton*, heat the vegetables in the sauce, arrange them around the *Canton*; put the shoulder blade, which must be scraped after it is boiled, and have the broad end notched to resemble feathers, in the tail of the *Canton*, and serve it.

Sage and Onion Forcemeat.—Pare six ounces of onion, and bring them to a boil in three different waters; soak eight ounces of stale bread in tepid water, and wring it dry in a towel; scald ten sage leaves; when the onions are tender, which will be in about half an hour, chop them with the sage leaves, add them to the bread, with one ounce of butter, the yolks of two raw eggs, one level teaspoonful of salt, and half a saltspoonful of pepper; mix and use.

ROAST HAM WITH MADEIRA SAUCE.

INGREDIENTS.

7 lbs. ham - - - - - - -	98 cents.
Carrots and turnips - - - - - -	10 "
Onions, bread, and seasonings - - -	3 "
One gill Madeira Wine - - - - -	13 "
Total - - - - -	$1.24 cents.

(1.) Choose a ham by running a thin-bladed knife close to the bone, and if the odor which follows the cut is sweet the ham is good; soak it in cold water for twenty-four hours, changing the water once. (2.) Scrape it well, and trim off any ragged parts; put it in enough cold water to cover it, with an onion weighing about one ounce, stuck with six cloves, and a *bouquet*, and boil it four hours. (3.) Take it from the fire and let it cool in the pot-liquor. (4.) Then take it up carefully, remove the skin, dust it with sifted bread or cracker crumbs, and brown it in the oven. Serve it either hot or cold: if hot, send it to the table with a gravy boat full of Madeira sauce, and a vegetable garnish made as below.

Madeira Sauce.—Put over the fire in a thick saucepan one pint of any rich, brown gravy, seasoned with salt and pepper to taste; the seasoning must depend on the flavor of the gravy: when scalding hot add quarter of a pint of Madeira wine, and stir till the sauce is thick enough to coat the spoon; then strain through a fine sieve, and serve hot.

Vegetable Garnish.—(1.) Pare some large carrots and white turnips, cut them in the shape of olives, and cloves of garlic; boil them in well salted boiling water, and then put them into cold water to retain their color until wanted. (2.) Heat them in the sauce, and then arrange them around the ham in alternate groups, with a little of the sauce poured over them.

CHAPTER V.

FIFTH LESSON OF THE PLAIN COOKS' COURSE.

POULTRY constitutes the substantial dish of most of the winter Sunday dinners of American families in moderate circumstances, and its preparation is a good test of a cook's skill; if she can draw her birds without mangling or soiling them, and then prepare them so as to combine an inviting appearance with an enjoyable flavor, she proves that she has pursued her art with taste and discretion. Nothing is more disagreeable than to find that a nice looking dish of poultry or game lacks delicacy or cleanliness of flavor; so it will be well for pupils to attend carefully to the instructions given in this lesson.

ROAST DUCK WITH WATERCRESSES.

INGREDIENTS.

3 lb. duck - - - - - - - -	45 cents.
1 pt. water cresses - - - - - -	5 "
Salad sauce - - - - - - -	5 "
¼ lb. cheese - - - - - - -	4 "
1 oz. butter - - - - - - -	2 "
2 eggs - - - - - - - -	2 "
Bread, herbs and seasonings - - - -	3 "
Total - - - - -	66 cents.

(1.) Pluck, singe and draw a duck as directed in the receipt for Chicken Curry on page 115. (2.) Twist the tips of the wings back under the shoulders, stuff the bird with forcemeat made according to receipt given below. (3.) Bend the legs as far up toward the breast as possible, secure the thigh bones in that position by a trussing cord or skewer; then bring the legs down and fasten them close to the vent. (4.) Pound the breast bone down, first laying a towel over it to prevent bruising it. Lay a thin slice of salt pork over the breast to baste it until sufficient drippings run from the bird, and put it in a hot oven. (5.) Baste it frequently, browning it on all sides by turning it about in the pan; use a clean towel to turn it with, *but do not run a fork into it or you will waste its juices ;* when it is half done season it with two teaspoonfuls of salt and one saltspoonful of powdered herbs. (6.) When it has cooked about fifteen minutes to each pound, dish it and keep it hot while you make a gravy by adding half a pint of water to the drippings in the pan, first taking off a little of the superfluous fat, and thickening it if desired with a teaspoonful of flour mixed with two tablespoonfuls of cold water; strain this sauce and serve it in a sauce-boat. The same directions for drawing, trussing and roasting will apply to other poultry and game. (7.) When the sauce is ready, or when the duck is done, if no sauce is to be used, lay the bird on a dish with a border of watercresses, slightly dressed with a tablespoonful of vinegar, two of oil, and a little pepper and salt, and send it to the table.

Forcemeat for Roast Poultry.—(1.) Steep eight ounces of stale bread in cold water for five minutes, and wring it dry in a clean towel. (2.) Meantime chop fine four ounces each of fresh veal and pork, or use instead, eight ounces good sausage meat, or grate eight ounces of good, rather dry cheese. (3.) Fry one ounce of onion in one ounce of butter to a light yellow color; add the bread, meat or cheese, season with a saltspoonful of powdered herbs, a teaspoonful of salt, a saltspoonful of pepper, and two whole eggs; mix well and use.

ROAST WILD DUCKS.

INGREDIENTS.

1 pair Mallard ducks - - - - -	$1.00
¼ lb. salt pork - - - - - - .	3 cents.
Lemon and seasonings - - - -	3 "
Total - - - - -	$1.06

Prepare a pair of ducks as directed in above receipt; do not stuff them, but tie over the breasts slices of pork or bacon; roast fifteen minutes to the pound; serve with gravy in a boat and quarters of lemon on the same dish. Wild ducks are usually served underdone. Canvas Back Ducks should be rare.

BOILED FOWL WITH OYSTER SAUCE.

INGREDIENTS.

3 lb. fowl - - - - - - - -	38 cents.
1 qt. oysters - - - - - - -	25 "
1 oz. butter - - - - - - -	2 "
Flour, seasoning, and parsley - - -	1 cent.
Total - - - - - -	66 cents.

(1.) Prepare a fowl in accordance with receipt for preparing roast duck on page 123, but do not stuff it. (2.)

Put it into boiling water enough to cover it, with a level tablespoonful of salt to each quart of water; skim until clear, and boil slowly until tender, about fifteen minutes to a pound. (3.) When nearly done, make an oyster sauce as directed below, and serve it on the same dish with the fowl, sprinkling it with a teaspoonful of chopped parsley.

Oyster Sauce.—Blanch one quart of oysters by bringing them to a boil in their own liquor; drain them, saving the liquor; wash them in cold water and set them away from the fire until you are ready to use them; stir one ounce of butter and one ounce of flour together over the fire until they form a smooth paste; strain into them enough of the oyster liquor and that in which the chicken was boiled, to make a sauce as thick as melted butter; season with a teaspoonful of salt, quarter of a saltspoonful of white pepper, and the same of grated nutmeg; put in the oysters and serve.

BONED BIRDS.
INGREDIENTS.

2 pigeons - - - - - - - -	25 cents.
¼ lb. sausage meat - - - - - -	3 "
Egg and seasoning - - - - - -	2 "
Total - - - - - -	30 cents.

(1.) Lay a bird on its breast on the table, and with a sharp knife make a clean cut down the length of the back. (2.) Without cutting through the skin cut towards and disjoint the wings. (3.) Next cut towards and disjoint the thighs, leaving the wing and thigh bones in the flesh. (4.) Now proceed to cut all the flesh from the carcass of the bird, keeping it entire, and being careful not to cut through the skin. (5.) When it is all removed, lay it skin down upon the table, and take out the wing and thigh bones without cutting through the skin. (6.) Season the flesh lightly with salt, pepper, and a little spice, stuff it with a piece of highly-seasoned sausage meat mixed with one egg, and roll the flesh over the forcemeat to imitate the form of the bird.   (7.) It may be tied tightly in a clean cloth, boiled two hours with herbs and spices, and served cold with a garnish of jelly.   Or it may be baked in a pie and served hot or cold.

BROILED BIRDS.
INGREDIENTS.

2 pigeons - - - - - - - - 25 cents.

(1.) Pluck and wipe clean with a damp cloth.   (2.) Split down the back and carefully remove the entrails without breaking them.   (3.) Broil the birds over a moderate fire for twenty minutes. lay each on a slice of toast, and serve them with *maître d'hotel* butter or watercresses.

CHICKEN *FRICASSÉE.*
INGREDIENTS.

3 lb. fowl - - - - - - - -	38 cents.
Flour. vegetables, and seasonings - - -	5 "
1 oz. butter - - - - - - -	2 "
Total - - - - - -	45 cents.

(1.) Dress a chicken and cut it in joints as directed in the receipt for Chicken Curry, on page 115.   (2.) Put it over the fire in boiling water enough to cover it, skim it as often as any scum rises, add a desertspoonful of salt, half a dozen peppercorns, half a carrot peeled, an onion peeled and stuck with ten cloves and a *bouquet.*   (3.) Simmer slowly until the chicken is tender, about an hour, and then take it up to keep hot while the sauce is made.   (4.) Strain out the vegetables, and set the broth to boil; mix one ounce of butter and one ounce of flour together over the fire until they become a smooth paste; then gradually add a pint and a half of the broth, stirring the sauce with an egg-whip until it is quite smooth; season it to taste with salt and pepper, put the chicken into it to heat, and then dish it on a hot platter.   Half a can of mushrooms greatly improves the flavor of the *fricassée.*

CHAPTER VI.

SIXTH LESSON OF THE PLAIN COOKS' COURSE.

THE pupils taking this lesson are desired to study the introductory matter of Chapter VIII., of the First Artisan Course, beginning on page 45, before practising these receipts.

BOILED POTATOES.

INGREDIENTS.

1 qt. potatoes - - - - - - -	3 cents.
Salt - - - - - - - - - -	1 cent.
Total - - - - - -	4 cents.

Boil according to receipt given on page 46.

POTATO *CROQUETTES*

INGREDIENTS.

1 qt. potatoes - - - - - - -	3 cents.
1 oz. butter - - - - - - -	2 "
3 eggs - - - - - - - -	3 "
Bread crumbs, seasonings and lard - -	5 "
Total - - - - -	13 cents.

(1.) Peel and boil the potatoes according to receipt given on page 46. (2.) Mash them through a fine colander, mix with them the butter and two yolks, and season them with salt to taste, and quarter of a saltspoonful each of white pepper and nutmeg. (3.) Dust the table thickly with bread crumbs, and beat up an egg with a tablespoonful of water. (4.) Dip the hands in cold water, form the potatoes in little rolls like corks, and toss them upon the cracker dust. (5.) Roll them first in the cracker dust, turning them lightly under the palm of the hand, dip them into the beaten egg, but do not wash off the cracker dust, and then roll them into shape. (6.) Fry them golden brown in smoking hot fat, lay them on brown paper a moment to free them from grease, and then serve them in a little pile on a napkin, or use them to garnish roast chicken or some meat dish.

KENTUCKY POTATOES.

INGREDIENTS.

1 qt. potatoes	3 cents.
½ pt. cream	10 "
Seasonings and butter	2 "
Total	15 cents.

Peel the potatoes, slice them, put them in layers in a baking dish with a little cream, season them with pepper, salt and nutmeg, and bake them an hour in a quick oven. Serve them hot.

STUFFED POTATOES.

INGREDIENTS.

Potatoes, cheese, butter, and seasonings	12 cents.

(1.) Wash the potatoes with a brush, and bake them only until they begin to soften, not more than half an hour. (2.) Cut off one end, scoop out the inside with a teaspoon into a saucepan containing two ounces of butter, one saltspoonful of white pepper, one teaspoonful of salt, and two ounces of grated Parmesan cheese; stir all these ingredients over the fire until they are scalding hot. (3.) Then fill the potato skins with the mixture, put on the ends, press the potatoes gently in shape, finish baking them in the oven, and serve them on a hot dish covered with a napkin, the potatoes being laid on the napkin. Observe never to cover a baked potato unless you want it to be heavy and moist.

BOILED GREEN PEAS.

INGREDIENTS.

½ peck of green peas	15 cents.
1 oz. butter	2 "
Seasonings and mint	3 "
Total	20 cents.

(1.) Put a saucepan two thirds full of water over the fire to boil, adding a tablespoonful of salt to every quart of water. (2.) Take the bruised or decayed pods from among the peas, wash the good ones in plenty of cold water, drain, and shell them. (3.) Throw the peas into the boiling water, with two sprigs of green mint, and boil them only until tender. Then drain them, and put them into cold water until wanted to prepare for the table. The action of the salt in boiling, and of the cold water in which the peas are subsequently placed, is to harden the surface sufficiently to prevent the escape of the coloring matter, and so to preserve the bright green hue of the vegetables. (4.) Five minutes before they are to be sent to the table they should be warmed quickly with a little butter, pepper, and salt, or with any sauce which is desired to dress them.

STEWED TURNIPS WITH *BÉCHAMEL* SAUCE.

INGREDIENTS.

1 qt. turnips	3 cents.
1 oz. butter	2 "
Flour, milk, and seasonings	2 "
Total	.7 cents.

(1.) Pare the turnips, cut them in half inch dice, and boil them until they begin to grow soft in boiling water with a tablespoonful of salt. (2.) Meantime make a *Béchamel* sauce as follows: stir together over the fire one ounce each of butter and flour until they bubble, gradually add half a pint of boiling water and a gill of milk, season with a level teaspoonful of salt, and quarter of a saltspoonful each of white pepper and nutmeg. (3.) Drain the turnips from the boiling water, put them into the sauce, simmer them until tender, and serve them in the sauce.

CHAPTER VII.

SEVENTH LESSON OF THE PLAIN COOKS' COURSE.

THE pupil is referred to page 40 for directions for choosing and boiling macaroni.

MACARONI WITH PARMESAN CHEESE.

INGREDIENTS.

½ lb. macaroni	8 cents.
1 oz. butter	2 "
1 " Parmesan cheese	2 "
Flour and seasonings	1 cent.
Total	13 cents.

(1.) Boil the macaroni as already directed. (2.) Make a white sauce by stirring together over the fire one ounce each of butter and flour until they bubble, adding half a pint of boiling water, and seasoning with a level teaspoonful of salt, and quarter of a saltspoonful each of pepper and nutmeg. (3.) After draining the macaroni from the cold water, put it into the sauce with an ounce of grated Parmesan cheese, stir it until thoroughly heated, and then serve it hot.

MACARONI À *L'ITALIENNE.*

INGREDIENTS.

½ lb. macaroni	8 cents.
1 oz. butter	2 "
1 " Parmesan cheese	2 "
Tomato sauce	5 "
Total	17 cents.

(1.) Boil the macaroni as directed. (2.) Make a Tomato Sauce as directed on page 74. (3.) Put the macaroni in a baking dish which can be sent to the table, in alternate layers with the Parmesan cheese and Tomato Sauce, brown

MACARONI À *LA MILANAISE.*

INGREDIENTS.

½ lb. macaroni	8 cents.
1 oz. butter	2 "
Tomato sauce	5 "
Chicken or tongue	10 "
Total	25 cents.

(1.) Boil the macaroni as already directed. (2.) Make a Tomato Sauce according to the receipt on page 74. (3.) Finish the dish as for the preceding dish, omitting the Parmesan cheese, and adding some cold chicken or tongue cut in dice, and enough gravy to moisten it.

CHAPTER VIII.

EIGHTH LESSON OF THE PLAIN COOKS' COURSE.

THE preparation of eggs is quite fully treated in Chapter IV. of the First Artisan Course, beginning on page 34, and pupils are referred to it for preliminary information. Several of the receipts given there are repeated here, on account of their importance to all classes of cooks.

POACHED EGGS.

See page 35 for receipt.

SCRAMBLED EGGS.

INGREDIENTS.

3 eggs	3 cents.
½ oz. butter	1 cent.
Seasonings	1 "
Total	5 cents.

Heat a clean frying pan, put the butter into it, then the eggs, broken into separate saucers, season lightly with salt and pepper, and stir briskly until the eggs are cooked to the proper degree. Serve them on a hot dish.

BAKED EGGS.

INGREDIENTS.

6 eggs - - - - - - - - -	6 cents.
½ oz. butter - - - - - - -	1 cent.
Seasonings - - - - - - - -	1 "
	——
Total - - - - -	8 cents.

Break the eggs separately, put them into a dish which can be sent to the table, season them lightly with pepper and salt, dot the surface with bits of butter, and bake the eggs until they are of the required consistency. Serve them hot.

HAM OMELETTE.

INGREDIENTS.

3 eggs - - - - - - - - -	3 cents.
2 oz. cooked ham - - - - - - -	4 "
Butter and seasonings - - - - -	1 cent.
	——
Total - - - - -	8 cents.

(1.) Chop the ham quite fine. (2.) Heat the omelette pan, put in a bit of butter as large as a walnut; then the eggs broken separately, and the ham, and finish as directed on page 36, for omelette.

OYSTER OMELETTE.

INGREDIENTS.

3 eggs - - - - - - - - -	3 cents.
Oysters - - - - - - - -	3 "
Butter and seasonings - - - - -	1 cent.
	——
Total - - - - -	7 cents.

(1.) Put a gill of oysters over the fire to come to a boil in their own liquor. (2.) When they just boil, drain them, put them in the middle of a plain omelette, fold it over and finish it as directed on page 36.

FINE HERBS OMELETTE.

INGREDIENTS.

3 eggs - - - - - - - - -	3 cents.
Herbs, butter and seasonings - - - -	5 "
	——

(1.) Chop fine a teaspoonful each of parsley, mushrooms, and any green herbs in season, and mix them with an omelette made as directed on page 36.

OMELETTE WITH PRESERVES.
INGREDIENTS.

3 eggs	3 cents.
Preserves	5 "
Butter and sugar	1 cent.
Total	9 cents.

Make an omelette as directed on page 36, put two table-spoonfuls of preserves into the middle, and finish it like the sweet omelette in the receipt on page 37.

CHAPTER IX.
NINTH LESSON OF THE PLAIN COOKS' COURSE.

THIS lesson is a repetition of the fourth lesson of the First Artisan Course, given on page 37, and so we refer the pupils to that part of the book for the directions.

CHAPTER X.
TENTH LESSON OF THE PLAIN COOKS' COURSE.

THIS lesson is devoted to good, but rather plain cake and pastry; and if pupils will take care to learn these receipts thoroughly, they will find but little difficulty in following out the more intricate methods of the next course.

FRUIT CAKE.
INGREDIENTS.

6 oz. sugar	5 cents.
6 " flour	2 "
2 " butter	4 "
5 eggs	5 "

¼ lb. raisins	-	-	-	-	-	-	-	3 cents.
¼ " currants	-	-	-	-	-	-	-	3 "
2 oz. citron	-	-	-	-	-	-	-	4 "
Total	-	-	-	-				26 cents.

(1.) Set two ounces of butter near enough to the fire to grow soft, without becoming oily. (2.) Line a cake pan with buttered paper. (3.) Seed the raisins, wash and dry the currants, and cut the citron in small, thin slices. (4.) Beat the sugar and two of the eggs to a cream; add two more eggs, and beat two minutes; then add the remaining egg, and beat two minutes more. (5.) Sift in the flour and beat the mixture smooth; then add the butter and fruit, beat one minute, and put into the pan. Bake in a moderate oven for about half an hour. Be careful not to burn the cake. Test it by running a clean broom straw into it when it seems nearly done; if the straw comes out clean the cake is sufficiently baked.

POUND CAKE.

INGREDIENTS.

½ lb. flour	-	-	-	-	-	-	-	2 cents.
½ " sugar	-	-	-	-	-	-	-	6 "
¼ " butter	-	-	-	-	-	-	-	8 "
6 eggs	-	-	-	-	-	-	-	6 "
Total	-	-	-	-				22 cents.

(1.) Line a cake pan with buttered paper. (2.) Put the butter, sugar, and one egg into a bowl and beat them with the hand to a cream; then add the rest of the eggs, one at a time, beating the cake with the hand two minutes after each egg is added. (3.) Flavor with twenty drops of Vanilla essence. (4.) Sift in the flour, beat smooth, put into the cake pan and bake about half an hour in a moderate oven. Test the cake with a clean broom straw.

The practice of beating the cake with the hand is in vogue with many excellent pastry cooks; extreme cleanliness is indispensable when this method is employed. The above receipt is that of one of the best *chefs* of the New York School of Cookery.

SPONGE CAKE.

INGREDIENTS.

6 oz. flour	2 cents.
6 " sugar	5 "
6 eggs	6 ".
Lemon rind	1 cent.
Total	14 cents.

(1.) Line a cake pan with buttered paper. (2.) Grate the yellow rind of half a lemon. (3.) Put the sugar and two eggs into a bowl, and beat them for two minutes; add another egg and beat two minutes; then add three yolks and beat three minutes. (4.) Beat the whites of three eggs to a stiff froth. (5.) Sift the flour into the cake, mix it smooth, add the whites, pour the cake into the buttered pan, and bake it in a moderate oven for about half an hour. Test the cake with a clean broom straw.

CRANBERRY PIE.

INGREDIENTS.

½ lb. flour	2 cents.
4 oz. butter	8 "
½ lb. sugar	5 "
1 qt. cranberries	10 "
Total	25 cents.

(1.) Pick over the berries, wash them in cold water, set them over the fire with enough cold water to cover them, and simmer them gently for fifteen minutes; add the sugar and simmer the berries until they are quite soft. Then rub them through a sieve with a wooden spoon, and cool them. (2.) Make a plain paste as directed in the receipt for Apple Tarts, on page 63; line a pie plate with it, building a rim of paste around the edge; fill with cranberry sauce, made as above, put some strips of paste across the top in diamond-shaped figures, and bake in a moderate oven.

APPLE PIE.
INGREDIENTS.

½ lb. flour - - - - - - - -	2 cents.
4 oz. butter - - - - - - - - -	8 "
1 qt. apples - - - - - - - - -	5 "
¼ lb. sugar - - - - - - - - -	3 "
Lemon - - - - - - - - -	1 cent.
Total - - - - -	19 cents.

(1.) The apples should be pared, cored, and sliced; sometimes they are stewed until tender with the sugar, and the yellow rind of half a lemon; and sometimes are simply sliced thin and baked in the pie. (2.) Line a pie plate with pastry made as directed on page 63, put the apples into it, cover it with pastry, and bake it brown in a moderate oven. Just before it is done dust it with powdered sugar, and return it to the oven for five minutes to glaze the surface.

CREAM *MÉRINGUE* PIE.
INGREDIENTS.

¼ lb. flour - - - - - - -	1 cent.
1 oz. corn-starch - - - - - - -	1 "
2 " sugar - - - - - - -	4 cents.
2 " butter - - - - - - - -	4 "
6 eggs - - - - - - - -	6 "
½ pt. milk - - - - - - - -	2 "
Total - - - - -	18 cents.

(1.) Mix together in a saucepan one ounce of corn-starch, two ounces of sugar, the yolks of two eggs, a tea-spoonful of Vanilla essence, and about half a pint of milk; put them over the fire, and stir them constantly until they have boiled about five minutes. (2.) Line a pie-plate with pastry made as directed on page 63, fill it with the cream, made as above, bake it in a moderate oven. (3.) Meantime beat the whites of four eggs to a stiff froth, and mix gently into it three ounces of powdered sugar. (4.) When the pie is done, spread the *méringue* on it, and set it in a moderate oven only long enough to just color the top. It

CHAPTER XI.

ELEVENTH LESSON OF THE PLAIN COOKS' COURSE.

THIS lesson treats of the dishes suitable for sick persons which are generally ordered by physicians in illness; and if studied in connection with Chapter XII, of the First Artisan Course, beginning on page 58, will give a fair variety of wholesome and nourishing dishes. It must always be remembered that no food or drink of any kind should be given in cases of dangerous illness, except under the direction of the doctor in attendance upon the patient.

MUTTON BROTH.

INGREDIENTS.

2 lbs. neck of mutton - - - - -	12 cents.
2 oz. pearl barley - - - - - -	2 "
Seasonings - - - - - - -	1 cent.
Total - - - - -	15 cents.

(1.) Pick over the barley, wash it well in cold water, and let it soak in hot water until wanted. (2.) Cut the meat from a lean neck of mutton, in small dice, put it over the fire in two quarts of cold water, and bring it slowly to a boil, skimming it carefully until it is quite clear. (2.) Add the barley to the broth, season it with a teaspoonful of salt, and let it simmer gently for two hours, until the barley is soft. (3.) If the invalid is not strong enough to eat the meat, remove it before serving the broth. Follow the advice of the physician upon this point, and in regard to seasoning the broth.

CHICKEN BROTH.

INGREDIENTS.

3 lbs. chicken - - - - - -	38 cents.
2 oz. rice and seasonings - - - - -	2 "
Total - - - -	40 cents.

(1.) Dress a chicken as directed for *fricassée*, on page 84, carefully removing every particle of fat; put it over the fire in three quarts of cold water and bring slowly to a boil, skimming it until it is clear. Pick over and wash the rice in cold water, add it to the broth with a teaspoonful of salt, and simmer it slowly for two hours. Serve the chicken in the broth if the patient is allowed by the doctor to eat a little of it. (2.) Make the broth as directed above, omitting the rice, strain it at the end of two hours, and serve it with Graham crackers.

BEEF TEA.

Use the directions for making Beef Tea, given on page 60.

BEEFSTEAK JUICE.

INGREDIENTS.

1 lb. tender sirloin steak	14 cents.
Toast	1 cent.
Total	15 cents.

Broil a juicy steak as directed on page 117; lay it on a hot platter, cut it in pieces, press out the juice, and pour it over a slice of toast, made as directed on page 58. Be very careful not to season the steak, except with a little salt, or use butter with the toast, unless both are allowed by the physician.

OATMEAL PORRIDGE.

INGREDIENTS.

¼ lb. oatmeal	2 cents.
Sugar, milk, and salt	3 "
Total	5 cents.

Stir the oatmeal into one quart of boiling water, with one teaspoonful of salt; let it boil gently one hour, stirring it occasionally to prevent burning. Use it either hot or cold with a little sugar and milk, if permitted by the phy-

CHOCOLATE.

INGREDIENTS.

1 oz. chocolate - - - - - - - -	2 cents.
½ pt. milk - - - - - - - - -	2 "
1 oz. sugar - - - - - - - - -	1 cent.
Total - - - - - - -	5 cents.

Grate one ounce of sweet chocolate, mix it smooth with three tablespoonfuls of cold milk, and stir it with the rest of the half pint of milk, which should be boiling. After adding the chocolate stir the beverage over the fire until all the grains are dissolved in the milk; then sweeten it and serve it.

ICELAND MOSS *BLANC-MANGE.*

INGREDIENTS.

½ oz. Iceland moss - - - - - -	3 cents.
1 qt. milk - - - - - - - -	8 "
Sugar and lemon - - - - - -	2 "
Total - - - - - -	13 cents.

(1.) Soak the moss over night in enough cold water to well cover it. (2.) Drain it, put it over the fire with enough cold milk to cover it, and simmer it gently for one hour, with the yellow rind of half a lemon. (3.) Sweeten it to taste, strain it through a fine sieve, and cool it in a mould. Serve it with milk and sugar.

CHAPTER XII.

TWELFTH LESSON OF THE PLAIN COOKS' COURSE.

VERY few cooks, even among professionals, understand how to cook properly for children. It is the common custom in this country for the little ones to be served at the same table and from the same dishes that are provided for the adults of the family. This is all wrong, but in this place we cannot discuss the reasons; we can only give directions for preparing a few simple and palatable dishes which are perfectly wholesome for children.

BAKED POTATOES.

INGREDIENTS.

1 qt. potatoes - - - - - - -	3 cents.
Butter and salt - - - - - - -	5 "
Total - - - - -	8 cents.

Choose smooth, even-sized potatoes, wash them well with plenty of cold water, and a brush or cloth, and put them into a quick oven to bake; they will cook in from twenty to thirty-five minutes, according to variety and ripeness; they are done when they yield easily to pressure between the fingers. They should be served the moment they are properly cooked, and should never be covered; if they stand after they are done they will become heavy, and if they are covered they will be watery. They should be eaten with a little butter and salt.

BROILED CHOPS.

INGREDIENTS.

1 lb. mutton chops - - - - -	12 cents.
½ oz. butter and salt - - - - -	1 cent.
Total - - - - -	13 cents.

Carefully study the directions for broiling meat, given on page 117, and cook the chops in accordance with them, first trimming off all superfluous fat. Put them on a hot dish, season them lightly with a little butter, pepper and salt, and serve them with baked potatoes.

BAKED APPLES.

INGREDIENTS.

1 qt. apples - - - - - - - -	5 cents.
3 oz. sugar - - - - - - - -	2 "
Spice and butter - - - - - -	1 cent.
Total - - - - -	8 cents.

Wash the fruit, remove the cores without breaking the

apples, and set them in a pan just large enough to hold
them; fill the cores with sugar, and put a very little spice
and a small bit of butter on each apple; put half a cup of
hot water in the pan, and bake the apples until tender in
a moderate oven. Do not break them in changing them
into the dish in which they are to go to the table; pour the
juice in the pan over them, and serve them either hot or
cold.

TAPIOCA PUDDING.

INGREDIENTS.

¼ lb. tapioca	3 cents.
4 oz. sugar	3 "
3 eggs	3 "
1½ pts. milk	6 "
Total	15 cents.

(1.) Put the tapioca over the fire in a pint of milk, and
let it heat and soften gradually, stirring it often enough to
prevent burning. (2.) When the tapioca is soft, beat together the eggs and sugar, add the cold milk and the tapioca, and bake the pudding about half an hour in a moderate oven. Use either hot or cold.

APPLES AND RICE.

INGREDIENTS.

1 qt. apples	5 cents.
½ lb. rice	5 "
¼ " sugar	3 "
Total	13 cents.

(1.) Pare, halve, and core the apples, put them over the
fire with the sugar and enough cold water to cover them,
and stew them gently only until tender, but do not let them
break. (2.) Meantime pick over the rice, wash it in cold
water, put it into plenty of boiling water containing a tablespoonful of salt, and boil it rapidly until tender. (3.)
Shake the rice out on a dish, form it into a mound with a
couple of forks, handling it lightly and quickly; lay the

apples on it and pour over them the syrup in which they were cooked.

APPLE CUSTARDS.

INGREDIENTS.

1 qt. apples - - - - - - -	5 cents.
6 oz. sugar - - - - - - - -	5 "
1 qt. milk - - - - - - - -	8 "
5 eggs . - - - - - - - -	5 "
Total - - - - -	23 cents.

Pare and core six apples, set them in a pan with a very little water, and stew them until tender; then put them in a pudding dish without breaking, fill the centers with sugar, and pour over them a custard made according to the receipt on page 72, of a quart of milk, five eggs, four ounces of sugar, and a very little nutmeg; set the pudding-dish in a baking-pan half full of water, and bake it about half an hour. Serve it either hot or cold at the noon dinner.

PART IV.

—

CHAPTER I.

FIRST LESSON OF THE LADIES' COURSE.

THIS course of lessons has been carefully adapted for the use of those ladies who desire to combine some of the elegancies of artistic cookery with those economical interests which it is the duty of every housewife to study. The first reading of the bills of fare may seem to indicate the necessity for the possession of considerable culinary skill on the part of our pupils; but four years' experience has proven that any intelligent lady who understands the simpler dishes of the preceding courses, need not hesitate to attempt the making of those included in the present one. There have been too many mysteries attached to culinary proficiency, and it has been our satisfaction to make most of them plain to our pupils; if they will only take pains to master the instruction we have already given in this book, they may begin this course of lessons with perfect confidence in their ability to surmount its seeming difficulties.

We believe that no explanation is needed of the foreign character of many of the dishes, because Americans are beginning to comprehend the economical and gastronomical advantages of European Cookery; we have not attempted to Anglicize the names, because in most instances they are indicative of the peculiarities of the different dishes.

—

Consommé à la Royale.
Baked Carp with Spanish Sauce.
Potatoes à la Royale.
Breast of Lamb with Béchamel Sauce.
Cauliflower au gratin.
Roast Beef.
Salade à la Romaine.
Apple Méringues.

CONSOMMÉ À LA ROYALE.

INGREDIENTS.

Consommé	31 cents.
8 eggs	8 "
Seasonings	1 cent.
Total	40 cents.

(1.) Make a *consommé* as directed on page 106, taking care that it is clear and bright, of a delicate straw color, and very lightly seasoned. (2.) Make a *Royale* paste as follows: beat together the yolks of eight eggs, half a pint of *consommé*, and quarter of a saltspoonful each of salt and grated nutmeg. Put this custard into a buttered, shallow mould, set the mould into a pan containing warm water enough to reach half way up its sides, cover it, and put it over a very slow fire, or into a moderate oven, until the custard is firm. Then cool it, turn it from the mould, cut it in long diamonds, in strips an inch long and quarter of an inch wide, or in half inch dice, and serve it in the hot *consommé*.

BAKED CARP WITH SPANISH SAUCE.

INGREDIENTS.

3 lbs. carp	45 cents.
Materials for Sauce	15 "
Total	60 cents.

(1.) Make a Spanish Sauce as directed on page 71, adding to it a teaspoonful of sugar, and using good stock instead of water to boil the vegetables in. (2.) Dress a carp, which is a species of large, gold-colored fish of rather dry flesh, for baking; lay it in a dripping pan on a few scraps of vegetables, season it with a teaspoonful of salt and half a saltspoonful of pepper, pour over it a gill of stock or gravy, and bake it half an hour. (3.) Strain a little of the Spanish Sauce on a dish, lay the fish in it without breaking, lay the potatoes *à la Royale* around it on the dish; garnish it with parsley, and send it to the table with more of the Sauce in a sauce boat.

POTATOES À LA ROYALE.
INGREDIENTS.

1 qt. potatoes - - - - - - - 3 cents.

Pare some large, sound potatoes, cut them in balls about three quarters of an inch in diameter, brown them in the oven, and use them with the Baked Carp.

BREAST OF LAMB WITH *BÉCHAMEL* SAUCE.
INGREDIENTS.

3 lbs. breast of lamb - - - - -	24 cents.
¼ " pork - - - - - -	3 "
1 oz. butter - - - - - -	2 "
1 lemon - - - - - - -	2 "
Vegetables and seasonings - - - -	2 "
Materials for sauce - - - - -	4 "
Total - - - - -	37 cents.

(1.) Bone a breast of lamb by cutting from the under part, and taking care not to mangle the flesh. (2.) Roll it up compactly and secure it with a stout cord. (3.) Put it into a saucepan with the butter, the pork sliced and laid in the bottom of the pan, the bones of the lamb and a few scraps of soup vegetables, laying the meat on the other ingredients, and squeezing the juice of one lemon over it. Cover it with hot water, season it with a teaspoonful of salt, a blade of mace, four pepper corns, and four cloves; lay a cloth over the saucepan, put on the cover, and simmer it gently for one hour, or until the lamb is tender. (4.) Make a *Béchamel* Sauce as directed on page 129, put a little of it on a dish, and lay the lamb on it, after removing the strings; pour some more *Béchamel* over it, and serve it hot.

CAULIFLOWER *AU GRATIN.*

INGREDIENTS.

1 cauliflower - - - - - - -	15 cents.
Béchamel sauce - - - - - - -	2 "
1 oz. Parmesan cheese - - - - -	2 "
Butter, bread crumbs and seasonings - -	2 "
Total - - - - -	21 cents.

(1.) Trim a cauliflower, and lay it top down in cold, salted water for one hour, to freshen it, and free it from insects. (2.) Put it to boil in boiling water enough to cover it, with a tablespoonful of salt, and boil it only until tender, about twenty minutes. (3.) Take it up without breaking, lay it on a *gratin* dish, or one that can be sent to the table, pour a gill of *Béchamel* sauce over it, dust it with sifted bread crumbs and grated Parmesan, dot it over with bits of butter, and brown it quickly. Serve it hot.

ROAST BEEF.

INGREDIENTS.

6 lbs. ribs of beef - - - - - -	96 cents.
Vegetables, flour, and seasonings - - -	4 "
Total - - - - -	$1.00

(1.) Have ribs of prime beef prepared by the butcher for roasting, all the bones being taken out if it is desirable to carve a clean slice off the top; secure it in place with stout twine; do not use skewers, as the unnecessary holes they make permit the meat-juices to escape. (2.) Lay it in the dripping pan on a bed of the following vegetables, cut in small pieces; one small onion, half a carrot, half a turnip, three sprigs of parsley, one sprig of thyme, and three bay leaves; *do not put any water in the dripping pan;* its temperature can not rise to a degree equal in heat to that of the fat outside of the beef, and can not assist in its cooking, but serves only to lower the temperature of the meat, where it touches it, and consequently to soften the surface and extract the juices. (3.) *Do not season it until the surface is partly carbonized by the heat,* as salt applied to the cut fibers draws out their juices. If you use a roasting oven before the fire, the meat should be similarly prepared by tying in place and it should be put on the spit carefully; sufficient drippings for basting will flow from it, and it should be seasoned when half done; when entirely done, which will be in from fifteen to twenty minutes to each pound of meat, the joint should be kept hot until served, but should be served as soon as possible to be good. (4.) When gravy is made, half a pint of hot water should be put into the dripping pan, after the vegetables have been removed, and the gravy should be boiled briskly for a few minutes, until it is thick enough, and seasoned to suit the palate of the family; some persons thicken it with a teaspoonful of flour, which should be mixed with a gill of cold water before it is stirred into the gravy.

SALADE À LA ROMAINE.

INGREDIENTS.

1 head of lettuce - - - - - -	5 cents.
Materials for *Romaine* dressing - - - - 5	"
Total - - - - -	10 cents.

(1.) Freshen a head of lettuce as directed on page 49. (2.) Tear the leaves apart with the fingers, but do not cut them, as that impairs their crispness and flavor; arrange the salad in a dish and pour over it the dressing made as follows. (3.) Grate half an ounce of onion, mix it with a teaspoonful of lemon juice, a saltspoonful each of salt and powdered sugar, a level saltspoonful each of white pepper and dry mustard, and then gradually stir into these ingredients three tablespoonfuls of oil and one of vinegar.

APPLE *MÉRINGUES.*

INGREDIENTS.

1 qt. small apples	5 cents.
¼ lb. powdered sugar	3 "
4 eggs	4 "
Butter and spice	1 cent.
Total	13 cents.

(1.) Pare the apples, remove the cores without breaking them, set them on a dish that can be sent to the table, fill them with sugar, lay a bit of butter and a very little spice on each one, and bake them just tender, but do not let them break. (2.) Beat the whites of four eggs to a stiff froth, stir three ounces of powdered sugar lightly into it, put it over the apples, rounding it well; just color it in a moderate oven. Use either hot or cold. The *méringue* will fall a little as it cools.

CHAPTER II.

SECOND LESSON OF THE LADIES' COURSE.

Purée of Salmon.
Filets of Bass à la Royale.
Julienne Potatoes.
Fricandeau of Veal.
Rizotta à la Milanaise.
Roast Ham with Champagne Sauce.
Celery à la Cardinale.
Crème Reversé.

PURÉE OF SALMON.

INGREDIENTS.

1 lb. salmon	25 cents.
2 qts. milk	16 "
2 oz. butter	4 "
Flour and seasonings	1 "
Total	46 cents.

(1.) Put the salmon to boil in boiling water with a level tablespoonful of salt to each quart of water; boil it fifteen minutes, then take it up, cool it, remove the skin and bones, and rub it through a sieve with a wooden spoon. (2.) Make a white soup as follows: put two quarts of milk over the fire to boil; mix together over the fire two ounces each of butter and flour until they begin to bubble, then gradually add the boiling milk; season the soup with a level teaspoonful of salt, and quarter of a saltspoonful each of white pepper and nutmeg, and let it come to a boil. (3.) As soon as the soup boils, stir the salmon *purée* into it, and serve it at once.

FILETS OF BASS *À LA ROYALE.*

INGREDIENTS.

2 lbs. bass - - - - - - - -	30 cents.
Materials for *marinade* - - - - -	5 "
Materials for batter - - - - -	5 "
Prawns and parsley - - - - - -	7 "
Lard for frying - - - - - -	3 "
Total - - - - - -	50 cents.

(1.) Prepare the *filets* of bass as directed for the *filets* of flounder on page 32; lay them for three or four hours in the following *marinade* or pickle, turning them over every twenty minutes. (2.) Make the *marinade* by mixing in a plate two tablespoonfuls each of oil and vinegar, a level teaspoonful of salt, and half a saltspoonful of pepper, and lay the *filets* in it. (3.) Make a frying batter as directed on page 51. Drop the *filets* into the batter, lift them out with a fork, and fry them golden brown in smoking hot fat. Lay them on brown paper for a moment to free them from fat, and serve them on a napkin, garnished with parsley and prawns.

JULIENNE POTATOES.

INGREDIENTS.

1 qt. potatoes - - - - - - -	3 cents.
Lard for frying - - - - - - -	3 "
Total - - - - -	6 cents.

(1.) Pare the potatoes, slice them thin with a crimping knife, and lay them in well-salted cold water for at least an hour. (2.) Wash them through two waters, and dry them on a clean towel. (3.) Fry them golden brown in smoking hot fat, lay them on brown paper a moment to free them from fat, and serve them hot.

FRICANDEAU OF VEAL.

INGREDIENTS.

2 lbs. veal - - - - - - - -	40 cents.
¼ lb. larding pork - - - - - -	5 "
Vegetables and seasonings - - - -	2 "
½ peck spinach - - - - - - -	20 "
Total - - - - -	67 cents.

(1.) Choose a thick, compact slice of veal from about the middle of the leg, and lard it as follows: cut the pork in strips an eighth of an inch thick, and two inches long; lay the veal on a folded towel on the left hand; put a strip of pork in the larding needle, and take a stitch with it in the upper surface of the veal; as you draw the needle out the strip of pork, or lardoon, will remain in the meat. Insert the lardoons in even rows along the cutlet, making as many rows as its width will permit. (2.) Put into a pan some scraps of vegetables and the trimmings of pork; lay the cutlet on them and cook it in a moderate oven, taking care not to let it burn, and seasoning it when half done, with white pepper and salt. (3.) Meantime dress the spinach as directed on page 109; just when the veal is done, warm the spinach with a tablespoonful of butter and a saltspoonful of salt; or take up the meat and keep it hot while you strain its gravy, and warm the spinach in it. (4.) Arrange the *purée* of spinach neatly on a dish, lay the *fricandeau* on the spinach and serve it hot.

RIZOTTA À LA MILANAISE.

INGREDIENTS.

½ lb. rice - - - - - - - -	5 cents.
1 oz. butter - - - - - - - -	2 "

½ pt. gravy - - - - - - - -	5 cents.
Cold tongue - - - - - - - - -	5 "
Fat for frying - - - - - - -	3 "
Total - - - - - -	20 cents.

There are several methods of cooking rice after the *Milanaise* style, any of which makes a delicious dish. (1.) Fry half a pound of dry, uncooked rice, with one ounce of chopped onion in a tablespoonful of butter, stirring it constantly until brown; then add a pint of gravy, season with salt, pepper, and cayenne, and stew fifteen or twenty minutes until the rice is tender. (2.) Boil the rice until tender in boiling water, and then drain it dry; fry it golden brown in plenty of smoking-hot fat, and then pour gravy over it. Cooked in either way and mixed with cold tongue, shredded apart with two forks, it is sometimes well shaken down in a buttered mould, heated in the oven, and turned out before serving. (3.) Cook as for number 2, substituting cold chicken for the tongue. The dish is excellent in any of these forms.

ROAST HAM WITH CHAMPAGNE SAUCE.
INGREDIENTS.

7 lb. ham - - - - - - -	98 cents.
Onions, bread crumbs and seasonings - -	3 "
½ pt. American champagne - - - -	25 "
Total - - - -	$1.26

(1.) Cook the ham as directed on page 121. (2.) Make the sauce as directed for Madeira Sauce, on page 122, substituting half a pint of native Champagne for the Madeira wine. Serve as directed on page 122.

CELERY À LA CARDINALE.
INGREDIENTS.

1 bunch of celery - - - - - -	15 cents.
3 eggs - - - - - - - - -	3 "
1 lemon - - - - - - - -	2 "
1 red beet - - - - - - - -	2 "
Oil, vinegar and seasonings - - - -	15 "
Total - - - - -	37 cents.

Choose the white, tender stalks of celery, wash them well, cut them in three-inch lengths, lay them in a pile in the middle of the salad bowl, and cover them with Cardinal Sauce. Decorate the salad with the young leaves of celery, arranging them so that light and dark leaves contrast prettily; and add, if desired, two cold hard-boiled eggs, cut in quarters.

Cardinal Sauce.—Wash a red beet without breaking the skin or cutting off the top or roots; boil it until tender in boiling water, well salted; peel it, chop it fine, rub it through a sieve with a wooden spoon, and put it on a saucer. Make a *mayonnaise** sauce as follows: put into a bowl the yolk of one raw egg, one level teaspoonful each of salt and dry mustard, one level saltspoonful of white pepper, the juice of half a lemon, and as much cayenne pepper as can be taken up on the point of a small penknife-blade. Mix these ingredients smooth with a wooden spoon; then add, drop by drop, stirring constantly, three gills of salad-oil and the juice of half a lemon. When the oil is two-thirds used begin to add vinegar, using in all four table-spoonfuls. When the *mayonnaise* is thick and smooth stir in enough of the beet, prepared as above, to make it a bright red color; then spread it thickly over the salad and keep it cool for use.

CRÈME REVERSÉ.

INGREDIENTS.

6 eggs	6 cents.
½ lb. powdered sugar	3 "
1 pt. milk	4 "
Flavoring	1 cent.
Total	14 cents.

(1.) Put one teaspoonful of powdered sugar in the bottom of a plain tin mould, set it on the stove and turn it about as the sugar melts, so that it can run evenly over the bottom of the mould. As soon as it browns slightly, take the

* In French *mayonnaise*, no mustard is used.

mould off the fire and let it cool. (2.) Make a custard by beating together six eggs, quarter of a pound of powdered sugar, one pint of milk, and one teaspoonful of the essence of Vanilla. (3.) Strain this custard into the mould, set the mould in a dripping-pan containing sufficient hot water to reach two-thirds up the sides of the mould, and bake the custard in a moderate oven about thirty minutes, or until it is quite firm. (4.) Then cool it, set it on the ice until it is very cold, and serve it cold. In turning it out of the mould, choose a dish the center of which will just cover the top of the mould, put it over the mould, and then, holding both firmly, so that they cannot slip, turn them over, the mould remaining upside down on the dish. Lift it off carefully, and the custard will remain on the dish. It is very pretty in appearance and very nice.

CHAPTER III.

THIRD LESSON OF THE LADIES' COURSE.

Mock Turtle Soup Stock.
Halibut Neck à la Créole.
Broiled Potatoes.
Salmon Croquettes.
Oyster Plant Sauté aux Fines Herbes.
Canton of Lamb à la Jardinière.
Salade à la Russe.
Cabinet Pudding.

MOCK TURTLE SOUP STOCK.

INGREDIENTS.

1 calf's head	50 cents.
Soup vegetables and seasonings	5 "
Total	55 cents.

(1.) Choose a fresh calf's head, which may be known by

the clear white skin. As the head gets stale the skin becomes discolored and muddy in appearance, and the odor betrays its age. Carefully remove all hairs, and wipe with a clean damp cloth. Lay the head upon its face, make a cut from the throat to the edge of the lower jaw; then cut the skin carefully from the head, keeping it as whole as possible, and lay it in cold water. (2.) Remove the tongue whole, and lay that in cold water. (3.) With a sharp meat-saw cut out that portion of the head between the ears and above the eyes, and lift the piece out carefully, so as to take out the brain without breaking it. Lay the brain in cold water, well salted, in a bowl by itself. (*See receipt for " Tongue and Brains," in next chapter.*) (4.) Cut the head through the center; remove the lining of the nasal passage and scald it thoroughly; then put it in the bottom of the soup-kettle. (5.) Roll the tongue in the skin, tie the roll loosely with twine, and lay it on the bones. Cover them with eight quarts of cold water. Set the kettle over the fire and bring the contents slowly to a boil, skimming off all the scum that rises. (6.) When the broth is quite clear, remove the kettle to the side of the fire, where it will boil slowly from one side. Pare and add to it one medium-sized carrot, one turnip, and one onion stuck with ten whole cloves. Tie up in a fine cloth three blades of mace, eight allspice, one large bay-leaf, and half a nutmeg broken up, and put into the soup. Make a *bouquet* by tying tightly together one ounce each of celery and parsley, one sprig each of thyme, savory, and tarragon, and the yellow rind of one lemon pared off in a thin strip, and add it to the soup, together with one ounce of salt and as much cayenne pepper as can be taken up on the point of a small penknife-blade. Boil slowly and steadily. (7.) When the skin and tongue are tender enough to pierce easily with a fork, which will be in about one hour, remove them, dip them for an instant in scalding hot water;

remove the skin from the tongue, lay them on a dish and cover them with a wet cloth, to keep them moist until wanted for use. Boil the soup six hours in all. (8.) Then strain it and let it cool. If you do not wish to use the head and brains until the soup is cool, put them in the bottom of the earthen jar or bowl into which the soup is strained. They will be perfectly preserved by this method.

HALIBUT NECK À LA CRÉOLE.

INGREDIENTS.

3 lbs. halibut neck - - - - - -	18 cents.
Tomatoes - - - - - - - -	5 "
1 oz. butter - - - - - - -	2 "
Vegetables and seasonings - - - - -	2 "
Total - - - - -	27 cents.

Halibut neck is esteemed quite highly by gourmands. It is generally much cheaper than the more solid parts of the fish, and is delicious when cooked as follows: wash and trim three pounds of halibut neck; put it into a dripping-pan, with two ounces of chopped onion, one teaspoonful of salt, one saltspoonful of chopped garlic, half that quantity of white pepper, and one pound of peeled sliced tomato, either fresh or canned; dust the fish well with powdered crackers or dried bread-crumbs, dot it over with one table-spoonful of butter, and bake it twenty minutes in a quick oven. When done, lay the fish on a hot platter, put the tomato, etc., around it, and garnish it with a few cresses or sprigs of parsley.

BROILED POTATOES.

INGREDIENTS.

1 qt. potatoes - - - - - - -	3 cents.
Butter and seasonings - - - - -	2 "
Total - - - - -	5 cents.

(1.) Wash the potatoes thoroughly, boil them in their jackets, and let them cool before peeling them, to keep them rather moist. (2.) Peel the potatoes, slice them half an inch thick, broil them on a buttered gridiron, and serve them hot with butter, pepper, and salt.

SALMON *CROQUETTES.*

INGREDIENTS.

½ lb. salmon	12 cents.
1 pt. milk	4 "
2 oz. butter	4 "
4 eggs	4 "
1 gill Madeira	13 "
Flour, seasonings, and bread crumbs	5 "
Lard for frying	3 "
Total	45 cents.

(1.) Tear some cold salmon in shreds with two forks. (2.) Chop a level teaspoonful of onion, put it over the fire in a saucepan with the butter, and let it begin to turn yellow. (3.) Stir two ounces of flour into the onion and butter, and when the mixture begins to bubble, gradually add one pint of boiling milk, and stir till smooth. (4.) Add the salmon, a level teaspoonful of salt, quarter of a saltspoonful each of white pepper and nutmeg, the yolks of four raw eggs, and a gill of wine, and mix over the fire for two minutes. (5.) Turn the *croquette* mixture out an inch thick on an oiled dish, and let it cool. (6.) Make up the *croquettes* as directed on page 87, fry them golden brown, and garnish them with fried parsley.

Fried Parsley is prepared by washing some nice sprigs of parsley, shaking it in a clean cloth until it is quite dry, and plunging it into fat heated to about 400° Fahr., only until it is crisp. Parsley is also crisped by laying it on paper before a clear fire, and turning it frequently, until it is done.

OYSTER PLANT *SAUTÉ AUX FINES HERBES.*

INGREDIENTS.

1 bunch oyster plant	10 cents.
1 oz. butter	2 "
Herbs and seasonings	3 "
Total	15 cents.

(1.) Scrape the oyster plant, splitting each root and laying it in cold water as soon as it is scraped, to keep it white, and when all is done, boil it in boiling water containing a tablespoonful of salt, until it is tender. (2.) Chop fine one tablespoonful each of parsley, onions and mushrooms, and heat them over the fire in a frying-pan with an ounce of butter. (3.) Meantime dry the oyster plant on a clean towel, and when the butter is hot, throw the oyster plant into the pan, and toss it about until it is brown. Season it lightly with salt and pepper, and serve it hot.

CANTON OF LAMB *À LA JARDINIÈRE.*

INGREDIENTS.

4 lbs. shoulder of lamb - - - - -	50 cents.
Materials for forcemeat - - - - -	5 "
Vegetables for garnish - - - - -	20 "
Total - - - - - -	75 cents.

(1.) Prepare a *canton* from a shoulder of lamb, as directed on page 120. (2.) Meantime, make the *jardinière* as follows: peel a carrot and a turnip, and cut them in diamonds; cut half a pint of string beans in the same shapes; cut half a pint of small flowerets from a cauliflower; use half a pint of green peas, or asparagus heads; boil all these vegetables separately in boiling water and salt until tender, and then lay them in cold water until wanted. (3.) When the lamb is done make the sauce as directed on page 121, heat the *jardinière* in it, and serve arranged around the *canton.*

SALADE À LA RUSSE.

INGREDIENTS.

Vegetables - - - - - -	10 cents.
Salad dressing - - - - - -	5 "
Total - - - - -	15 cents.

(1.) Shell one pint of green peas, pare one carrot and two white turnips, slice them one inch thick, stamp them in little cylinders with a small tin tube, and boil them as directed in the previous receipt. (2.) Arrange them neatly on a salad dish and dress them with the following salad sauce: mix together one tablespoonful of vinegar, three of oil, half a level teaspoonful of salt, and a very little pepper. Pour it over the salad just before you serve it.

CABINET PUDDING.

INGREDIENTS.

¼ lb. candied cherries - - - - -	20 cents.
2 oz. citron - - - - - - - -	4 "
¼ lb. macaroons - - - - - -	15 "
Sponge cake - - - - - - - -	10 "
1 pt. milk - - - - - - - -	4 "
½ oz. gelatine - - - - - - -	3 "
1 lemon - - - - - - - -	2 "
3 oz. powdered sugar - - - - - -	2 "
Total - - - - -	60 cents.

(1.) Soak the gelatine in two tablespoonfuls of cold water until it is soft, and then put it over the fire in a saucepan with the milk, sugar, and the yellow rind of the lemon cut very thin, and let it heat thoroughly, stirring occasionally until the gelatine and sugar are dissolved. (2.) Cut the citron in thin slices. Butter a plain pudding mould rather thickly with cold butter, and ornament the bottom and sides by placing some of the fruit against them in some pretty shape. (3.) Place the remaining fruit and the cake in the mould in alternate layers, and then strain the milk into the mould. Set it where it will cool and grow firm, which will be in four or five hours, and then turn it out of the mould and serve it cold.

CHAPTER IV.

FOURTH LESSON OF THE LADIES' COURSE.

Mock Turtle Soup.
Crimped Cod à la Colbert.
Parisienne Potatoes.
Calf's Tongue and Brains with Tartar Sauce.
Jerusalem Artichokes.
Artichokes with Butter Sauce.
Calf's Head à la Poulette.
Anchovy Salad.
Omelette Soufflée—Chocolate Soufflée.

MOCK TURTLE SOUP.

INGREDIENTS.

Calf's Head stock - - - - - - - -	———
1 oz. butter - - - - - - - -	2 cents.
2 eggs - - - - - - - -	2 "
1 lemon - - - - - - - -	2 "
1 gill of Madeira wine - - - - -	13 "
Soup vegetables and seasonings - - -	3 "
	———
Total - - - - -	22 cents.

When the stock is quite cold, the fat which has collected upon the surface must be removed, and then the stock will be ready to finish as follows:

(1.) Take out the skin and tongue, and heat the stock. (2.) Cut the best part of the skin into regular pieces about two inches square, and save it, with the ears, for Calf's Head *à la Poulette.* Cut the rest of the head in half inch dice. (3.) Put an ounce of butter and half an ounce of flour in a thick saucepan over the fire, and stir until light brown. When the flour and butter are brown gradually add one quart of the stock to them, stirring the mixture until it is smooth; then add to it a small bay-leaf, a small onion stuck with three cloves, two ounces of carrot, and the following seasonings: two sage leaves, one small blade of mace, one sprig of thyme, and three sprigs each of parsley and marjoram. Boil all these ingredients slowly for half an hour; then strain and add to the soup stock, which must meantime have been set by the side of the fire, to boil very gently. If any scum rises, remove it instantly, for the soup should be clear and bright. Reserve a quart of the stock for Calf's Head *à la Poulette*; then put in the dice of Calf's Head already cut; if the soup is not brown color it with a little caramel. Boil two eggs hard, cool them, remove the shells and whites, chop the yolks in small dice, and put them into a soup tureen, with one gill of Sherry or Madeira wine and the juice of one lemon, and pour the soup over them. Thin slices of lemon may be passed with the soup.

CRIMPED COD *À LA COLBERT.*
INGREDIENTS.

2 lbs. codfish - - - - - - -	12 cents.
Egg and bread crumbs - - - - -	2 "
Materials for *maître d'hotel* butter - -	5 "
Vegetables and seasonings for sauce - - -	5 "
1 gill white wine - - - - - - -	13 "
Fat for frying - - - - - - -	3 "
Total - - - - - -	40 cents.

(1.) Skin the codfish, remove the bones, and cut the fish in small thin slices; lay them in well salted cold water for one hour. (2.) Meantime make a fish essence by boiling the skin and bones with half a carrot and an onion sliced, a *bouquet* of herbs, six cloves, two bayleaves and a pint of hot water; boil the essence rapidly until it is reduced to a gill, then add the wine, strain it, and keep it hot by setting the saucepan containing it into another half full of boiling water. (3.) Bread the slices of fish and fry them as directed on page 33; spread them lightly with *maître d'hotel* butter, made as directed on page 34, and serve them on a little of the fish essence on a hot dish.

PARISIENNE POTATOES.

INGREDIENTS.

1 qt. potatoes	3 cents.
Fat for frying	3 "
Parsley and salt	1 cent.
Total	7 cents.

(1.) Pare a quart of potatoes, cut them in balls about an inch in diameter, either with a knife or with a round vegetable scoop, laying them in cold water as fast as they are cut, and saving all the trimmings in water for mashed or *Duchesse* potatoes. (2.) When all the balls are cut, drop them into salted boiling water, only until they begin to grow tender; then drain them, lay them for a moment on a clean, dry cloth, and fry them a golden brown in smoking hot fat; drain them on brown paper, sprinkle them with chopped parsley, and salt and serve them hot.

CALF'S TONGUE AND BRAINS WITH TARTAR SAUCE.

INGREDIENTS.

Calf's tongue and brains	——
Materials for sauce	5 cents.
Vinegar and parsley	1 cent.
Total	6 cents.

The method of preparing the tongue has already been described in the receipt for Mock Turtle Soup, on page 159. The brain, in the same receipt, was directed to be laid in salted water. After it has been in the water one hour, the thin skin or membrane covering its soft inner substance must be removed so carefully as to avoid breaking it. It should then be put into a saucepan over the fire, with one quart of cold water, one teaspoonful of salt and one tablespoonful of vinegar, and allowed to parboil fifteen minutes. It will then be ready for use.

The tongue and brains are generally served cold—the

tongue being laid in the center of a dish, the brains cut in two pieces and placed at the sides of the tongue, and some Tartar Sauce put around them on the base of the dish. Some bits of parsley may be used for garnishing the dish.

Tartar Sauce.—Put the yolk of a raw egg into a bowl with one level teaspoonful of dry mustard, one level salt-spoonful of salt, and as much cayenne pepper as can be taken up on the point of a small penknife-blade; stir these ingredients with a wooden salad-spoon or spatula until they are smooth; then add, a few drops at a time, one gill of salad oil and three tablespoonfuls of lemon-juice, stirring quickly all the time. When the sauce is thick and smooth, add the following ingredients to it and keep it cool until wanted for use; one tablespoonful each of chopped parsley, capers and gherkin, and one teaspoonful of chopped onion.

JERUSALEM ARTICHOKES.

INGREDIENTS.

1 qt. artichokes - - - - - -	20 cents.
1 oz. butter - - - - - - - -	2 "
Flour, vinegar and seasonings - - -	3 "
Total - - - - -	25 cents.

(1.) Scrape the artichokes, throwing them into two quarts of cold water containing a gill of vinegar, to keep them white; boil them in boiling water well salted, only until tender, and then put them into a *Béchamel* Sauce, made as directed on page 41. Serve them hot.

ARTICHOKES WITH BUTTER SAUCE.

INGREDIENTS.

3 artichokes - - - - - - -	50 cents.
3 oz. butter - - - - - - - -	6 "
Flour and seasonings - - - , -	1 cent.
Total - - - - -	57 cents.

(1.) Wash the artichokes, which somewhat resemble large thistle heads, in cold water, changing the water several times; trim the leaves and the bottoms, or stalk ends, and put them with the leaves down in plenty of well salted boiling water. Boil them until tender, from half an hour to an hour and a half, according to the age of the artichoke; to test them, pull out a leaf; if it comes away easily the artichoke is .done. (2.) When they are done, drain them on a sieve, and then let them lay in cold water for five minutes. Take each artichoke successively in the left hand, and pressing the leaves apart at the top with the handle of a tablespoon, remove the choke, or fibrous substance in the center of the leaves. (3.) Put the artichokes again in boiling water to heat while the sauce is being made. (4.) Make a *Béchamel* sauce as directed on page 129, and add to it two ounces of butter and a tablespoonful of lemon juice. (5.) Drain the artichokes from the hot water, dish them on a napkin, put a tablespoonful of the butter sauce in each one, and send the rest in a sauce-boat to the table with them.

CALF'S HEAD *À LA POULETTE.*

INGREDIENTS.

Calf's head - - - - - - - -	——
2 oz. butter - - - - - - -	4 cents.
3 eggs - - - - - - - - -	3 "
Parsley, flour, and seasonings - - -	3 "
Total - - - - -	10 cents.

(1.) Put the pieces of the head reserved in making the Mock Turtle Soup, over the fire to heat in a quart of the stock. (2.) Make a sauce as follows: stir together in a saucepan over the fire two ounces or tablespoonfuls each of butter and flour until they are smoothly blended; then gradually add a pint of hot stock, stirring until smooth; season with quarter of a saltspoonful of grated nutmeg, a saltspoonful of salt, or more if required by taste, and as much cayenne pepper as can be taken up on the point of a small penknife-blade. Let the sauce begin to bubble after it is seasoned, then move it to the side of the fire, and stir in the yolks of three eggs, one at a time. Then put in the calf's head. *Do not let the sauce boil,* or it may curdle. (3.) When ready to use, dish with the ears in the middle, a little raised; sprinkle a little chopped parsley over it, and garnish it with sprigs of parsley.

ANCHOVY SALAD.

INGREDIENTS.

Anchovies	20 cents.
5 eggs	5 "
Parsley, oil, vinegar, and seasonings	5 "
Total	30 cents.

(1.) Soak the anchovies over night in cold water. (2.) Remove the scales and bones, and cut them in thin pieces. (3.) Boil five eggs hard; cool them; remove the shells, cut three of them in quarters for the garnish, and chop two fine, keeping the whites and yolks separate. (4.) Lay the anchovy *filets,* eggs, and parsley in alternate layers upon a salad dish, dress with two tablespoonfuls of oil and one of vinegar, and serve the salad.

OMELETTE *SOUFFLÉE.*

INGREDIENTS.

4 eggs	4 cents.
3 oz. powdered sugar	2 "
Vanilla flavoring	1 "
Total	7 cents.

(1.) Mix to a cream the sugar, the yolks of two eggs, and a teaspoonful of Vanilla essence. (2.) Beat four whites to a stiff froth. (3.) Gently stir the yolks and sugar into the whites, put the mixture by the tablespoonful on a buttered *gratin* dish, or *soufflée* pan, and bake it golden brown in a moderate oven, dusting it with powdered sugar when it is half done; serve it the instant it is done, or it will fall.

CHOCOLATE *SOUFFLÉE.*

INGREDIENTS.

4 eggs	4 cents.
3 oz. powdered sugar	2 "
½ oz. chocolate	1 "
Total	7 cents.

(1.) Grate the chocolate and mix it with the yolks and sugar. (2.) Beat the whites to a stiff froth, and finish the *soufflée* as directed in the previous receipt.

CHAPTER V.

FIFTH LESSON OF THE LADIES' COURSE.

Cream of Beets.
Oysters à la Poulette.
Saratoga Potatoes.
Fried Oysters.   Broiled Oysters.
Red Haricots Sauté à la Bordelaise.
Baron of Lamb with Mint Sauce.
Salade à la Macedoine.
Cream Fritters.

CREAM OF BEETS.

INGREDIENTS.

1 red beet	2 cents.
2 qts. milk	16 "
2 oz. butter	4 "
Flour and seasonings	1 cent.
Total	23 cents.

(1.) Boil a red beet and rub it through a sieve as directed in the receipt for Celery *Salade à la Cardinale,* on page 151. (2.) Make a white soup as directed for *Purée* of Salmon, on page 149. (3.) Stir into the white soup enough of the *purée* of beets to color it to a delicate pink, and serve it at once.

OYSTERS À LA POULETTE.

INGREDIENTS.

1 qt. oysters - - - - - - - -	25 cents.
1 oz. butter - - - - - - -	2 "
1 lemon - - - - - - - -	2 "
3 eggs - - - - - - -	3 "
Oil and seasonings - - - - - -	3 "
Total - - - - -	35 cents.

(1.) Examine the oysters to see that no shell adheres to them. (2.) Strain the broth and set it over the fire to come to a boil. (3.) Mix together over the fire one ounce each of butter and flour until they bubble; gradually stir in the oyster liquor, and season the sauce with a teaspoonful of salt, and quarter of a saltspoonful each of white pepper and nutmeg; stir in three raw yolks, one at a time, two tablespoonfuls of oil, and the juice of a lemon. (4.) Put the oysters into the sauce, let them heat until their edges begin to curl, and then serve them at once, as they spoil by standing.

SARATOGA POTATOES.

INGREDIENTS.

1 qt. potatoes - - - - - - -	3 cents.
Fat for frying - - - - - - -	3 "
Total - - - - -	6 cents.

(1.) Peel a quart of potatoes, cut them in very thin slices, and lay them in cold water and salt for an hour or more. (2.) Then dry them on a towel, throw them into a deep kettle of smoking hot fat, and fry them light brown; take them out of the fat with a skimmer into a colander, scatter over them a teaspoonful of salt, shake them well about, and turn them on a platter to serve.

FRIED OYSTERS.

INGREDIENTS.

1 qt. oysters - - - - - - -	25 cents.
Fat for frying - - - - - - -	3 "
Egg and bread crumbs - - - - -	2 "
Total - - - - -	30 cents.

(1.) Lay the oysters on a clean towel, dry them slightly, bread them as directed on page 33, and fry them golden brown in smoking fat; lay them for a moment on brown paper, to free them from grease, and serve them hot, garnished with a few sprigs of parsley.

BROILED OYSTERS.

INGREDIENTS.

1 qt. oysters - - - - - - -	25 cents.
Eggs and bread crumbs - - - - -	2 "
Materials for *maître d'hotel* butter - -	5 "
Total - - - - - -	32 cents.

Prepare the oysters as directed in the preceding receipt, broil them on an oiled gridiron, over a moderate fire, and serve them with some *maître d'hotel* butter, made as directed on page 34.

RED HARICOTS *SAUTÉ À LA BORDELAISE.*

INGREDIENTS.

1 pt. Red Haricot beans - - - - -	6 cents.
2 oz. butter - - - - - - -	4 "
Herbs and seasoning - - - - - -	2 "
Total - - - - - -	12 cents.

(1.) Dress the beans as directed on page 44, boiling an onion stuck with six cloves, and a *bouquet* of herbs with them. (2.) When they are soft, but not broken, drain them, put them into a frying-pan containing two ounces of butter, and a tablespoonful each of chopped parsley and any green herb in season; add a teaspoonful of salt, and a level saltspoonful of pepper, and toss them over the fire until they are hot. Turn them out on a hot dish, sprinkle them with chopped parsley and serve them hot.

BARON OF LAMB WITH MINT SAUCE.

INGREDIENTS.

6 lbs. lamb - - - - - - -	$1.50
Vegetables and seasonings - - - -	5
Mint, sugar, and vinegar - - - -	5
Total - - - - -	$1.60

A baron of lamb is the entire loin, not divided at the back bone, and the upper part of both legs.

Lay the lamb in a dripping-pan on a little bed of vegetables, made of an ounce of carrot and turnip sliced, one slice of onion, one sprig each of thyme and parsley, and one bay leaf. Put it into a quick oven long enough to brown, then season it with salt and pepper, and finish baking it in a moderate oven, cooking it in all twenty minutes to a pound. While it is roasting, make the following sauce.

Mint Sauce.—This sauce is made both hot and cold, the vinegar being scalded with the sugar when the sauce is to be hot; otherwise the process is the same as for cold sauce. For the latter put one tablespoonful of chopped mint and two of soft sugar into half a pint of vinegar, and stir until the sugar is dissolved. Serve it in a gravy-boat.

SALADE À LA MACEDOINE.

INGREDIENTS.

1 qt. small white turnips - - - - -	5 cents.
½ pt. green peas, or beans - - - - -	3 "
Beet, carrot, celery - - - - - -	2 "
Materials for sauce - - - - -	10 "
Total - - - - -	20 cents.

(1.) Boil a red beet as directed for Cardinal Sauce, on page 152. (2.) Pare the turnips and hollow them out like little cups. (3.) Slice the carrot half an inch thick, and stamp it out in small cylinders with a tin tube. Cut four small white stalks of celery in half inch lengths. Shell the peas, or use canned ones. (4.) Put all these vegetables over the fire, in boiling water in separate vessels with half a teaspoonful each of salt and sugar, and boil them only until tender; then throw them into cold water in separate vessels until wanted for use. (5.) Meantime, make a *mayonnaise* as directed for Cardinal Sauce, omitting the *purée* of beet which colors it. (6.) Drain the vegetables which form the *macedoine*, dry them on a clean towel, arrange them in a mound on a salad dish, and cover them with the *mayonnaise*. The salad may be ornamented with hard boiled eggs, bits of celery leaf, and some of the *macedoine*, if desired.

CREAM FRITTERS.

INGREDIENTS.

1½ pts. milk - - - - - - -	6 cents.
4 oz. corn starch - - - - - - -	4 "
3 " butter - - - - - - -	6 "
8 " powdered sugar - - - - - -	5 "
4 eggs - - - - - - -	4 "
Bread crumbs and flavoring - - - -	2 "
Total - - - - -	27 cents.

(1.) Dissolve the corn starch in half a pint of milk. Place a pint of milk on the stove to heat. Separate the yolks of three eggs from the whites. (2.) As soon as the milk boils up add to it the sugar, corn starch, butter, yolks, and a teaspoonful of flavoring, stirring the yolks in one at a time, and beating the cream till it is smooth with an egg whip; let it simmer gently for five minutes and then pour it out, about an inch thick, on an oiled dish and let it cool. (3.) Dust the table thickly with bread crumbs, lay the cream upon it and cut it in diamonds. (4.) Beat one egg and the remaining whites just enough to mix them, and use them to bread the pieces of cream. Fry them in smoking hot fat, and lay them on brown paper to free them from grease. (5.) Arrange them on a dish, dust them with powdered sugar, and serve them.

CHAPTER VI.

SIXTH LESSON OF THE LADIES' COURSE.

Potage à la Reine.
Broiled Trout with Maître d'Hotel Butter.
Duchesse Potatoes.
Canton de Rouen.
Celery à la Villeroi.
Breast of Lamb à la Maréchale.
Chicken Salad.
Rice Croquettes with Vanilla Cream Sauce.

POTAGE À LA REINE.

INGREDIENTS.

4 lbs. chicken - - - - - - -	50 cents.
Soup vegetables and milk - - - -	5 "
1 pound rice - - - - - -	10 "
Total - - - - -	65 cents.

(1.) Dress a chicken as directed on page 123; cut off the legs and thighs without separating them, and put it into a saucepan with four quarts of cold water, and a teaspoonful of salt; bring it slowly to a boil, skimming until it is clear. (2.) Add a carrot, an onion stuck with six cloves, a *bouquet* of herbs, a tablespoonful of salt, and quarter of a saltspoonful each of white pepper and grated nutmeg, and boil until the chicken is tender; then take it up, cut off the white meat from the breast, and free it from fat and skin, and use it for the soup, saving the rest of the chicken for the salad. (3.) Strain the soup, return it to the fire with the white meat of the chicken, and the rice well washed; boil these ingredients slowly until they are tender enough to be rubbed through a sieve with a wooden spoon. (4.) Return the soup to the fire to heat, adding half a pint of boiling milk, and stirring until it is scalding hot, *but do not let it boil*; it is then ready to serve. (5.) If it needs to stand set the saucepan containing it in another partly filled with some boiling water to keep the soup hot.

BROILED TROUT WITH *MAÎTRE D'HOTEL* BUTTER.

INGREDIENTS.

2 lbs. trout - - - - - - -	50 cents.
Materials for *maître d'hotel* butter - - -	5 "
Total - - - - -	55 cents.

Dress a trout, splitting it down the back, broil it over a moderate fire on an oiled gridiron, cooking the inside first, and serve it with some *maître d'hotel* butter, made as directed on page 34.

DUCHESSE POTATOES.

INGREDIENTS.

1 qt. potatoes - - - - - - -	3 cents.
1 oz. butter - - - - - - - -	2 "
2 eggs and seasonings - - - - -	3 "
Total - - - - -	8 cents.

(1.) Boil one quart of potatoes and mash them through a fine colander with the potato masher; mix with them one ounce of butter, one level teaspoonful of salt, half a saltspoonful of white pepper, quarter of a saltspoonful of grated nutmeg, and the yolks of two raw eggs. (2.) Turn the potato out on a plate, and then form it with a knife into small cakes, two inches long and one inch wide; lay them on a buttered tin, brush them over the top with white of egg, and color them golden brown in a moderate oven.

CANTON DE ROUEN.

INGREDIENTS.

Legs and thighs of chicken - - - -	———
Parsley, pork and seasonings - - -	2 cents.
¼ lb sausage meat - - - - -	3 "
Vegetables for *Macedoine* - - - -	10 "
½ pt. *Béchamel* sauce - - - -	5 "
Total - - - - -	20 cents.

(1.) Lay the legs and thighs of the chicken, which must be cut off without separating them, on the table, with the skin down; remove the thigh bone, and half the leg bone, cutting them away from the flesh with a sharp knife to avoid mangling it. Trim off the ends of the leg bone just below the knee joint, to make them resemble a duck's bill. Stuff the thighs with a little delicately seasoned forcemeat or sausage, and sew them up; turn them over and pat them into the shape of a bird, securing the leg bone in place for the head, with a trussing needle, and tying it securely. Lay the *cantons* in a pan on some scraps of pork and vegetables, season them lightly with salt and pepper, and bake them one hour in a moderate oven. (2.) Prepare some vegetables as directed for the *salade à la Macedoine*, on page 168. (3.) Make a *Béchamel* sauce as directed on page 129, and heat the vegetables in it. (4.) When the *cantons* are done remove the strings, dish them on a bed made of the vegetables and sauce, and serve them hot.

CELERY *À LA VILLEROI.*

INGREDIENTS.

½ bunch of celery - - - - - -	8 cents.
Materials for batter - - - - - -	5 "
Fat for frying - - - - - -	3 "
	———
Total - - - - -	16 cents.

(1.) Trim the celery stalks, cut them in two inch lengths, boil them until tender in boiling water and salt. Dry them on a clean towel, dip them in frying batter, made as directed on page 51, and finish them like the Parsnip Fritters, described on the same page.

BREAST OF LAMB *À LA MARÉCHALE.*

INGREDIENTS.

1 breast of lamb - - - - - -	25 cents.
Vegetables, herbs, and seasonings - - -	3 "
Egg and bread crumbs - - - - -	2 "
Fat for frying - - - - - - -	3 "

½ pt. Spanish sauce - - - - - - 5 cents.
Mushrooms - - - - - - - - 5 "

Total - - - - - 43 cents.

(1.) Put a breast of lamb over the fire in boiling water to boil, with a *bouquet* of herbs, an onion stuck with six cloves, half a carrot, and a turnip, and boil it until the bones can be pulled out easily. When the lamb is tender enough, remove all the bones, press it flat between two platters, under a weight, and let it cool. (2.) Make half a pint of Spanish Sauce as directed on page 71, and put half a pint of mushrooms in it to heat. (3.) Bread the breast of lamb by dipping it first in sifted bread crumbs, then in beaten egg, and again in crumbs, and fry it in smoking hot fat. (4.) Pour the sauce on a dish, and lay the lamb on it with the mushrooms around it.

CHICKEN SALAD.
INGREDIENTS.

Cold chicken - - - - - - - ——
Olives and capers - - - - - - 10 cents.
Materials for *Mayonnaise* - - - - 15 "
Celery or lettuce - - - - - - - 5 "
3 eggs - - - - - - - - 3 "

Total - - - - - - 33 cents.

(1.) Free the cold chicken remaining from the soup, from fat, skin and bone, and cut it in half-inch dice. (2.) Trim and wash the salad, break it in small pieces, and dry it on a clean towel. (3.) Mix the chicken and salad in a salad bowl, and dress it with a tablespoonful of oil, a teaspoonful of vinegar and half a saltspoonful of salt and pepper. (4.) Make a *Mayonnaise* as directed in the receipt for Cardinal Sauce, omitting the beet coloring, and cover the salad with it. Decorate the salad with olives, capers and hard boiled eggs cut in quarters.

RICE *CROQUETTES*, WITH VANILLA CREAM SAUCE.

INGREDIENTS.

½ lb. rice - - - - - - - - -	5 cents.
1 oz. butter - - - - - - - -	2 "
4 " sugar - - - - - - - -	3 "
½ pt. milk - - - - - - - -	2 "
4 eggs - - - - - - - - -	4 "
Flour, cracker dust, and fat for frying -	7 "
Total - - - - -	23 cents.

(1.) Boil half a pound of well washed rice in one quart of boiling water, with a level tablespoonful of salt until just tender; drain it, put it into half a pint of milk with half the yellow rind of a lemon, or two inches of stick cinnamon, and two ounces of sugar, and boil for half an hour, stirring it occasionally to prevent burning. (2.) Take it from the fire, stir in, one at a time, the yolks of three eggs, and return to the fire for two minutes to set the egg; then spread the rice on an oiled platter, laying it about an inch thick, and let it get cool enough to handle. (3.) When it is cool enough, turn it out of the platter upon some cracker dust spread on the table, cut it in strips one inch wide and three inches long, roll them into the shape of corks, dip them first in cracker, then in beaten egg, then in crackerdust, and fry them golden brown in plenty of smoking hot fat; lay them on a napkin for a moment to free them from grease, put them on a dish, dust a little powdered sugar over them, and serve them with Cream Sauce. (4.) Stir one ounce each of butter and flour together over the fire until they bubble; then add half a pint of boiling milk, one ounce of sugar, and a teaspoonful of Vanilla Essence, and serve as soon as it boils up, with the *croquettes*.

CHAPTER VII.

SEVENTH LESSON OF THE LADIES' COURSE.

Mock Terrapin Soup.
Bouillabaisse.
Potatoes au gratin.
Calf's Liver, à la Bordelaise.
Macaroni à la Napolitaine.
Braized Beef à la Printanière.
Salade à la Suede.
French Pancakes.

MOCK TERRAPIN SOUP.

INGREDIENTS.

Calf's liver	—
2 qts. stock	12 cents.
½ pt. Spanish sauce	5 "
3 eggs	3 "
1 gill Madeira wine	13 "
Flour, oil and seasonings	2 "
Total	35 cents.

(1.) In preparing the calf's liver *à la Bordelaise*, take off the smallest lobe, or division, and bring it to a boil in boiling water, with a tablespoonful of salt and a *bouquet* of herbs; when it is done chop it in quarter inch dice. (2.) Heat two quarts of stock and half a pint of Spanish Sauce, made as directed on page 71; add the liver to it, and keep it hot over the fire. (3.) Make some egg-balls as follows: rub the yolks of two hard boiled eggs through a sieve with a wooden spoon, and mix them with a teaspoonful of oil, a very little salt and pepper, the yolk of a raw egg and enough flour to make a stiff paste; roll this out about half an inch thick, cut it in strips, and then in dice, and roll them into little balls under the palm of the hand; poach the egg-balls in boiling water for five minutes, and then put them into the soup. (4.) When ready to use the soup, add the wine to it, and pour it into the tureen. Thin slices of lemon are passed with this soup, as with Mock Turtle.

BOUILLABAISSE.

INGREDIENTS.

1 lb. cod fish	8 cents.
1 " perch	15 "
1 " bass	15 "
2 gills oil	10 "
1 gill of white wine	13 "
Onion, flour and seasonings	3 "
Bread and lemon	3 "
3 eggs	3 "
Total	70 cents.

(1.) Chop a small onion and fry it golden brown in a gill of salad oil; stir into it two ounces of flour until it bubbles; add one clove of garlic chopped fine, a tablespoonful of saffron, a gill of wine, a *bouquet* of herbs, and two quarts of boiling water, and simmer while the fish is being fried. (2.) Dry the fish, which should be sliced, on a clean towel, roll it in flour, season it with pepper and salt, fry it brown in a gill of oil, and lay it on brown paper to free it from grease. (3.) Cut some stale bread in half-inch dice, fry them golden brown and put them into the soup tureen. (4.) Mix the yolks of three raw eggs with two gills of the soup, and then stir them into the rest of the soup, with the juice of a lemon. Put the fish into the tureen and strain the soup over it. Serve it at once.

POTATOES *AU GRATIN.*

INGREDIENTS.

1 qt. potatoes	3 cents.
½ pt. *Béchamel* sauce	5 "
1 oz. Parmesan cheese	2 "
Bread and seasonings	2 "
Total	12 cents.

Slice some cold boiled potatoes, warm them in half a pint

of *Béchamel* sauce, put them into a *gratin* dish, or one that can be sent to the table, season them with salt and white pepper, dust them thickly with bread crumbs and grated Parmesan cheese, and brown them quickly in a hot oven.

CALF'S LIVER *À LA BORDELAISE.*

INGREDIENTS.

1 calf's liver - - - - - - - -	50 cents.
¼ lb. larding pork - - - - - -	5 "
Soup vegetables - - - - - -	5 "
Total - - - - -	60 cents.

(1.) After cutting off the smaller lobe of the liver to use for Mock Terrapin Soup, lard it as directed in the receipt for *Fricandeau* of veal on page 150. (2.) Lay it in a dripping pan on a bed of soup vegetables and the scraps of larding pork, season it with a teaspoonful of salt and a quarter of a saltspoonful of pepper, add a little boiling water or stock to baste it with every twenty minutes, and bake it an hour and a half in a moderate oven. (3.) When it is done take it from the pan and keep it hot while the sauce is being made by passing the vegetables and dripping through a sieve with a wooden spoon. Serve the sauce on the dish with the liver.

MACARONI *À LA NAPOLITAINE.*

INGREDIENTS.

½ lb. macaroni - - - - - - -	8 cents.
½ pt. Spanish sauce - - - - - -	5 "
Cold game - - - - - - -	10 "
Bread crumbs and Parmesan cheese - -	2 "
Total - - - - - -	25 cents.

(1.) Boil the macaroni as directed on page 40. (2.) Cut any remains of game in half inch dice. (3.) Make a Spanish Sauce as directed on page 71. (4.) Grate an ounce of Parmesan cheese, and sift an equal quantity of bread crumbs with it. (5.) Put the macaroni, sauce, and game in layers in a dish suitable to be sent to the table, dust it thickly with the cheese and bread crumbs, and brown it quickly in a hot oven. Serve it hot.

BRAIZED BEEF À LA PRINTANIÈRE.

INGREDIENTS.

4 lbs. flank of beef	40 cents.
1 qt. small turnips	5 "
½ pint green peas	5 "
Parsley and seasonings	5 "
Total	55 cents.

(1.) Trim the fat and skin from the flank of beef, season it with two teaspoonfuls of salt, and quarter of a saltspoonful of pepper, roll it up compactly, and tie it tight. Put it into a saucepan on a bed of vegetables, with a gill of vinegar and ten whole cloves, cover it with broth or boiling water, put a clean cloth over the top of the saucepan and fit on the lid. Let the beef simmer slowly for three hours, or until quite tender. (2.) Pare the turnips, scoop them out in the form of little cups, boil them only until tender in well-salted boiling water, and then lay them in cold water until wanted. Boil the peas in the same way, and lay them in cold water. When the vegetables are wanted, heat the turnips in boiling water, warm the peas with a teaspoonful of butter, and fill the turnip cups with them. (3.) When the beef is tender lay it on a dish, remove the string, strain the gravy over it, arrange the little cups of peas around it, and garnish it on each side with tufts of parsley.

SALADE À LA SUEDE.

INGREDIENTS.

Cold potatoes	2 cents.
Olives and capers	5 "
2 pickled herrings	2 "
Apple, egg, and pickled beet	3 "
Oil, vinegar, and seasonings	5 "
1 pt. oysters	13 "
Total	30 cents.

(1.) Skin and slice the herrings. (2.) Peel and slice the potatoes, apple, and beet. (3.) Put them into a salad bowl, and dress them with two tablespoonfuls of oil, one of vinegar, a teaspoonful of salt, and quarter of a saltspoonful of pepper. (4.) Lay one pint of freshly opened oysters around the salad, and fill the center with the olives, capers, and a hard boiled egg sliced.

FRENCH PANCAKES.

INGREDIENTS.

6 eggs	6 cents.
½ lb. flour	2 "
¼ " butter	8 "
½ pt. milk	2 "
3 oz. sugar	2 "
Jelly	10 "
Total	30 cents.

(1.) Beat together till smooth six eggs and half a pound of flour. (2.) Melt four ounces of butter, and add it to the batter with one ounce of sugar, and half a pint of milk, and beat till smooth. (3.) Put by the tablespoonful into a hot frying-pan, slightly greased, running the batter evenly over the surface of the pan by tipping it about; fry the pancake light brown, spread it with jelly, roll it up, dust it with powdered sugar, and serve hot.

CHAPTER VIII.
EIGHTH LESSON OF THE LADIES' COURSE.

Mi-Carême Soup.
Halibut filets à la Maréchale.
Potatoes à la Crème.
Curry of Duck, à l'Indienne.
Kale with Butter Sauce.
Roast Turkey.
French Salad.
Cream Cakes. Chocolate Éclairs.

MI-CARÊME SOUP.
INGREDIENTS.

2 lbs. flounder - - - - - -	12 cents.
1 qt. milk - - - - - - -	8 "
2 oz. butter - - - - - -	4 "
Bread, flour and seasonings - - - -	2 "
Soup vegetables, lettuce and beet - -	5 "
Total - - - - -	31 cents.

(1.) Remove the *filets* of the flounder as directed on page 32. (2.) Pare a carrot, turnip, and onion; make a *bouquet* of herbs; put these vegetables over the fire in a quart and a half of cold water, with the *filets*, and a teaspoonful of salt, and bring them to a boil. Then remove the *filets* carefully, lay them between two platters to cool, and let the vegetables simmer slowly. (3.) Stamp half a dozen lettuce leaves in little rounds with an apple corer, and throw them into well salted boiling water for one minute; then drain them and put them into cold water until needed. (4.) Stamp similar rounds from thin slices of a cold beet, boiled as directed in the receipt for Cream of Beets, on page 165. (5.) Stamp the *filets* in the same sized rounds; put them aside until wanted for use, and rub the remains of the *filets* through the sieve with a wooden spoon. (6.) Put one quart of milk over the fire to boil. (7.) Stir together over the fire two ounces each of butter and flour until they bubble; gradually add the boiling milk, and one quart of the water in which the vegetables have been simmering; season the soup with quarter of a saltspoonful each of white pepper and grated nutmeg, adding a little more salt if it is required; stir in the *purée* made from the trimmings of the *filets*, and mix the soup smooth with an egg whip. (8.) When ready to use the soup, add the rounds of fish, lettuce and beet, and serve instantly, so that the brightness of the contrasting colors may not be impaired.

HALIBUT *FILETS À LA MARÉCHALE.*

INGREDIENTS.

1 lb. Halibut - - - - - - -	20 cents.
3 eggs - - - - - - - - -	3 "
Bread crumbs and lard for frying - -	5 "
2 oz. butter - - - - - - - -	4 "
Flour, mushrooms and seasonings - -	5 "
Total - - - - - -	37 cents.

(1.) Make an *Allemande* Sauce as follows: stir two ounces of butter and one and a half ounces of flour over the fire until they bubble, add half a pint of boiling water, or the essence from a can of mushrooms; season with a level saltspoonful of salt, quarter of a saltspoonful each of white pepper and nutmeg, and boil the sauce three minutes, stirring it constantly. Remove it from the fire, stir in the yolks of two eggs, return it to the fire, and stir it two minutes longer; it will then be ready for use. (2.) Cut the halibut in *filets* quarter of an inch thick, an inch wide, and about three inches long; cover one side with the *Allemande* Sauce, lay that side down on an oiled platter, and let the *filets* stand five minutes to harden the sauce. Then, without moving them, cover the upper side with the sauce, and let them stand five minutes. (3.) Dust the table thickly with bread crumbs, beat up an egg, bread the *filets*, and fry them golden brown in smoking hot fat. Lay them for a moment on brown paper to free them from grease, and serve them on a folded napkin, garnished with parsley.

POTATOES À LA CRÈME.

INGREDIENTS.

1 qt. potatoes - - - - - - - -	3 cents.
2 oz. butter - - - - - - - -	4 "
Milk, lemon-juice and seasonings - - -	3 "
Total - - - - -	10 cents.

(1.) Boil some new potatoes as directed on page 47, peel and slice them thin; put them into a sauce-pan with a gill of milk, two ounces of butter, a teaspoonful of lemon juice, a saltspoonful of salt, and quarter of a saltspoonful each of white pepper and nutmeg, and toss them over the fire till hot. *Croûtons* of fried bread may be used as a garnish, if desired.

CURRY OF DUCK À L'INDIENNE.

INGREDIENTS.

3 lb. duck - - - - - - - -	45 cents.
½ " rice - - - - - - -	5 "
Cocoanut and apple - - - - -	5 "
Curry, butter, flour and seasonings - - -	5 "
Total - - - - -	60 cents.

Make the curry as directed on page 115, adding a cupful of grated cocoanut, and a tart apple, peeled, cored, and sliced. Cook and serve the rice as directed in the same receipt.

KALE WITH BUTTER SAUCE.

INGREDIENTS.

½ peck purple kale - - - - -	20 cents.
2 oz. butter - - - - - -	4 "
Flour and seasonings - - - - -	1 cent.
Total - - - - -	25 cents.

(1.) Boil as directed for Green Vegetables on page 50, and serve with Butter Sauce made as follows. (2.) Stir together over the fire two ounces of butter and one of flour until they bubble, then add half a pint of boiling water, and season with a teaspoonful of salt, and quarter of a salt-spoonful of white pepper. (3.) Chop the kale, and warm it in the sauce before serving.

ROAST TURKEY.
INGREDIENTS.

7 lb. Turkey	$1.40
½ " cheese	8
Bread, herbs and seasonings	5
Butter, egg and onion	3
Total	$1.56

(1.) Dress a turkey as directed in the receipt for Chicken Curry on page 115; twist the tips of the wings back under the shoulders; stuff the bird with a forcemeat made as directed on page 124. Bend the legs as far up toward the breast as possible; secure the thigh bones in that position by a cord or skewer, and then fasten the legs down close to the vent. (2.) Roast the bird as directed in the receipt for Roast Duck, on page 123, making the gravy as for that dish.

FRENCH SALAD.
INGREDIENTS.

1 pt. watercress	5 cents.
1 head lettuce	5 "
Materials for Salad Dressing	5 "
Total	15 cents.

(1.) Thoroughly cleanse the cress and lettuce, shake them dry in a clean towel, arrange them in a salad bowl, and pour over them the following dressing. (2.) Mix together a tablespoonful of vinegar, two of oil, a level teaspoonful of salt, and quarter of a saltspoonful of pepper; pour it over the salad and serve it at once. The salad wilts by standing after it has been dressed.

CREAM CAKES.

INGREDIENTS.

8 eggs - - - - - - - -	8 cents.
1 oz. butter - - - - - - - -	2 "
Flour and corn starch - - - - -	3 "
1 pt. milk - - - - - - - -	4 "
Sugar and flavoring - - - - -	3 "
Total - - - - -	20 cents.

(1.) Put one ounce of butter over the fire to melt in one pint of water; when the water boils beat into it four ounces of flour, and let it cook five minutes, stirring it constantly to prevent burning. (2.) Remove it from the fire and beat six eggs into it, two at a time. When thoroughly mixed and beaten, put the batter by the tablespoonful on a baking-sheet, first buttered and then floured; brush the tops of the puffs with beaten egg, and bake them in a moderate oven about half an hour. (3.) Cool them, cut them open at one side, and fill them with Pastry Cooks' Cream, made as follows. (4.) Mix together in a sauce-pan two ounces of corn starch, two ounces of powdered sugar and the yolks of two eggs; then gradually stir in a pint of milk, put the cream over the fire and stir it constantly until it has boiled five minutes. Remove it from the fire, flavor it with a teaspoonful of Vanilla Essence, pour it into a bowl to cool, and then fill the puffs with it.

CHOCOLATE *ÉCLAIRS.*

INGREDIENTS.

Materials for Cream Cakes - - - -	20 cents.
Chocolate and sugar - - - - -	5 "
Total - - - - -	25 cents.

(1.) Make the batter for the *éclairs* as directed for Cream Cakes, putting it upon the baking-pan in strips three inches long and an inch and a half wide. When baked and cooled, fill them with Pastry Cooks' Cream, brush the tops with Chocolate Icing, made as directed in the following receipt, let them cool, and use them. (2.)

Make a Chocolate Icing as follows: put four ounces of sugar and a gill of water over the fire and boil and skim it until it reaches what is called the "crack," which may be decided by dipping a small stick first into the boiling sugar, and then into cold water; if the sugar forms a clear, brittle candy it is ready for the chocolate. Check the boiling at once by dipping the sauce-pan containing the sugar into another partly filled with cold water; now stir in an ounce of finely grated and sifted chocolate, and brush the *éclairs* with it. Dry them in the mouth of a rather cool oven, cool them, and serve them.

CHAPTER IX.

NINTH LESSON OF THE LADIES' COURSE.

Purée of Celery.
Eels en Matelotte.
Potatoes à la Maître d'Hotel.
Galantine of Chicken.
Asparagus Peas.
Braized Capons with Tongue.
Lobster Salad.
Cumberland Pudding with Rum Sauce.

PURÉE OF CELERY.

INGREDIENTS.

1 bunch celery - - - - - - -	15 cents.
2 oz. butter - - - - - - -	4 "
2 qts. milk - - - - - - -	16 "
Flour and seasonings - - - - -	1 cent.
Total - - - - - -	36 cents.

(1.) Make a White Soup as directed in the receipt for *Purée* of Salmon, on page 148. (2.) Trim six of the white stalks of celery, boil them until tender in well salted boiling water, rub them through a sieve with a wooden spoon, and blend the *Purée* with the Soup. Serve it as soon as it is done; or if it is to be kept hot, set the sauce-pan containing it into another partly filled with boiling water.

EELS *EN MATELOTTE.*

INGREDIENTS.

2 lbs. eels	- - - - - - - - -	24 cents.
2 oz. butter	- - - - - - -	4 "
½ pt. button onions	- - - - - -	3 "
Bread, flour and seasonings	- - - -	2 "
Wine	- - - - - - - - -	5 "
Total	- - - - -	38 cents.

(1.) Clean the eels, cut them in two inch lengths, put them over the fire and bring them to a boil in plenty of cold water containing a tablespoonful of salt, an onion stuck with ten cloves, and two tablespoonfuls of vinegar. (2.) Boil them fifteen minutes, take them up, dry them on a clean cloth, roll them in flour and fry them brown in a sauce-pan with two ounces of butter. (3.) When they are brown add a *bouquet* of herbs and a pint of boiling water; season the *matelotte* with a teaspoonful of salt, and quarter of a saltspoonful of pepper. (4.) Peel a pint of button onions, toss them over the fire until brown with a teaspoonful each of butter and sugar, and then add them to the *matelotte* and simmer it one hour. If the sauce evaporates, add enough boiling water to make up the original quantity. When the *matelotte* is done, add a glass of wine to it, and serve with some *croûtons* of fried bread.

POTATOES *À LA MAÎTRE D'HOTEL.*

INGREDIENTS.

1 qt. potatoes	- - - - - - -	3 cents.
Maître d'Hotel butter	- - - - -	3 "
1 pt. broth	- - - - - - -	3 "
Total	- - - - -	9 cents.

Boil the potatoes as directed on page 47. Pare them, cut them in quarter inch slices, and put them into a saucepan with some *maître d'hotel* butter, made as directed on page 34, and a pint of broth. Toss them over the fire till hot, and serve them at once, or the butter may become oily.

GALANTINE OF CHICKEN.

INGREDIENTS.

4 lbs. chicken - - - - - - -	50 cents.	
2 " forcemeat - - - - - - - -	24 "	
¼ " larding pork - - - - - -	5 "	
¼ " cold tongue - - - - - -	10 "	
1 gill wine - - - - - - -	13 "	
2 eggs - . - - - - - - - -	2 "	
Soup vegetables and seasonings - -	4 "	
Total - - - -	$1.08	

(1.) Bone the chicken as directed in the receipt for Boned Birds on page 125. (2.) Put the carcass over the fire in four quarts of cold water, with a *bouquet* of herbs, an onion peeled and stuck with ten cloves, a carrot and turnip peeled, and bring it to a boil, skimming it clear. (3.) Either make a forcemeat of one pound each of fresh veal and pork, finely minced, or use an equal quantity of nice sausage meat. Season the forcemeat highly with a teaspoonful of mixed ground cloves, nutmeg, mace and allspice, a teaspoonful of salt, and a saltspoonful of peppei; add to it the wine, two raw eggs, the larding pork and tongue cut in one inch dice, and mix it thoroughly. (4.) Lay the flesh of the chicken on the table, skin down; put the forcemeat on it, and fold the chicken up over it in the form of the bird. Roll it tightly in a strong, clean cloth, tie it with tape in the center, and near the ends of the roll; fasten the ends firmly with strong twine, taking care to make the roll compact and perfectly secure. Put the chicken into the water containing the carcass, and boil it slowly for three hours, replenishing the stock with boiling water, so as to have the chicken entirely covered with it. The conclusion of this receipt is given in the next lesson.

ASPARAGUS PEAS.

INGREDIENTS.

1 bunch asparagus - - - - - -	15 cents.
Butter and seasonings - - - - - - -	3 "
Total - - - - -	18 cents.

(1.) Thoroughly wash a bunch of young green asparagus, cut it in half inch lengths as far down the stalk as it is tender, and boil it as directed for Green Vegetables on page 50. (2.) When ready to use it, heat it over the fire with one ounce of butter, half a level teaspoonful of salt, and quarter of a saltspoonful of pepper, and serve it at once before the color changes.

BRAIZED CAPONS WITH TONGUE.

INGREDIENTS.

1 capon - - - - - - - - -	75 cents.
2 small tongues - - - - - - -	20 "
Soup vegetables and herbs - - - - -	5 "
1 pt. broth - - - - - - - -	3 "
1 gill wine - - - - - - -	13 "
1 oz. butter - - - - - - -	2 "
Flour and seasonings - - - - -	2 "
Total - - - - -	$1.20

(1.) Prepare a capon for boiling as directed in the receipt for Boiled Fowl on page 24, and put it over the fire to simmer gently in sufficient boiling water to cover it, with a *bouquet* of herbs, a carrot and turnip peeled, an onion stuck with ten cloves, a level tablespoonful of salt, and ten peppercorns. Keep enough boiling water in the sauce-pan to cover the capon and tongues all the time they are cooking. (2.) Wash two small fresh calf's tongues, put them with the capon to simmer until both are tender, about two hours. (3.) Put a handful of any green herbs in season into boiling water and salt, boil them three minutes, drain them, lay them in cold water for five minutes to set their color. Chop them fine and rub them through a sieve with a wooden spoon; use them to color the sauce, which is made as follows. (4.) Stir together over the fire one ounce each of butter and flour until they bubble; add the wine and half a pint of the broth from the capon, and stir until smooth. Season the sauce lightly with a salt-spoonful of salt and quarter of a saltspoonful each of pepper and nutmeg, and add the *purée* of herbs to it, when it is required for use. (5.) When the capon and tongues are done, dish them on a little of the sauce laid on the bottom of a platter, placing a tongue on each side of the capon; garnish the dish with parsley, and send the remainder of the sauce to the table in a sauce-boat, with dish of capon.

LOBSTER SALAD.

INGREDIENTS.

1 lobster - - - - - - - -	25 cents.
Materials for *Mayonnaise* - - - -	10 "
Eggs, olives, and capers - - - - -	5 "
Lettuce and salad dressing - - - -	10 "
Total - - - - -	50 cents.

(1.) Boil a lobster as directed on page 31. Remove it from the shell, throwing away the intestine which runs through the center of the tail, and the stomach, often called the "lady," a hard, round membrane lying near the head of the lobster. If there is any coral, green fat, or spawn, save them to decorate the salad with. (2.) Wash the lettuce, shake it dry in a towel, tear it apart with the fingers, and arrange it in the salad bowl with the lobster, reserving the white inner leaves for decoration; pour over the salad a dressing made of two tablespoonfuls of oil, one of vinegar, a saltspoonful of salt, and quarter of a saltspoonful of pepper. (3.) Make a *Mayonnaise* as directed in the receipt for Cardinal Sauce, on page 152; cover the salad with it, and decorate it with olives, capers, the coral or spawn, the white lettuce leaves, and two hard boiled eggs cut in quarters. Serve it as soon as it is

CUMBERLAND PUDDING WITH RUM SAUCE.

INGREDIENTS.

6 oz. bread crumbs - - - - - - -	2 cents.
6 " currants - - - - - - - -	4 "
6 " suet - - - - - - - - -	3 "
6 " apples - - - - - - - - -	2 "
8 " sugar - - - - - - - -	5 "
4 " citron - - - - - - - - -	8 "
6 eggs - - - - - - - - -	6 "
Orange and lemon - - - - - - -	4 "
1 gill rum - - - - - - - - -	13 "
Total - - - - - -	47 cents.

(1.) Shred and chop the suet. Pick over and wash the currants. Pare and chop the apple. Cut the citron in thin slices. Grate the rind of the orange and lemon, and squeeze their juice into separate cups. (2.) Put all these ingredients, except the lemon juice, into a bowl; add the bread crumbs, eggs, six ounces of sugar, and a teaspoonful of salt, and mix them together thoroughly. (3.) Put the pudding into a buttered mould, set it in a saucepan containing boiling water enough to reach two-thirds up its sides, set it over the fire, and steam it three hours. Then turn it from the mould, dust it with powdered sugar, and serve it with Rum Sauce, made as follows. (4.) Melt two ounces of sugar over the fire with the lemon juice and a gill of boiling water, add the rum, and use the sauce at once.

CHAPTER X.

TENTH LESSON OF THE LADIES' COURSE.

Game Consommé à la Désclignac.
Carp à la Chambord.
Potatoes à la Provençale.
Galantine of Chicken.
Oyster Patties.
Shoulder of Lamb à la Financière.
Shad-roe Salad.
Macedoine of Fruits.

GAME *CONSOMMÉ À LA DÉSCLIGNAC.*

INGREDIENTS.

1 partridge or prairie hen	50 cents.
1 rabbit	25 "
¼ lb. ham	3 "
1 knuckle of veal	10 "
Soup vegetables	5 "
7 eggs	7 "
Total	$1.00

(1.) Make a *consommé* as directed on pages 105 and 106, substituting the veal, ham, a partridge, and a rabbit for the soup meat, and clearing it perfectly. (2.) Make a *Royale* Paste, as directed on page 144, and add it to the *consommé* as directed in the receipt for *Consommé à la Royale.* Serve as soon as the paste is added.

CARP *À LA CHAMBORD.*

INGREDIENTS.

3 lbs. carp	45 cents.
¼ lb. larding pork	5 "
½ " button mushrooms	25 "
1 gill wine	13 "
1 oz. butter	2 "
Vegetables, flour and seasonings	3 "
Total	93 cents.

(1.) Dress a carp for baking, remove the skin from the upper side, and lard it as directed in the receipt for *Fricandeau* of Veal, on page 150. (2.) Lay it in a dripping-pan on a little bed of herbs and vegetables, season it with a teaspoonful of salt and quarter of a saltspoonful of pepper, and bake it half an hour in a moderate oven. (3.) Mix together over the fire one ounce each of butter and flour until they bubble; add half a pint of boiling water gradually, stirring the sauce smooth with an egg whip, season it with a teaspoonful of salt, and half a saltspoonful each of white pepper and nutmeg; add the button mushrooms and wine, and simmer gently, closely covered, for twenty minutes. (4.) When the carp is done transfer it to a platter without breaking it, pour the sauce over it, garnish it with parsley, and serve it hot.

POTATOES À LA PROVENÇALE.

INGREDIENTS.

1 qt. potatoes - - - - - - -	3 cents.
1 oz. butter - - - - - - - -	2 "
Shallot and seasonings - - - - -	2 "
	___
Total - - - - - -	7 cents.

(1.) Cut a quart of cold boiled potatoes in little balls with a vegetable scoop or knife. (2.) Chop one shallot, which is a small onion of intense flavor, and fry it pale yellow in an ounce of butter. (3.) Put the potato balls into the frying-pan with the shallot and butter, and toss them over the fire until they are pale brown. Sprinkle them with a little salt, and serve them hot.

GALANTINE OF CHICKEN (TO FINISH).

INGREDIENTS.

Chicken - - - - - - - - -	___
2 eggs - - - - - - - - -	2 cents.
2 oz. gelatine - - - - - - -	15 "
½ pt. wine - - - - - - - -	25 "
	___
Total - - - - - -	42 cents.

(1.) When the chicken has boiled three hours, take it up, remove the cloth, wash it in cold water, and tie the chicken up again in it; put it between two platters, under a heavy weight, and let it stand over night to cool. (2.) Strain the stock in which it was boiled, and let that stand over night, so that all the fat can be removed. (3.) Remove all the fat, put the stock over the fire, add to it two ounces of gelatine dissolved in a pint of cold water, and clarify it as directed in the receipt for *consommé*, on page 106. Strain it through flannel until perfectly clear; pour it into two shallow moulds; color one dark brown with Caramel, and cool until the jelly is firm. (4.) Lay the *Galantine*, or boned chicken on a dish, and garnish it with the jelly, cut in fanciful shapes. Serve it cold. Boned Turkey is prepared in the same way.

OYSTER PATTIES.

INGREDIENTS.

½ lb. flour	2 cents.
½ " butter	16 "
1 qt. oysters	25 "
Materials for sauce	10 "
Total	53 cents.

Make a Puff Paste as follows: some ice, a round, smooth roller about two feet long and two and a half inches in diameter, and a smooth stone or marble slab, are the sole extraneous aids to the manipulator's skill. (1.) Wet the slab with a little water, lay upon it half a pound of butter; work out all the salt and buttermilk by kneading it with both hands, and then keep out about an ounce of the butter, fold the rest in a floured napkin, and lay it upon some ice. (2.) Next dry the slab thoroughly, sift upon it half a pound of fine, white flour, form this in a circle or well, putting aside about two ounces to dust the slab with; into the well drop the ounce of butter reserved, and the yolk of one egg, and work them to a cream with the tips of the fingers; to this gradually add the flour from the well, with enough ice-cold water poured on from time to time, as required to form a dough about the consistency of short-cake (*about one cup of water, more or less, will be used, according to the body of the flour;*) now work the paste about on the slab until it leaves it clean and free, and does not cling to the fingers; take it up in a ball and dust the slab lightly with flour, lay on the paste, flatten it down, and beat it with the roller for five minutes, turning and doubling it constantly; this process toughens it so that the butter will not break through in the subsequent manipulations. (3.) Now raise the paste and dust the slab again with flour; lay the paste on it, and roll out to a square of about eight inches; turn *the face of the paste,* or the part which has been next the roller, down upon the slab, lay upon it the lump of cold butter, and fold the paste up and over it so as to cover every part; turn the ball thus formed upside down, roll it out gently and evenly until the butter is incorporated with the paste, taking care not to break through the latter, as all the air-cells that can be gathered unbroken in the paste assist its rising; now turn the sheet of paste gently about on the slab, so that every part may be rolled to the same thickness of about one-quarter of an inch; in turning the paste, lift its outer edge and gently lap it over the roller towards you, being sure not to tear it, roll it gently inward, keeping it around the roller, and lifting it clear from the board when you wish to turn it or change its position in any way; when you wish to replace it upon the slab, gently unwind it from the roller, letting the face, or part next the roller, fall upon the slab. (4.) *The paste is now ready for forming the flakes; to do this, turn the face down, fold it in three thicknesses lengthwise, lay it in a long pan floured, set this in a larger pan of ice, and place upon it a third pan filled with ice, so that the paste will be completely surrounded with ice; let the pans stand for five minutes in the ice-box, or in the coolest place you can command, always bearing in mind that the cooler the paste is kept the better it will be.* Repeat the process described between the asterisks six times in succession, every time setting the paste in ice for five minutes, every time turning the face of the paste with the folds down to the slab, and every time folding in an opposite direction, or the butter will lie at one side, and the paste will rise unevenly in baking. (5.) To finish. After the sixth time of folding, roll the paste out to the thickness of one-quarter of an inch, and cut out in shape with a sharp tin cutter of the size required, marking a circle an inch in diameter on the top of each with a small pastry cutter. For small tarts, or patties, have the paste one quarter of an inch thick; for large ones, or *vol-au-vents,* have it about one third thicker; for patties use two layers of paste, put one over the other after cutting out, and wet the under layer with a soft brush dipped in cold water; brush the top of the second layer with an egg beaten up; this is called *dorée,* or gilding, and the process gives the pastry a beautiful golden glaze. In forming *vol-au-vents,* or large pastries, use three or even four thicknesses of the paste, putting them together as for patties, brushing the under layers with cold water, and gilding the top. (6.) Lastly, wet the baking-pan with water instead of greasing it, lay the paste upon it, set it for five minutes upon the ice in order that the layers may adhere, and put in a moderate oven five minutes, so that all the air-cells will have a chance to expand; then finish at a heat of about 300° Fahr., and be sure that the patties are done before taking them from the oven, or they will fall. (7.) Cut a little circle in the center of the patties, and fill them with Oysters *à la Poulette,* made as directed on page 166.

SHOULDER OF LAMB À LA FINANCIÈRE.

INGREDIENTS.

3 lbs. shoulder of lamb - - - - -	36 cents.
½ can of mushrooms - - - - - -	18 "
1 gill wine - - - - - - -	13 "
1 oz. butter - - - - - - -	2 "
Eggs, bread crumbs and seasonings - -	5 "
2 qts. broth - - - - - - -	24 "
¼ lb. larding pork - - - - -	5 "
Total - - - - -	$1.03

(1.) Trim off the end of the knuckle, and bone the shoulder as directed for *Canton* of Lamb on page 120. (2.) Stuff it with a forcemeat made as directed on the same page. (3.) Sew it up in the form of a cushion, lard it as directed in the receipt for *Fricandeau* of Veal, lay it in a saucepan on a bed of the trimmings of the larding pork and some scraps of vegetables and herbs; cover it with broth and simmer it for four hours. (4.) When it is tender lay it on a dish after removing the string, garnish it with the following sauce, put a paper frill on the end of the bone, and serve it hot. (5.) Make the sauce by stirring together over the fire one ounce each of butter and flour until they bubble, then adding half a pint of the broth from the lamb, the mushrooms and the liquor in which they were preserved, the wine, and a slight seasoning of salt, nutmeg and pepper. Cock's-combs and truffles are part of the regular *Financière ragoût*, but they are expensive and difficult to obtain.

SHAD-ROE SALAD.

INGREDIENTS.

1 shad-roe - - - - - - - -	10 cents.
1 head salad - - - - - - -	5 "
1 pt. tomatoes - - - - - - -	3 "
Lemon juice, oil, and seasonings - - -	5 "
Total - - - - - -	23 cents.

Boil the roe, separate the grains by washing them in vinegar, place them in a salad bowl, with one head of tender lettuce and one pint of ripe tomatoes cut thin; dress them with two tablespoonfuls each of oil, lemon juice, and strained tomato pulp, seasoned with cayenne pepper. Serve the salad as soon as it is made.

MACEDOINE OF FRUITS.

INGREDIENTS.

½ pt. currant jelly - - - - -	20 cents.
½ " orange " - - - - - -	20 "
½ " wine " - - - - - -	20 "
½ " lemon " - - - - - -	20 "
¼ lb. candied cherries - - - - -	25 "
¼ " " oranges - - - - -	25 "
¼ " " grapes - - - - -	25 "
¼ " " currants - - - - -	25 "
Total - - - - -	$1.80

A *macedoine* of fruits may be made of any fresh fruit in season, or of candied fruits of contrasting colors; the effect of the dish depends upon the contrast of color which it affords. The jellies must be melted separately, and one poured into an oiled mould and allowed to become firm. Some of the fruit should be laid upon it, then another jelly poured in and allowed to set. More fruit and jelly should be added until all are used, and then the mould should be set upon the ice until the *macedoine* is perfectly firm. It may then be turned from the mould and served.

CHAPTER XI.

ELEVENTH LESSON OF THE LADIES' COURSE.

Potage à la Hollandaise.
Scallops of Sturgeon aux Fines Herbes.
Potatoes with Sauce Piquante.
Chicken Sauté à la Maréngo.
Brussels Sprouts à la Maître d'Hotel.
Roast Pigeons.
Shrimp Salad.
Pudding Diplomatique.

POTAGE À LA HOLLANDAISE.

INGREDIENTS.

1 knuckle of veal - - - - - -	10 cents.
Carrot, turnips, seasonings and herbs - -	3 "
1 pt. green peas - - - - - -	5 "
1 " string beans - - - - - - -	5 "
1 " milk - - - - - - - -	4 "
6 eggs - - - - - - - - -	6 "
2 oz. butter - - - - - - -	4 "
Total - - - - -	37 cents.

(1.) Make a clear stock as directed on page 105, from the knuckle of veal. (2.) Cut the carrot and turnip in the shape of olives; cut the string beans in diamonds, and shell the peas; boil all these vegetables till tender, in separate vessels, in boiling water and salt, and put them into cold water to keep their color. (3.) Beat the yolks of six eggs with half a pint of milk, and gradually add them to the soup, stirring it smooth over the fire; season it lightly with salt and pepper; put the vegetables into it to heat, and serve it hot, at once, so that they will not lose their color.

SCALLOPS OF STURGEON *AUX FINES HERBES.*

INGREDIENTS.

2 lb. sturgeon - - - - - -	20 cents.
Materials for *Marinade* - - - -	15 "
Oil for frying - - - - - - -	15 "
Fried parsley - - - - - - -	5 "
Total - - - - -	55 cents.

(1.) Make a *Marinade* as directed on page 118, adding another gill of oil to it and lay the sturgeon in it for two days. (2.) Cut the sturgeon in small slices, dry them on a clean towel, and toss them over the fire till brown, with the following ingredients, which must first be made hot: a tablespoonful each of chopped parsley and mushrooms, a level teaspoonful of chopped onion, and a gill of oil. (3.) Arrange the scallops neatly on a dish, and garnish them with parsley which has been washed, dried, and dipped for one minute in hot oil to crisp it.

POTATOES WITH *SAUCE PIQUANTE.*

INGREDIENTS.

1 quart of potatoes - - - - -	3 cents.
1 oz. butter - - - - - - -	2 "
Onions, pickle, capers and vinegar - - -	5 "
1 pint of broth - - - - - -	5 "
Total - - - - -	15 cents.

Cut some cold boiled potatoes in slices, toss them over the fire in a sauce made according to the directions given on page 95, substituting a pint of broth for the boiling water, and serve them hot.

CHICKEN *SAUTÉ À LA MARÉNGO.*

INGREDIENTS.

3 lbs. chicken - - - - - -	38 cents.
½ can mushrooms - - - - -	18 "
1 gill wine - - - - - - -	13 "
Flour, oil and seasonings - - - -	5 "
Total - - - - -	74 cents.

(1.) Prepare a chicken as directed for Chicken Curry on page 115. (2.) Brown it in a sauce-pan with a gill of oil, and stir in an ounce of flour; when the flour is brown add one teaspoonful of salt, quarter of a saltspoonful of pepper, one clove of garlic and a *bouquet* of herbs; put in the mushrooms, and enough boiling water to cover the chicken, and simmer it until it is tender. (3.) When the chicken is tender, add the wine, see if the seasoning is palatable, and serve the dish with a garnish of *croûtons* of fried bread.

BRUSSELS SPROUTS *À LA MAÎTRE D'HOTEL.*

INGREDIENTS.

1 qt. Brussels Sprouts - - - - -	20 cents.
Materials for *maître d'hotel* butter - - -	5 "
Total - - - - - -	25 cents.

Cleanse the sprouts in plenty of cold water and salt, boil them as directed for Green Vegetables on page 50, and when ready to use them, warm them over the fire with some *maître d'hotel* butter, made as directed on page 34. String beans may be cooked and served in the same way, the beans being cut in diamonds, or slivers, before cooking.

ROAST PIGEONS.

INGREDIENTS.

6 pigeons - - - - - - -	75 cents.
¼ lb. larding pork - - - - - -	5 "
Materials for sauce - - - - - -	5 "
Total - - - - -	85 cents.

(1.) Pluck the birds and dress them, reserving the livers, but do not wash them. (2.) Tie a slice of larding pork over the breasts, and roast them twenty minutes. (3.) Meantime chop the livers, and put them over the fire to simmer with the grated rind of one lemon, half a pint of broth or water, one ounce of butter, a tablespoonful of chopped parsley, a teaspoonful of salt, and quarter of a saltspoonful of pepper. When the livers are done, add the lemon juice, and serve the sauce in a sauce-boat. Garnish the pigeons with watercresses.

SHRIMP SALAD.
INGREDIENTS.

1 pint of shrimps	15 cents.
1 head lettuce	5 "
Materials for *Mayonnaise*	15 "
Total	35 cents.

(1.) Boil the shrimps five minutes in boiling water and salt; remove the heads and hard shells, and arrange them in a salad dish with the lettuce, which must be well washed, and dried by shaking in a clean towel. (2.) Chop a tablespoonful of parsley, mix it with a *Mayonnaise*, made as directed on page 152, and dress the salad with it.

PUDDING *DIPLOMATIQUE.*
INGREDIENTS.

Sponge Cake	25 cents.
¼ lb. raisins	3 "
¼ " currants	3 "
2 oz. citron	4 "
6 eggs	6 "
1 pt. milk	4 "
4 oz. sugar	3 "
1 " butter	2 "
Total	50 cents.

(1.) Stone the raisins, slice the citron, wash and dry the currants. (2.) Slice the cake, put it into a plain mould, well buttered, in layers with the fruit, and pour over them a custard made as follows. (3.) Beat six eggs with a pint of milk, four ounces of sugar, and a teaspoonful of Vanilla essence, and pour the custard over the pudding; put an ounce of butter on the top in small bits, set the mould in a sauce-pan, containing enough boiling water to reach two-thirds up the sides of the mould, and simmer the pudding an hour. (4.) Make a sauce by dissolving a teaspoonful of corn starch in a cup of cold water, adding two table-

spoonfuls of currant jelly and a glass of wine to it, and
bringing it to a boil. (5.) When the pudding is done,
turn it out of the mould, dust it with powdered sugar, and
send it to the table with the sauce in a sauce-boat.

CHAPTER XII.

TWELFTH LESSON OF THE LADIES' COURSE.

Purée of Carrots.
Turban of Flounders à la Hollandaise.
Potatoes sauté à la Barigoule.
Mutton Cutlets à la Milanaise.
French Beans sauté aux Fines Herbes.
Filet de Bœuf à la Macedoine.
Italian Salad.
To Glacé Fruits and Nuts.
Gâteau de Princesse Louise.

PURÉE OF CARROTS.

INGREDIENTS.

1 pt. green peas	5 cents.
Carrots	5 "
4 oz. sausage meat	3 "
1 " butter	2 "
Flour and seasonings	1 cent.
Total	16 cents.

(1.) Pare and slice the carrots and boil them in two
quarts of boiling water till tender enough to rub through a
sieve with a wooden spoon. Return the *purée* thus made
to the water in which the carrots were boiled. (2.) Mix
one ounce each of butter and flour together dry, and stir
them into the *purée* to keep it from settling. (3.) Boil a
pint of green peas in boiling water and salt till tender,
wash them in cold water to set their color, and put them

into the soup tureen. (4.) Meantime make the sausage meat into balls about quarter of an inch in diameter, toss them over the fire in a frying-pan until they are brown, and put them into the tureen with the peas. (5.) Season the soup with two teaspoonfuls of salt and quarter of a saltspoonful of pepper; pour it into the tureen upon the peas and force-meat balls, and serve it at once.

TURBAN OF FLOUNDERS À LA HOLLANDAISE.

INGREDIENTS.

2 lbs. flounders - - - - - -	12 cents.
½ pt. *Hollandaise* Sauce - - - - -	10 "
Total - - - - -	22 cents.

(1.) *Filet* the flounders as directed on page 32; roll each *filet* up, secure it in place with a little wooden skewer, and set them on a dish that can be sent to the table. (2.) Make a *Hollandaise* Sauce as directed on page 111, pour it over the *filets,* or *turbans,* as they are called when rolled, and bake them fifteen minutes in a moderate oven.

POTATOES SAUTÉ À LA BARIGOULE.

INGREDIENTS.

1 qt. potatoes - - - - - - -	3 cents.
Oil and seasonings - - - - - -	10 "
Total - - - - -	13 cents.

Cut cold boiled potatoes in the shape of olives, and toss them over the fire till brown in hot olive oil with a table-spoonful of chopped green herbs; drain them on brown paper, and serve them hot.

MUTTON CUTLETS À LA MILANAISE.

INGREDIENTS.

1 lb. mutton cutlets - - - - - -	16 cents.
¼ " macaroni - - - - - -	4 "
2 oz. Parmesan cheese - - - - -	4 "
Bread crumbs, egg, and fat for frying - -	6 "
Total - - - - -	30 cents.

(1.) Trim the cutlets free from fat, bread them as directed in the receipts for fried *filets* on pages 32 and 33, mixing a little grated Parmesan cheese with the bread crumbs, and fry them light brown in half an ounce of butter, seasoning them with a teaspoonful of salt. (2.) Meantime, boil the macaroni as directed on page 40, put in a mound in the center of a dish, dust it with the rest of the grated Parmesan, arrange the cutlets around it, and serve the dish hot.

FRENCH BEANS *SAUTÉ AUX FINES HERBES.*

INGREDIENTS.

1 pt. string beans - - - - - - -	5 cents.
Butter and herbs - - - - - - - - 5	"
Total - - - - -	10 cents.

Cook the beans as directed in the receipt for boiling Green Vegetables on page 50; toss them over the fire till hot with an ounce of butter, a tablespoonful of chopped green herbs, a teaspoonful of chopped onion, a saltspoonful of salt, and quarter of a saltspoonful of pepper; serve them hot.

FILET DE BŒUF À LA MACEDOINE.

INGREDIENTS.

3 lbs. of *filet* of beef - - - - -	$1.50
Soup vegetables - - - - -	5
1 qt. stock - - - - - - - -	.12
¼ lb. larding pork - - - - - -	5
1 pt. string beans - - - - - -	5
Cauliflower and asparagus - - - -	.10
Carrots and turnips - - - - -	5
Total - - - -	$1.92.

(1.) Lard the *filet* as directed in the receipt for *Fricandeau* of Veal. Lay it in a sauce-pan on a bed of scraps of vegetables and trimmings of larding pork. Cover it with stock and simmer it an hour, or until tender. (2.) Meantime cut the carrots and turnips in the form of olives, the beans in diamonds, half a cauliflower in little branches, half a bunch of asparagus in asparagus peas, and cook them in separate vessels, as directed in the receipt for Green Vegetables on page 50. When the *filet* is done, heat these vegetables separately in a little of the broth it has been cooked in, dish it and arrange them around it in little groups; strain over it enough of the broth to moisten it, and serve it hot.

ITALIAN SALAD.

INGREDIENTS.

1 pt. green peas	5 cents.
1 " string beans	5 "
Carrot, turnip and beet	3 "
Cauliflower and asparagus	10 "
Oil, vinegar and seasonings	5 "
Total	28 cents.

(1.) Shell the peas. Cut off the asparagus heads. Cut the beans in diamonds. Peel and slice the carrot and turnip, and cut them in cylinders quarter of an inch thick and an inch long. Cut the cauliflower in little branches. (2.) Boil all these vegetables and lay them in cold water to preserve their color, as directed on page 50. (3.) Boil the beet as directed in the receipt for Cardinal Sauce on page 152, and cut it in cylinders like the carrot and turnip. (4.) Arrange all the vegetables on a salad dish, dress them with two tablespoonfuls of oil, one of vinegar, a teaspoonful of salt and quarter of a saltspoonful of pepper, and serve the salad.

TO *GLACÉ* FRUIT AND NUTS.

INGREDIENTS.

1½ lbs. of loaf sugar	20 cents.
½ " Malaga grapes	10 "
2 oranges	4 "
¼ lb French chestnuts	15 "
Total	49 cents.

(1.) Slit the chesnut shells, roast the nuts about twenty minutes, and then peel off the shells and skins. Cut the grapes in small bunches. Peel and quarter the oranges, taking care not to break the inner skin, and dry them by the fire. (2.) Put the sugar into a copper sugar boiler, with three gills of cold water, and bring it slowly to a boil. As often as the sugar boils up lift the boiler an instant to check the boiling, and when it falls wipe the sugar from the sides of the boiler with a clean, wet cloth. Have a bowl of cold water by the fire, and when the sugar boils up in large air bubbles dip a little stick into it, and then quickly into the cold water; if the sugar crackles and breaks easily away from the stick it has boiled to the proper point. It may be necessary to test it several times, and care should be taken not to let it boil an instant longer than necessary. The moment the proper point is reached take the boiler from the fire and *glacé* the fruit. (3.) Have each nut and piece of fruit stuck on a thin skewer; dip the fruit into the sugar, and lay the skewer on a sieve so that the fruit hangs over the edge, and so that no two pieces touch. The sugar will harden quickly, and then the fruit may be laid on a dish until required for use. The grapes may be held by the stem and moved about in the sugar until they are covered with it. (4.) A clear day should always be chosen for preparing fruit in this way, because dampness softens the sugar and makes it run.

GÂTEAU DE PRINCESSE LOUISE.

INGREDIENTS.

Sponge Cake sheet - - - - - -	10 cents.
Material for Cream Cakes - - - -	25 "
1 pt. cream - - - - - - - -	20 "
Sugar and flavoring - - - - -	5 "
½ lb. *glacé* fruit and nuts - - - - -	40 "
Total - - - -	$1.00

(1.) Make a *paté-choux* paste and cream as for Cream Cakes; put part of the paste on the baking pan in a hollow ring as large as a dinner plate, and the rest by the teaspoonful in little puffs; bake them, and fill them with the cream as directed in the receipt for Cream Cakes. (2.) *Glacé* some nuts and fruit as directed in the previous receipt. (3.) Cut the sponge cake sheet to fit the outer edge of the rim of *paté-choux* paste, and fasten the rim to it with a little of the *glacé*. (4.) *Glacé* the little puffs, and fasten them upon the rim; ornament it profusely with the *glacé* fruit and nuts. (5.) Sweeten and flavor the cream to taste, and whip it to a stiff froth, taking off the froth as fast as it appears firm, and draining it upon a sieve. (6.) When it is half done color the remainder bright pink with a few drops of raspberry or strawberry syrup, and finish whipping it, draining it on a second sieve. (7. When all the cream is whipped fill the *gâteau* with it, blending the white and pink cream tastefully; keep the *gâteau* very cold until wanted for use.

PART V.

APPENDIX.

CHAPTER I.

THE PHYSIOLOGY OF NUTRITION.

THE principles of economy which form the basis of the system of instruction followed in the N. Y. School of Cookery underlie the mere culinary treatment of food. In order to comprehend the possibilities of frugal living, some study must be made of the proportionate nutritive value and economy of the best known alimentary substances. This appendix is designed to present these facts to pupils in a form sufficiently popular to admit of their application to every-day use.

To make our system perfectly clear, we must ask attention for an outline which at first sight may seem rather prosaic, but which will be found not only indispensable to the success of our teaching, but will grow interesting as it is developed and practically illustrated. We shall successively discuss the following points:

The physiological composition of the body and the elements necessary to the maintenance of health which are supplied to it through the medium of food.

The requisite amount and variety of food.

The action of the digestive organs upon food.

The economic value of food.

The alimentary action of condiments.

Beverages and their nutritive values.

The effect of cookery upon food.

PHYSIOLOGICAL COMPOSITION OF THE BODY.

Experimental physiology plainly indicates those substances which enter into the composition of our bodies, and thus clearly points out the elements we must supply to it through the medium of food. In order to fully explain our meaning, we briefly recapitulate Dr. Edward Smith's summary of physical constituents:

Flesh and blood are composed of water, fat, fibrin, albumen, gelatin, and the compounds of lime, phosphorus, soda, potash, magnesia, silica, iron, and some extractive matters.

Bone contains cartilage, gelatin, fat, and the salts of lime, magnesia, soda, and potash, combined with phosphoric and other acids.

Cartilage consists of chondrin, which resembles gelatin, together with the salts of sulphur, lime, soda, potash, phosphorus, magnesia, and iron. .

Bile has in its substance water, fat, resin, sugar, cholestrin, some fatty and organic acids, and the salts of potash, iron, and soda.

The brain is made up of water, albumen, fat, phosphoric acid, osmazome, and salts.

The liver unites water, fat, and albumen, with phosphoric and other acids, and lime, iron, soda, and potash.

The lungs are formed of a substance resembling gelatin, another analogous to casein; and albumen, fibrin, cholestrin, iron, water, soda, and various fatty and organic acids.

CORRESPONDING ELEMENTS PRESENT IN FOOD.

All these elements exist in our common foods. Thus we find water in the different beverages, in fruits, succulent vegetables, eggs, fish, meat, cheese, the cereals, and even in fats.

Fat exists in butter, lard, drippings, milk, eggs, cheese,

fish, meat, the cereals, the leguminous vegetables, nuts, cocoa, and chocolate.

Sugar abounds in fruits and vegetables, and is more or less apparent in milk and cereals. Starch, which in the process of digestion is changed into glucose or grape sugar, is present in vegetables and cereals.

Fat, starch, and sugar are the principal heat foods, and are found chiefly in vegetables and cereals.

Fibrin, albumen, casein, gelatin, and gluten are the chief nitrogenous, or flesh foods, and are found both in ani' l and vegetable substances, the greater proportion of the four first elements being present in flesh, and the latter in vegetables.

The various salts exist in both animal and vegetable foods. Phosphorus, lime, and magnesia are found in meat, fish, the cereals, and potatoes. Soda is largely present in common salt, but also exists in common with potash in many vegetables. Potash is present in meat, fish, milk, vegetables, and fruits. Iron abounds in flesh, and vegetables. Sulphur is found in fibrin, albumen, and casein.

SUITABLE CHOICE OF DIET.

Upon the first consideration of this subject, it might seem possible that errors in judgment might arise pending selection from such varied food resources; but it is the fact that different races of men habitually use those foods which are best suited to enable them to resist the physical waste caused by labor or climate. Nature has given us an unerring guide to a proper choice of diet. An unperverted appetite is the voice of the physical system making known its needs, and it may always be trusted to indicate the foods necessary to the preservation of health. Of course, the amount of nutriment required by individuals will vary with their occupations and habits, as well as with their mental conditions; but this does not preclude the desirability or necessity for fixed dietaries and specific bills of fare. It only involves discrimination in their use. For, while, on the one hand, circumstances and occupation affect the choice of food, on the other, serious physical disarrangements can be largely counteracted by the judicious selection of alimentary substances.

AMOUNT AND VARIETY OF FOOD REQUISITE TO HEALTH.

Plenty of nutritious food is required early in the morning, for two reasons; the hours of sleep are those in which the vital forces draw upon the nourishment stored in the blood for their reënforcement, and the activity of the digestive organs demands a fresh supply of alimentary matter for distribution throughout the system. The following is our plan for the dietary of healthy adults.

BREAKFAST.

One pint of hot coffee or cocoa, or half a pint of chocolate, with a palatable addition of milk and sugar; quarter of a pound of bread, made of whole meal, (*i. e.*, Graham flour,) if possible; one ounce, or less, of butter; some warmed-over potatoes, and two eggs, or quarter of a pound of fresh or salt meat or fish. Cereals in any form are a valuable addition to this meal.

DINNER.

A mid-day dinner is preferable, when it is possible to obtain it, because the burden of the day's labor is not yet done, and the system demands abundant nourishment in order to accomplish it. The repast should consist of half a pint of soup, or three ounces of fish and a quarter of a pound of meat, accompanied by an equal quantity of bread and half a pound of vegetables. A plain, nutritious pudding and some fruit may conclude the meal. A little strong coffee or cheese may be often used with advantage to digestion.

SUPPER.

When the dinner is eaten at noon, the supper, or tea, should consist of a pint of tea or milk, with sugar, bread and butter, and a couple of ounces of meat or cheese, as a relish; some farinaceous food, and plain biscuit or crackers. Rich cake and pickles should be avoided. At all times this meal should be light and eaten early in the evening, so that the labor of digestion can be completed before the hour of retiring.

There are many persons who, from choice or occupation, dine at a late hour. In that case the meal should not be later than seven o'clock, and should be comparatively light if the digestion is at all impaired; for an accumulation of undigested food in the stomach and intestines will preclude the possibility of a comfortable or healthy slumber.

ACTION OF THE DIGESTIVE ORGANS ON FOOD.

We are all sensible of the attractions which a well-spread table possesses for a hungry man; but we do not always remember the fact that the delicate food which has exercised the skill of both caterer and cook is only the comparatively raw material which we are forced to draw upon for the daily supply of our physical needs.

The labor of procuring food and preparing it for the table fails to answer the end for which it was undertaken, unless, after the eating, we can derive from it those elements we need to maintain us in health and strength. All nutriment must travel the road from the stomach to the blood without hindrance, in order to meet the requirements of life.

The importance of this part of the subject must be apparent to the most careless observer, and after what we have already said regarding the close relation between food and health, we think all our pupils and readers will follow us with interest in our endeavor to give a popular *resumé* of the workings of the digestive system. If we have studied this particular branch of physiology at school, many of us have forgotten it, as we do forget most of the abstract knowledge of school before we have been a year away from it; but the revival of some of its points is absolutely necessary if we want to know the meaning of life and intend to enjoy it.

THE USE OF APPETITE.

It is a pernicious habit of thought which leads persons to disregard the claims of appetite. Those vain reasoners who seek to cast discredit upon this wonderful human mechanism, which is the greatest work in nature, by decrying our physical attributes and disregarding our daily necessities in ostensible care for our spiritual or intellectual parts, are quite sure to pay the penalty of their indifference or neglect. The wrong they do themselves and others recoils upon their own heads. Before half their allotted term of life has expired they are unable to perform its functions, and they lose their hold upon it before their time.

WHY FOOD MUST BE DIGESTED.

Food is generally of a solid consistency and needs to undergo definite changes before its nutriment can be imparted to the blood. Not only must some of its elements be changed, but it must also be reduced to a semi-liquid state. Even in the case of substances which solidify in the temperature of the stomach, or of the foods with which they are combined in cooking—such as milk, blood and eggs—they must undergo reliquefaction before they can be digested. Hence, the first office of the digestive organs is to disintegrate the particles of food and resolve them into a sort of emulsion, which the absorbent system can take up and transmit to the blood, where nutriment is stored preparatory to the renewal of the wasted atoms of the body.

Digestion is a complicated process, not confined solely to that much-abused organ, the stomach. That part of our bodies called the alimentary canal, through which the food must pass during digestion, consists of many compartments, united to each other by tubes and openings. Each compartment has its own specific work to do in the process of changing food into nutriment: This process begins in the mouth, where food is masticated and subjected to the action of the saliva.

MASTICATION.

Mastication, or chewing our food, is the only part of digestion which is left to our discretion. It is also the one which is indifferently performed in many cases, and thus becomes the fruitful parent of countless bodily ills. When food is "bolted," instead of being thoroughly masticated, it reaches the stomach in lumps of different sizes, instead of being reduced to that even moist pulp upon which the gastric juices of the stomach can act. It is taxed beyond its powers in reducing these lumps of food to the consistency it must acquire before it can leave the stomach. The soft coats and yielding tissues of that organ are forced to do the grinding and tearing work intended for the teeth. The time of digestion is greatly lengthened, and from this overtaxation spring the first seeds of dyspepsia. When food is properly divided by the teeth, the second step toward digestion takes place in the mouth. It is called insalivation, or the proper mixture of the alkaline saliva with food.

INSALIVATION.

Insalivation serves a double purpose, by moistening food and helping to dissolve its most soluble parts. It would be impossible by simple mastication to reduce food to that semi-liquid condition in which it can be acted upon by the fluids of the stomach; and, hence, we can understand at once the important office of the saliva, which flows freely into the mouth during mastication, and mingles with the food, until it is reduced to a soft paste. The saliva, by softening and partly dissolving food, enables the organs of taste to distinguish flavors. The longer we chew a morsel of food, and the more thoroughly we mix it with the saliva, the more we heighten its flavor and increase our own enjoyment. This fact alone should teach us the importance of thorough mastication, for it is an obvious proof that Nature designed the process to be pleasant enough to induce us to prolong it. Insalivation mingles globules of air with our food. These contain oxygen, the universal promoter of chemical changes in the system, and thus begin the transformation of food, or its digestion, which is its change into the elements of nutriment which are to be mingled with the blood. It also partly transforms starch into glucose, or grape sugar. This change is arrested during the passage of food through the acid gastric juice of the stomach, and is resumed under the influence of the alkaline intestinal fluids. A familiar instance of this elementary change may be cited in the case of bread, which, being chewed long enough to become well mixed with the saliva, acquires a very sweet taste, from the fact that the starch it contains has undergone the partial change into sugar.

The flow of saliva seems to depend upon either the sight or the thought of food. Even the idea of a palatable meal "makes the mouth water." The quantity of the secretion depends upon the character of food. Brinton gives the average proportion as follows: with the use of juicy fruit, four per cent.; with meat, about fifty per cent., and with hard bread or crackers, as much as one hundred and fifty per cent. The use of spices augments the secretion of saliva.

ENTRANCE OF FOOD INTO THE STOMACH.

Mastication and insalivation are followed by deglutition, or swallowing. The food passes from the mouth into a tube or canal, called the œsophagus, which has the power of circular contraction, and forces its contents down into the stomach, which is a pouch-shaped enlargement of the alimentary canal. The largest part lies under the œsophagus, on the right side of the body, and the smaller end, connected with the small intestine, is situated toward the left. The stomach generally holds about three pints, but is larger when the food is of a coarse texture and bulky consistency.

On entering the stomach, the food is carried around it by a kind of churning motion, which is caused by the action of two layers of muscles, running lengthways and cross-ways, and capable of expansion and contraction in all directions. The object of the motion is to change the relative position of the particles of food, so that they are brought successively into contact with the digestive fluid, and prepared for passage into the small intestine by being reduced to a semi-liquid consistency. The food traverses the stomach in about three minutes, and the motion continues from one to three hours, during which time the gastric juice is poured out and mingled with it, until all its nutritive properties available in stomach digestion are converted into the milky substance called chyme. In this condition some portions of it are absorbed by the stomach, as we shall now explain.

GASTRIC JUICE AND STOMACH DIGESTION.

The gastric juice is a compound fluid made up of several substances, the chief of which are pepsin and lactic acid. It is secreted by the walls of the stomach when food is introduced into it; but not when the stomach is empty. It affects only that class of elements which we have made familiar under the name of nitrogenous foods, such as the lean part of flesh, the gluten of bread and cereals, the casein of milk, the albumen or gluten of vegetables, the fiber of fish, and the white of eggs. Neither starch, sugar, nor oil undergo any chemical change of elements in the stomach. Starch is hydrated or gelatinized by the moisture and heat of the stomach, which is about 100 degrees, and the fats are melted by the same temperature. The cellular tissue of fat meat is dissolved and the oil set free, while the lean is converted into chyme. The gluten of bread and the albumen or casein of cheese are digested, while the starch of the former and the oil of the latter remain undigested until they reach the small intestine. The absorption of food really begins in the stomach, where some of its extremely liquid portions pass at once into the blood by a process known as osmosis; that is, the passage of fluids through animal membranes.

INTESTINAL DIGESTION.

From the stomach the chyme and undigested food pass into the duodenum, or upper part of the small intestine, which is the third compartment of the alimentary canal. Here the starch is acted upon by the mixed intestinal and pancreatic fluids, and entirely changed into sugar and prepared for absorption. These fluids are capable of digesting any nitrogenous matters which may have escaped the action of the gastric juice. The fats and oils, both animal and vegetable, now remain to be digested. Heretofore, as we have already said, they have only been melted; now they pass the upper part of the small intestine and unite with the pancreatic juice, which changes the oil globules into a white, opaque fluid, called chyle, which can be absorbed.

The different elements of food, converted by the digestive fluids into this semi-liquid state and prepared for absorption, may be classified as follows.

1. Albumenoid substances, or chyme, which is produced by the action of the gastric juice upon nitrogenous matters in the stomach.

2. Glucose, or grape sugar, the formation of which is begun in the mouth by the alkaline action of the saliva, suspended in the stomach by the acid reaction of the gastric juice; and completed in the duodenum by the alkaline intestinal fluids.

3. Chyle or lymph, an oily, milk-white emulsion, yielded by fats under the action of the intestinal fluids.

HOW NUTRIMENT IS ABSORBED INTO THE BLOOD.

There are two kinds of absorption, osmotic and lacteal. We have already referred to the osmotic absorption, which takes place in the stomach, and is continued in the intestine wherever chyme or glucose is present, and the lacteal absorption of chyle, which is performed by a set of vessels terminating all along the inner surface of the intestine. Thence the nutritive matters enter the receptacle for chyle, which lies in the abdominal cavity, close to the spine. Here the large vessel called the thoracic duct takes up the nutritive fluid, carries it upward, and discharges it into the general circulation through the left sub-clavian vein, which lies in the left side of the neck, under the collar-bone.

HOW NUTRIMENT IS ASSIMILATED WITH THE BLOOD.

Assimilation is the mingling of the nutritive fluid with the blood. Some physiologists believe that the albumenoid substances and glucose lose their identity during their passage through the thoracic duct, so that when its contents arrive at the entrance to the general circulation, they are already so perfectly prepared for assimilation with the blood that the union results in a well-nourished fluid, capable of revivifying the body. The chyle which passes into the circulation by this medium, is not assimilated to any great extent during its passage through the thoracic duct; and that part of it which is absorbed through the membranes of the intestines by the capillaries passes directly through the liver, with but little change of elements. Thence the oily matters are carried to the right side of the heart, and subsequently into the lungs. There they lose their identity, unless they have been used in excessive quantities, when they remain perceptible in the blood until they are gradually withdrawn to meet the requirements of nutrition.

THE MECHANICAL PART OF DIGESTION.

The churning movement already spoken of as taking place in the stomach, is the beginning of the mechanical part of digestion which is known as peristaltic action. This action is continued in the intestines wherever food comes in contact with their mucous membrane. This contact causes a local irritation, from the effects of which the circular muscular fibers of the intestine contract, and the diameter of the intestine is decreased at that point until its contents are forced downward into another section. The contraction follows the downward passage of the food, while the part originally contracted is relaxed to its former proportions. Thus a slow, creeping motion is continued from above downward. At the same time the straight muscular fibers of the intestine, which pass from end to end of it, draw its contracted portions upward, and then lower them as they relax, thus causing a peculiar writhing, worm-like motion, which perfects the downward movement of the food.

During the passage of the food through the alimentary canal its nutritive matters are undergoing absorption, so that by the time it has reached the end of the small intestine nothing remains but the indigestible portions, which cannot be converted into food. These pass into the large intestine, where they become feces.

THE USE OF WASTE MATTER IN FOOD.

Nature, being a rigid economist, permits nothing to exist without a use. These indigestible portions facilitate digestion in two ways: first, by increasing the volume of food, and rendering it less compact and solid, they expose it more thoroughly to the action of the digestive fluids; and, second, by increasing peristaltic action by the irritation they cause during their passage through the alimentary canal. If it were not for the presence of this waste matter, peristaltic action would almost entirely cease, as the nutritive portions of food are constantly being absorbed during their passage through the stomach and small intestine; constipation would follow, and Nature would lose a valuable agent for removing the worn-out matter which accumulates in the body. This fact proves that food ought not to be all nutrition and capable of entire absorption, if it is to serve the purposes of health.

CONSTIPATING AND RELAXING FOOD.

For the reasons given above, we can see the comparative value of constipating and relaxing foods. All highly concentrated nutriments, such as eggs, milk, meat, and the gluten of wheat, belong to the first class, because they afford no indigestible matter to promote the action of the bowels. The relaxing foods are preparations of unbolted flour, rye and corn breads, and fruit and vegetables.

CHAPTER II.

THE CHEMISTRY OF FOOD.

THE chemical composition of various articles of food so closely indicates their economic value that the study of these two points must be identical.

The present limit of space precludes the admission of special tables of analysis of different alimentary substances, but their general characteristics can be ascertained clearly enough from the following matter to answer the ordinary requirements of our pupils and readers. We shall treat simultaneously the chemical composition and the economic value of food.

In considering the economic value of food we must fix upon some well-known article in general use as the standard to which we can compare others. For instance, beef being the best-known and most important animal food, we shall choose it as the standard for that class of substances.

Wheaten flour and dried peas will serve as the represent-atives of vegetable aliments. The comparison would be closer if we could take lentils as our standard, as it will be seen by a glance at the following table that they are the most nutritious of all vegetables. However, we name wheat because it is much more familiar to the public generally. This table of the nitrogenous (*i. e.*, the flesh-forming) value of different foods is compiled from the catalogue of the Food Gallery at South Kensington, England.

About an equal quantity of nitrogenous elements exists in

				Cost about	
8 ounces (½ lb.) of		lean beef			6 cents.
10 "		dried lentils - - - -		7	"
11 "		dried peas or beans - -		5	"
12 "		cocoa-nibs - - - -		20	"
14 "		tea - - - - -		40	"
15 "		oatmeal - - - -		5	"
1 pound	1 ounce	wheat flour - - -		4	"
1 "	1 "	coffee - - - - -		30	"
1 "	2 "	rye meal - - - -		5	"
1 "	3 "	barley meal - - - -		5	"
1 "	5 "	Indian meal - - - -		5	"
1 "	13 "	buckwheat flour - - -		10	"
2 "	— "	wheaten bread - -		10	"
2 "	6 "	rice - - - - -		20	"
5 "	3 "	cabbage - '- - -		10	"
5 "	3 "	onions - - - - -		15	"
7 "	13 "	parsnips - - - -		15	"
8 "	15 "	turnips - - - - -		9	"
10 "	7 "	potatoes - - - -		10	"
15 "	10 "	carrots - - - - -		15	"

We must not attach too much importance to the seeming value of tea, coffee, and cocoa, as indicated by this table, unless we intend to consume with our half pound of meat nearly a pound dry weight of either at one meal. We use such comparatively small quantities of these articles of diet that their real nutritive value is very low, their alimentary use being due to the sense of warmth and comfort which we derive from them. We must also remember that the above weights are supposed to be of the dry, uncooked material, and that the process of cooking alters their weight considerably. Take, for instance, the two first articles, meat and lentils. The half pound of meat in boiling will lose about one-fourth of its substance, while the lentils will be augmented at least three times in volume, so that it will be seen that the quantity of food when cooked must be considered, as well as its price.

VALUE OF DIFFERENT MEATS.

The different kinds of meat vary greatly, so far as their comparative nutriment is concerned. We get nearly three times as much carbon, or heat-food, from equal weights of fat salt pork or bacon as from the same quantity of beef, while the amount of nitrogen, or flesh-food is nearly equal. This fact will show at a glance that a poor man would exercise the greatest economy in buying the fat bacon, on account of its excess of carbon, and in combining it in cooking with vegetables which contain an excess of nitrogen, such as peas, cabbage, etc. We need only to refer to the foregoing table to prove the importance of peas, beans, and lentils in this connection, and to justify our persistent recommendation of them to those persons who wish to choose economical as well as wholesome food. In buying pork and bacon, excessively salt brands should be avoided, because all the salt used in excess of that required to preserve the meat extracts many of its valuable juices and mineral salts, especially if it is kept in brine. Meats cured partly by smoking are preferable to the pickled sorts, for this reason, as well as for the valuable antiseptic effect of the smoke.

The flesh of young animals contains less nutriment than that of full-grown ones, and its shrinkage in cooking is greater, on account of the water it presents. In full-grown meats the waste in boiling or stewing, with the pot closely covered, is about one pound in four; in baking, one pound and a quarter; in roasting before the fire, one pound and a half. The waste is much greater in careless cooking, when the oven-door is left open or the cover is not kept on the pot. The flesh of mountain sheep and cattle is said to be richer in nitrogenous elements than any other, and, consequently, preferable, when tender.

PERCENTAGE OF FAT AND BONE.

The different joints of meat vary in economic value according to the quantity of fat and bone which they contain, as well as the density or looseness of their texture. The latter point is important. A piece of meat of a loose, fibrous texture shrinks more in cooking in proportion to its weight than one that has a close, firm fiber. The fat of a full-fed healthy animal is about one-third of its entire weight, and varies in its distribution, the largest quantity being present in the loin. The percentage of fat is a little less than one-half in prime mutton and three-fourths in fat pork. Game and poultry are much leaner than meat.

The percentage of bone varies in different joints. For instance, there is very little bone in the loin and upper part of the leg, nearly one-half the entire weight in the shin, and about one-tenth in the other parts of the carcass. The proportion of bone in prime mutton and pork is much less than that present in beef, because the bones are much smaller and the amount of fat greater. Bones are exceedingly useful in the preparation of soups and stews; especially the bones of the leg, which contain the marrow. Experiments made by Dr. Edward Smith proved that three pounds of bone would yield as much carbon, and six pounds as much nitrogen as one pound of meat. The bones were chopped fine and boiled slowly for nine hours. These facts prove the use that can be made of a part of the animal very generally considered as refuse, especially for soup.

EDIBLE ENTRAILS.

Another very important part of the animal structure is

too often thrown aside as useless, except perhaps for the fat it yields in the mass. We refer to the edible entrails, such as the haslet, tripe, etc. This portion of the animal yields quite as much nitrogen as the solid flesh, and some parts of it—the liver, for instance—much more. In Europe, where the meat supply is more limited than in this country, this fact is understood, and these organs are very generally used as food. We have thrown all our influence into the scale of public opinion on this point, in order to induce people to satisfy themselves by experiment of the actual nutritive value of this sort of food. Combined with potatoes, onions, cereals, or leguminous vegetables, the nutritive value equals, and in some cases exceeds that of meat, while the cost is far less.

We have been thus explicit in regard to meat because it is so highly and so unduly esteemed as an article of food, especially by the poorer classes, who attach an exaggerated importance to it; probably because they do not have all they want of it, and also because they do not understand the real nutritive worth of vegetable foods.

FISH, EGGS, MILK, AND CHEESE.

Estimating the nitrogenous elements present in fish on the basis of the South Kensington Food Catalogue, we find that a pound of red-blooded fish is equal to about eight pounds of potatoes, and that its value as food is less than that of meat. On the other hand it is much more abundant and cheaper, and many varieties are well-flavored and palatable. It, therefore, becomes an important article of diet, especially upon the seaboard and in lake and river towns.

The nutritive value of milk and eggs is very generally understood; and the point to be considered in relation to them is their price, which varies with the season.

Cheese is an exceedingly valuable food. It has long been held at its true value in Europe, and is beginning to be properly estimated in this country, as its recent addition to our army ration-list proves. From two to four ounces of cheese, with plenty of bread, makes a hearty meal, even for a laborer. Its actual nutritive merit depends upon the percentage of fat and casein which it contains. It is at its best stage when it is about six months old, and has begun to lose its value when it has become sharp or bitter. Cream cheese is the most nutritious. That which has been improperly made or badly kept is not so good as the prime quality. English dairy and American factory cheese of good brands are the best for economic use.

ECONOMIC AND NUTRITIVE VALUE OF THE POTATO.

By reference to the preceding table of food values, it will be seen that potatoes occupy a comparatively low position in the scale; but it is, nevertheless, the fact that they are one of the most valuable and economical of foods. Dr. Edward Smith says that in the west of Ireland laborers are allowed 10 1-2 pounds of potatoes per day as a ration, together with plenty of buttermilk; an abundant supply, when we consider the fact that 8 pounds of potatoes contains all the nitrogen a man needs for health, and more than enough carbon. As compared with wheat flour, potatoes contain 770 grains of carbon and 24 grains of nitrogen to a pound; while wheat flour contains to each pound 2,000 grains of carbon and 120 grains of nitrogen. The average cost of a pound of potatoes is 1 cent, and of a pound of medium quality of flour, 4 cents. The economic comparison can easily be made, even considering the variation from this standard of cost which must occur at different seasons.

The mild and agreeable flavor of the potato, its wholesome character, and the possibility of combining it with various other foods, make it a favorite vegetable; while the advantage of being able to obtain it at any season of the year makes it invaluable to the household purveyor. It is best however in summer autumn and winter. When

the spring approaches a change of elements takes place
preparatory to germination or sprouting, and its nutritive
value is diminished.   New potatoes, if not full grown, are
less nutritious than mature ones.   Waxy potatoes are less
digestible than mealy ones, but more hearty, because of the
length of time they remain in the stomach.   Potatoes that
are a little underdone are more satisfactory to the appetite
for this reason; and it is the case that in localities where
potatoes form the staple diet of the laboring classes they
are preferred rather underdone—(*i. e.,* "with a bone in
them.")

The different methods of cooking potatoes do not affect
their nutritive value, but there is a greater waste in some
than in others.   For instance, unless raw potatoes are
large and very carefully peeled, the loss will be nearly one-
fourth; while if they are peeled after cooking the waste
will not exceed one-fifteenth.   Again, if potatoes are boiled
in their jackets, they will not waste more than one ounce
in a pound; while if they are baked the loss will be about
one-fifth, even if they are eaten the moment they are done,
and if they are allowed to stand and shrivel, the waste is
nearly one-fourth the entire weight.

ALIMENTARY ACTION OF CONDIMENTS.

While young people do not require condiments,
either to stimulate taste or appetite, they are very useful to persons whose digestion and desire for food is impaired.

We give salt the first rank among condiments, on account of its important bearing on the general health.   A
grown person absolutely requires from a quarter to half an
ounce of salt daily to keep him in good health.   The actual value of salt cannot be more forcibly illustrated than
by citing that oft-quoted old Dutch punishment of con-
demning criminals to a diet of unsalted food.   The effects
are said to have been unmitigated physical torture, ending

in death. On the other hand, its excessive use hinders destructive assimilation.

All condiments increase our relish for food by stimulating the flow of saliva and gastric juice and by enhancing the flavor of the food. When this effect is produced, the pleasure of eating is greatly increased. We digest our food more readily and assimilate it more perfectly, so that we really derive more nutriment from well-seasoned food than from that which is so insipid as to create disgust with the first taste.

Many condiments possess actual medicinal properties, in addition to that which we have already attributed to salt. Pepper is a carminative stimulant, and its action is to aid digestion, and to prevent or abate flatulence. The spices which enter into many of the table-sauces properly included among condiments are grateful stomachics, which assist digestion, and dispel nausea. Ginger is especially valuable as a stimulating tonic, particularly in hot weather and in very warm climates. Lemon juice and vinegar, used in moderation, increase the solvent properties of the gastric juice.

In very hot climates condiments are used habitually and excessively, and are believed to counteract the languor produced by the extreme heat, as well as to fortify the system against the approach of local diseases, such as fevers caused by malarious influences. In Asia asafœtida is largely used as a condiment, especially in the mountain districts. Its flavor is based upon the same alliaceous principle which marks the taste of onions, shalots, leeks, and garlic. These vegetables may be ranked as condiments, for they are generally used simply for seasoning purposes.

As we have already indicated, all condiments should be used with reference to their direct effects upon individuals, and always in moderation.

WATER AND OTHER BEVERAGES.

The action of water upon the system is marked and important, and it is necessary that all students of cookery should understand its effect upon food when it is used with it.

Water is indispensable to the healthy operation of our physical functions. It enters into the composition of the body to the extent of, at least, two-thirds of its substance; and the blood, the great circulating medium by which the nourishment derived from food is distributed throughout the entire system, contains nine-tenths of water. This fluid condition is necessary, both to the blood and to the secretion, in order to enable them to supply the body with new material, to repair its daily waste, and also to afford an avenue for the discharge of its worn-out particles. Water enters also into the composition of the solid portions of the body. The muscles and cartilages contain it to the extent of more than one-half their substance, and the bones and teeth to about one-tenth part. The best scientific authorities fix the quantity of water or fluid required by a healthy adult at about five pints a day.

The quantity of water taken into the system during a given time cannot be estimated by that which is drank, for no ordinary food is without a large proportion of it; and absolutely dry food should have at least four times its quantity of water used with it. The following table of the proportion of water present in ordinary foods has been compiled from the deductions of the eminent English authorities, Smith and Church.

PER CENTAGE OF WATER IN 100 POUNDS OF FOOD.

Lettuce	96 pounds.	Parsnips	81 pounds.
Onions	91 "	Grapes	80 "
Beer	90 "	Potatoes	76 "
Skim milk	90 "	Fish (fresh)	74 "
Carrots	89 "	Fowl	73 "
Cabbages	89 "	Lean meat	73 "
New milk	88 "	Eggs	72 "
Apples	83 "	Liver	70 "
Beets	82 "	Fat and lean beef	50 "

Fish (dried) - -	50 pounds.	Flour - - - -	14 pounds.
Fat and lean mutton -	42 "	Rice - - - -	13 "
Bread - - - -	40 "	Indian corn meal -	13 "
Cheese - - -	34 "	Crackers - - -	13 "
Bacon - - - -	22 "	Butter - - - -	10 "
Peas and beans (dried)	14 "	Pure lard and drippings	1 "

Thus we see that we receive a large proportion of our supply of fluid in combination with our solid food; and where we make use of soups and stews we obtain an additional quantity. Even vegetables and meats, when cooked in water, absorb more or less of its bulk, especially if these substances are dried.

It must be remembered that the above table is only approximate. The quantities of water present in different articles of food vary with their age and method of preservation. For instance, freshly-gathered vegetables contain the maximum quantity of water, and those which have been stored some time in a dry place the minimum. Fresh meats which are exposed to the action of the air lose a portion of their moisture by evaporation.

PURITY OF WATER.

Since water enters so largely into the composition of our daily nourishment, it is important that it should be pure, in order to serve the purposes for which it is designed in the wise economy of Nature.

Water is usually obtained from springs and rivers, and always contains more or less organic impurities, together with certain inorganic matters, such as the mineral salts. When the quantity of the latter present in a gallon of water does not exceed thirty grains, its use will be innocuous. Where water for domestic uses is kept in cisterns or tanks lined with lead, or where it passes through leaden pipes, it is apt to be impregnated with the salts of lead to an extent capable of producing lead-poisoning. For this reason, where the water passes through lead pipes, it should be run long enough before using to insure a supply of fresh water, which has not lain for any length of time in the pipes; and where lead-lined reservoirs are employed to hold it, they should be freshly filled at least once a day.

Soft or rain-water is much more susceptible to the action of lead than hard water.

Another metallic substance which is frequently imparted to water in its passage through cisterns and pipes is iron. This is not absolutely injurious, but it imparts a disagreeable color and taste.

QUALITY OF WATER FOR DRINKING AND COOKING.

Drinking water should appear clear and colorless when seen in small quantities, and should present a pale-blue or bluish-green tint in the mass. It should have no smell and its taste should be pleasant and refreshing. This last quality in water is largely due to the gases which it contains when freshly drawn from its natural reservoir, and which are present in it in the form of air. These gases are nitrogen, oxygen and carbonic acid. A familiar illustration of this point may be made by comparing the appearance and taste of a glass of fresh spring water with some which has been long boiled. The first will be clear and sparkling, almost exhilarating; the second dull, tasteless and insipid. This fact should be remembered in the making of tea and coffee. If we want them prime, we must make them the instant the water boils, before it has had an opportunity to lose all its valuable gases by continued ebullition. Cool, fresh water is more wholesome than that which has been standing in a warm or close room or exposed to the rays of the sun.

Much of the success of cooking depends upon the water which is used during the process. Hard water coats the surface of meat or vegetables boiled in it with lime to such an extent as to render them difficult of digestion. Very soft water, which contains no mineral salts, is not healthy either for cooking or drinking, on account of this deficiency. Medium soft water helps the solution of the hard substance of food during the process of cooking, especially in the preparation of soups and stews. It also serves as a valuable solvent of animal and vegetable food during the process of digestion. Salt added to soft water hardens it to a sufficient extent for the effect to be decidedly apparent in the cooking of vegetables. This is especially to be observed with green vegetables, where the addition of salt to the water in which they are boiled maintains the firmness of their texture to such a degree as to preserve both color and flavor. Those which are boiled in unsalted soft water are soft, discolored and tasteless.

Onions boiled in soft water without salt lose nearly all their flavor and aroma; peas and beans boil to a pudding in a very short time; and even the solid roots, such as turnips and beets, lose their firmness and flavor to an unpleasant degree. It is impossible to restore either taste or consistency by salting them after they have been cooked in this way.

TEA.

The physiological action of this pleasant beverage is so well known that any extended discussion of it would seem superfluous. We shall, therefore, only recall some of the chief facts connected with it. We all know that it causes cheerfulness, clearness of mind, wakefulness, and nervousness, while it increases the action of the skin and lungs, and lowers the heart's pulsations. It is certainly a welcome accessory to every well-spread board. In fact, it is one of those luxuries which custom clothes in the garments of necessity.

There, is, however, in connection with tea, one point which should not be forgotten. We have already said that the body requires immediate nourishment early in the morning; and for that reason tea, which retards the action of the natural functions, should be banished from the breakfast table, and should appear at lunch and after dinner. Certain rules should be followed by habitual tea drinkers, if they wish to use their favorite beverage without injurious effects. They should use a moderate quantity of tea. Always make the infusion with boiling water, and employ milk as an adjunct, and sugar, if liked. Especially should they remember that high-priced teas are less desirable for general use than the medium qualities, both on account of their price, and because, owing to their purity and strength, they abound in deleterious properties. A judicious mixture of several kinds of tea is often advisable. An excellent English mixture, which combines cheapness with fineness of flavor, is composed of one pound of Congo tea with a quarter of a pound each of Assam and Orange Pekoe. The usual mixture of black and green tea is four parts of black to one of green.

COFFEE.

The action of coffee is so similar to that of tea that we need not consider it separately; it will be sufficient to remark that the chief points of difference are lessening the action of the skin, increasing the action of the heart, and when used very strong, aiding digestion to some extent.

This favorite beverage is so seldom well made that we advise our readers to remember the following points. The best method for making coffee is that which yields a clear, fragrant infusion, whose very aroma cheers and exhilarates. Intense heat is necessary to the extraction of all the valuable properties of the berry; but actual boiling dissipates the fragrant volatile oil and extracts the tannic acid of the coffee. This acid, in combination with the cream or milk usually served with coffee, hardens the albumen which they contain into an indigestible compound, which is excessively irritating to the delicate internal membranes. Therefore, in making coffee, we must endeavor to secure the requisite strength without risking a corresponding lack of flavor and extraction of tannic acid. We have tried various coffee-pots, ranging from French percolators down to earthen biggins, and we are satisfied that good coffee can be made in any pot, cup, or pitcher.

The right proportion of good coffee is one ounce and a half of the pure berry, ground very fine, to each quart of water. The water must be *boiling* when it is poured on the coffee, *but must not boil afterward*. The vessel in which the beverage is made must stand near enough to the fire to maintain a temperature of about 200° Fahr. for five or ten minutes before using. If it is made in a pot containing a strainer, it will be clear; if it is made in an ordinary pot or pitcher, it should be stirred for three minutes, in order to thoroughly saturate the grounds with the boiling water, and so cause them to sink. If the coffee is allowed to stand for about ten minutes to settle, it can be poured off carefully without disturbing the grounds, and will be as clear as wine.

COCOA AND CHOCOLATE.

Next to coffee these two beverages find favor at the breakfast table, while they are much more nutritious. Both these articles are made from the kernels of a tropical fruit, about the size of a cucumber, the fleshy part of which is sometimes used to produce a vinous liquor; they are produced from the seeds of the cocoa palm, and from a kind of ground nut. These kernels consist of gum, starch, and vegetable oil; and are marketed in four different forms, as cocoa shells, which are the husks of the kernel; cocoa nibs, which consist of the crushed nuts; ground cocoa, which is the kernels ground fine, and chocolate.

Chocolate is the finely ground powder from the kernels, mixed to a stiff paste with sugar, and sometimes a little starch. It is very nutritious; when it is difficult to digest, remove from its solution the oily cake which will collect upon the surface as it cools. It is so nutritious that a small cake of it, weighing about two ounces, will satisfy hunger; for that reason it is a good lunch for travelers.

Both cocoa and chocolate are very nutritious, and are free from the possible injurious influences of tea and coffee.

NUTRITIVE BEVERAGES.

There are some conditions of illness in which sufficient nutriment can be supplied to the body by means of certain nourishing drinks, such as egg-tea, beef-tea, Iceland-Moss chocolate, milk-punch, and egg-nogg. These beverages should always be administered under the direction of a physician in cases of serious illness; and, used judiciously, are exceedingly valuable. The excessive use of teas and gruels tends to injure weak digestive organs; especially is this fact true of gruels; when they are rapidly swallowed they are unaffected by the alkaline action of the saliva, which, as we have already said, begins the digestion of the starch of which they are largely composed. If their starchy portion has not been affected by the saliva, they pass through the stomach into the small intestine with their elements unchanged, and severely tax that portion of the digestive system.

THE EFFECT OF COOKERY ON FOOD.

The object of cooking is to prepare food so that its nutritive elements may be changed by the process of digestion into healthy blood. The application of heat greatly facilitates this process; heat is applied to food either by placing it in close proximity to the fire, as in broiling and roasting; by the use of hot air, as in baking; of hot vapor as in steaming, or of hot water as in boiling and stewing. All cooked food is more wholesome if eaten while it is hot than after it has been allowed to get cold. The temperature of the stomach is 102° Fahr., and when anything is introduced into it which lowers that temperature, digestion is suspended; and the temperature must be regained before digestion can recommence. This overtaxes the whole system. The fact that hot food is a physical economy should never be forgotten. Food should not be used while cold unless the system is very much heated, and even then the quantity should be limited; for as we have already explained, food cannot be digested until its temperature corresponds with that of the stomach.

The best method of cooking animal food is that which retains all its juices, and disintegrates its fibers so that it can be easily digested; the juices contain the flavors and the valuable mineral salts which make meat palatable and nutritious; in order to preserve them it is necessary to coagulate the albumen of the cut surfaces by excessive heat, so as to prevent their escape; for that reason, in broiling or roasting, the meat should be exposed to the intense heat of the open fire until the surface is browned, and then so far withdrawn that there is no danger of burning, and allowed to finish cooking slowly.

In boiling and stewing it should be plunged into boiling water, boiled for five minutes, and then the utensil containing it should be removed to the side of the fire so that the meat can simmer until it is done; by this process the flavoring and salts of the meat are preserved in it. When it is desirable to extract them for soup, or beef tea, the object is best served by soaking the meat for a short time in cold water, putting it over the fire in the same water, and bringing it slowly to the boiling point, which can be maintained until the soup is done; the importance and economy of soup as food is not yet fully understood in this country. The trimmings of meat, or bones, or even vegetables, will, if properly prepared, make a wholesome and hearty meal, that will go farther towards maintaining health and strength than any other article of diet of equal pecuniary value. When vegetables alone are used for food it should be remembered that they take more time for complete digestion, and must be supplied in greater quantities than animal food.

In making wheat and other cereals into bread, three different methods are employed; leavening, or raising by means of fermentation, as in ordinary home-made or bakers' bread; the rapid introduction of carbonic acid gas by means of baking-powders; and the mechanical introduction of air, as in ærated bread; the latter is undoubtedly the best means if it can be properly accomplished, as none of the nutritive elements of the flour are lost by it.

Thus we see that good cookery economizes food by preparing its elements for direct absorption into the system; in many instances it increases the bulk and nutritive values of various aliments, as, for instance, in soups and stews. It gives that variety of flavor and diversity of form upon which the appetite so largely depends; in a word, it insures the fulfilment of the requirements of health, while it gratifies our gastronomic tastes.

CHAPTER III.

DIETARY FOR SCHOOLS.*

The correspondence of this office with boarding schools and orphan asylums reveals not only the necessity of instruction in cookery, but the need of supplying certain practical information at once that can be furnished at present in no form so well as by the specific suggestions of dietaries, which recognize the condition with respect to age, etc., of those for whom they are designed. The following have therefore been supplied on request by Miss Juliet Corson, Superintendent of the New York School of Cookery,

To plan dietaries which can be applied to special uses, it is necessary to study several leading points: first, the age, sex, and occupation of those for whom the dietaries are intended; second, the climate in which they live, whether warm or cold, and the location of their dwelling, whether upon a mountain or plain; third, a due variation of aliment, and that containing sufficient water and waste matter to supply the demands of the system without overtaxing the digestive organs; fourth, the selection of foods locally well known, and their provision in quantities adequate to the requirements of the consumers.

PHYSICAL TRANSITION DURING CHILDHOOD.

At the period of childhood the transformation of the nutritive elements of food into that healthy and well nourished blood which is the source of physical and mental

---

*Reprinted from Circular No. 4, 1879, of the Bureau of Education, Department of the Interior, Washington, D. C. This Dietary was prepared at the request of the Hon. John Eaton, U. S. Commissioner of Education, and its publication was ordered by the Hon. Carl Schurz, Secretary of the Interior.

strength goes on with greater rapidity and persistence than at any other time of life; hence the importance to children more than to grown persons of an abundant supply of wholesome food. The underfeeding of a child is equivalent to the deliberate destruction of his mental faculties as well as the ruin of his health. It is a sure means of giving him a weak mind and a defective constitution, of making him an inefficient member of society, and of sending him to an untimely grave. Facts warrant us in saying that the parent, guardian, or instructor who permits a child to suffer from innutrition is as much his destroyer as if life were ended at one blow. Bad effects can undoubtedly be produced by over-feeding, but they can usually be easily remedied, while the effect of under-feeding cannot always be counteracted.

ADOLESCENCE.

Especially from the age of twelve years up to eighteen, the greatest and most unremitting care is demanded, if children are to grow up into healthy and well developed men and women. This is a time of rapid growth and marked physical changes; and these conditions are attended with the exhaustion of all that reserve force which may have been accumulated during a well nourished childhood.

It often is the case at this period of life that the appetite fails perceptibly or becomes abnormal; the task of meeting such contingencies is imperatively imposed upon those having the charge of the youth of either sex. Exercise in the open air and freedom from vexatious or severe study should be secured; the action of the skin and bowels should be carefully regulated, and the supply of nutritious food, especially of flesh-forming materials, should be ample.

The ordinary occupation at this time of life is study,

and even the lighter studies are more arduous than the greatest amount of open air exercise or any manual labor which is not excessive; so that even under the most favorable physical conditions the system must be well nourished.

EFFECT OF CLIMATE AND SEASON.

In cold climates and during the winter season an abundance of heat food is required. A well housed and warmly clad person requires less food than one thinly clad and exposed to the severity of the elements. The inhabitants of hilly regions consume more heat food than those who live in the lowlands, and a greater quantity of all kinds of food. The system demands the most generous supply of food when the season is coldest, as in midwinter.

NECESSITY FOR WATER AND WASTE IN FOOD.

The important part which water holds in the nourishment of the body can readily be comprehended if we remember that it constitutes at least two-thirds of the entire substance of the body, and nine-tenths of the volume of the blood. Its office is to assist in the digestion and distribution of food elements, and to forward the elimination of the worn out particles of the body. All flesh foods contain more or less of it, and all concentrated and dried foods should be cooked with a liberal addition of water. Soups and stews, which are exceedingly wholesome and nutritious, usually contain about three-fourths of water.

In addition to water, a healthy type of food must afford considerable waste matter or innutritious particles. If food is too highly concentrated or composed entirely of nutritive elements, it cannot keep up the natural and healthy action of the digestive organs; a certain proportion of waste is indispensable.

The woody fibre of vegetables and the bran or husks of

cereals are waste matter; they are not consumed in the system, but serve to render food less compact, thus facilitating its mingling with the gastric juices; and the stimulus caused by their presence in the bowels promotes the excretion of the worn out particles of the body.

Foods containing a wholesome quantity of waste matter are called relaxing foods, and include bread made from unbolted flour, rye, and corn meal, and fresh fruits and vegetables. Foods composed almost entirely of nutritious elements, such as eggs, milk, meat, and fine white flour, are constipating in their effect upon the system.

CONDIMENTS AND STIMULANTS.

The value of all condiments, except salt, when used with food consists in their action in promoting the appetite and stimulating the digestive organs; as both appetite and digestion are usually normal in youth, condiments are not required and should be used sparingly. Salt, however, is indispensable to health, and should be supplied in a sufficient quantity to meet the demands of an unperverted appetite; a vigorous youth requires, carefully blended with his food, about half an ounce of salt per diem.

Alcoholic stimulants are absolutely injurious to the expanding system, because their tendency is to retard that change of tissue so essential to the process of growth. Where physical debility is marked, stimulants may be valuable, but they should be used only by direction of a physician.

ACTION OF TEA AND COFFEE.

The action of tea and coffee upon the system is a theme prolific of discussion, but the fact is conceded by the best authorities that both these agreeable beverages, when used in moderation, exercise a pleasantly stimulating and "staying" influence; that is, they so far retard the process of destructive assimilation as to render the sensation of hunger less acute, and to reserve a certain amount of strength even 'during hard labor. In youth, the change of the nutriment contained in food into well nourished blood should never be retarded, and sufficient strength should be supplied by food to meet all the demands of the body; therefore the action of tea and coffee is undesirable.

FOOD VALUE OF COCOA AND CHOCOLATE.

Cocoa and chocolate have a somewhat similar stimulating effect, but as they also possess considerable fat and nutriment, their moderate use in youth is less objectionable than the use of tea and coffee.

MILK AS A NUTRIENT.

But the proper beverages for youth are moderately cool water, of the temperature of about 45° F., and plenty of sweet, pure milk.

Actual scientific experiments, made in England by Dr. Ferguson, an inspector of factories, establish the fact that between the ages of thirteen and sixteen children grow nearly four times as fast, and become correspondingly strong, on milk for breakfast and supper, as when ordinarily strong tea and coffee are used. With plenty of milk, about one quart per diem, and bread enough to satisfy the appetite, a child would be well nourished; but after reaching the age of seven years, the physical requirements of children are best met by a plain mixed diet.

PROPER TEMPERATURE OF FOOD.

The temperature at which food is eaten should approach that of the stomach, about 100° F., so that the process of digestion may not be impeded. Food cannot be digested until it is heated to this temperature; and, unless the necessary heat is artificially supplied before its introduction into the stomach, that organ must be taxed to afford

it.   This fact accounts for the unwholesome effect of
ice cold water upon the process of digestion.   Too
great a degree of heat in food is also injurious to the digestive organs, by causing irritation and weakness, besides
tending to destroy the teeth.

VARIETY OF FOOD NECESSARY TO HEALTH.

Monotony of diet is to be avoided because it restricts
the supply of food elements essential to good health; but
unfounded fancies about new or peculiar articles of food
should be corrected firmly and kindly, unless some physical idiosyncrasy justifies their indulgence.   Because the
equal and adequate nourishment of the body influences
the formation of both mind and character, the utmost care
should be given to the selection of the diet; and where vi-
tality is impaired even in a slight degree, means must be
employed to increase the desire for food.

A wholesome and abundant variety of food can be obtained in almost any civilized locality: broiled and roasted
meats, poultry and fish cooked so as to preserve all their
natural juices, rice, macaroni, eggs plain boiled and rather
soft, milk, and sugar, are all common and healthy foods;
all seed-bearing fruits are excellent, especially apples,
pears, grapes, and berries; such succulent vegetables as
potatoes, spinach, green corn, onions, celery, lettuce, carrots, peas, and beans are wholesome, plentiful, and cheap.
Sago, arrowroot, and tapioca, unless combined with plenty
of milk and eggs, are of but little use, except during illness,
when some bland, simple food is required to satisfy the
slight alimentary needs of the system.

EFFECTS OF INDIGESTIBLE FOODS.

Such indigestible articles as fat meat, rich pastry, hot
bread, unripe fruit and vegetables, tea, coffee, spices,

condiments, pickles, and stimulants, should be avoided.
Children fed upon such articles often appear plump, but
their muscles will be found to be soft, their bones small
and weak, and their systems predisposed to inflammatory
affections.

To counteract the deleterious effects of such diet, plenty
of lean meat, fish, oatmeal, graham bread, eggs, milk, ap
ples, onions, celery, asparagus, cauliflower, spinach, and
salad vegetables should be given. The breakfast should be
given soon after rising, the dinner at noon, and the supper
at least two hours before retiring.

PHYSICAL INDICATIONS OF COMPLETE NUTRITION.

If the supply of food answers all physical requirements,
both body and mind will be well developed in proportion
to the age; the eyes will be bright, the cheeks rosy, the
form plump, and the spirits exuberant. Any degree of
health short of this shows that the amount of nutriment
assimilated is insufficient to satisfy the daily demands of
the system, and permit that accumulation of force required for the vigorous development of the growing body.

When educational exigencies seem to interfere with this
reserve of vital force, they should be alternated with a sufficient degree of open air exercise to insure it, and the
proportion of milk, eggs, meat, and bread in the daily fare
should be increased; especially milk should be supplied in
a quantity satisfactory to the appetite.

STUDYING BEFORE BREAKFAST.

Studying before breakfast is not conducive to general
good health, but a moderate degree of open air exercise
will promote an appetite. If part of an hour must be filled
with some studious occupation, it should be judiciously
combined with relaxation; a short walk in some rural
locality, or a visit to the green-house, would afford
occasion for botanical instruction combined with healthy

exercise; and in rainy weather, music, drawing, and light gymnastics offer a choice of suitable occupations for both teacher and pupils.

NECESSITY FOR EARLY BREAKFASTS.

The experiments of Dr. Edward Smith and other eminent investigators prove that the greatest vital action takes place in the early part of the day, that the digestion and assimilation of food are most easily and naturally performed at that time, and consequently that the most nutritious food should then be supplied in abundance.

The danger of overeating at breakfast is provided against by the fact that it is usually composed of simple viands plainly cooked. A healthy child never finds that a hearty breakfast causes indigestion; the activity of the system makes ample provision for the use of all the nourishment it can obtain; it is only towards evening that the force of the vital functions is diminished and that the system becomes unable to assimilate an excess of nutriment.

If the rising hour is about six in the morning, the breakfast should not be later than seven; if the meal is likely to be delayed beyond that hour, a cup of milk and a slice of bread should be taken after dressing. The use of this slight refreshment does not warrant the deferring of the breakfast proper until ten or eleven o'clock.

The breakfast should consist of such plain fare as bread, butter, eggs, or fish, all simply prepared, and plenty of milk. The healthy appetite should be completely satisfied at this meal. for, as we have already said, the vital actions are keenest from rising until noon, and the long fast of the night has depleted the system of the nutriment derived from food during the previous day.

MIDDAY DINNERS BEST FOR HEALTH.

Equally important with a hearty breakfast is a full and

wholesome early dinner of freshly cooked warm meat and vegetables, plenty of bread, and some plain pudding or fruit; these should be well masticated, and accompanied by about half a pint of fresh, cool water as a drink. The meal may be varied with nutritious soups, stews of fresh meat, and red blooded fish.

LIGHT AND EARLY SUPPERS.

The supper should be composed of light and digestible aliments, in quantity sufficient to satisfy the appetite, and should be eaten at least two hours before retiring.

Abundantly nutritious suppers for boys may be made up of bread, milk porridge, a little tapioca or sago pudding made with milk and eggs, or a custard, together with a glass of milk or of moderately cool water. Bread with stewed fruits, as apples or prunes, serve to vary the meal pleasantly, without overtaxing the digestive powers.

For girls, a little warm milk or a cup of weak cocoa may be added with advantage.

Suppers for both boys and girls should be composed of the most digestible foods, because it is imperative to health that the hour for retiring should be early, and digestion should be well advanced before that time. When any unusual exertion or excessive fatigue seems to demand a heavier repast, sufficient time for digestion should be allowed before retiring; if fish is used, sleep should be deferred at least two hours; meat and eggs digest in about three hours, and consequently the bedtime should be graduated accordingly.

NECESSARY DAILY QUANTITY OF FOOD.

Boys from fifteen to twenty years of age require nearly as much food as men; that is, about six pounds per diem.

Girls of the same age require about four pounds. Nutritious soups are especially useful when there is any indication of malnutrition in either sex.

For both boys and girls the character of the food should be largely determined by the appetite, unless it has become very much perverted. Girls are far more apt to be "notional" about their food than boys, and should be much more closely watched.

DAILY DIETARIES.

The facts already cited warrant us in outlining the following dietaries for the youth of both sexes; of course the quantities must be varied to suit individual cases, but the supply should always be ample and appropriate :

Dietary for Children from 6 to 10 Years of Age.

Bread.	Milk.	Butter.	Meat.	Vegetables.	Pudding.	Fruit.
Unlimited.	One pint, or soup half pint.	2 oz.	5 oz., or fish 8 oz.	8 oz.	6 oz.	4 oz.

Dietary for Children from 10 to 14 Years of Age.

Bread.	Milk.	Butter.	Meat.	Vegetables.	Pudding.	Fruit.
1 lb.	1 1-2 pints, or soup 1 pint.	3 oz.	8 oz., or fish 12 oz., or eggs 3 oz.	12 oz.	8 oz.	8 oz.

Dietary for Youths from 14 to 20 Years of Age.

Bread.	Milk.	Butter.	Meat.	Vegetables.	Pudding.	Fruit.
1 1-2 lbs.	1 1-2 pints, or soup 1 pint.	4 oz.	12 oz., or fish 16 oz., or eggs 5 oz.	1 lb.	8 oz.	8 oz.

TABLE OF COMPARATIVE FOOD VALUES.

The following table, compiled from South Kensington estimates, gives some idea of the relative nutritive value of those articles of food in general use throughout the United States; a little study will afford hints for the variation of everyday fare. The figures represent a fair average, but of course are not arbitrary, because the same kind and quantity of food presents different nutritive qualities at different seasons of the year: for instance, juicy fruits are best at the point of ripening; succulent vegetables just before flowering; roots and tubers at their early maturity; and meats and poultry in the winter, when they are generally full grown, and when the temperature permits their preservation until the hardness of fibre which exists in very recently killed meats has passed away.

The following table shows what proportions are yielded of one pound of articles named:

	Heat food.	Flesh food.	Mineral salts.	Water.
Bread............	10 oz.	2 oz.	1-6 oz.	3 5-6 oz.
Meat	3 oz.	3 oz.	1-4 oz.	9 3-4 oz.
Cheese	4 1-2 oz.	5 1-2 oz.	1-2 oz.	5 1-2 oz.
Milk...	1 1-2 oz.	1-2 oz.	1-6 oz.	13 5-6 oz.
Eggs	1 1-2 oz.	2 1-2 oz.	1-4 oz.	11 3-4 oz.
Fish....... ....:	1 oz.	2 1-2 oz.	1-4 oz.	12 1-4 oz.
Poultry.....	2 oz.	1 1-2 oz.	1-2 oz.	12 oz.
Fresh fruit .... } Juicy vegetables .... }	2 oz.	1 oz.	1-2 oz.	12 1-2 oz.
Wheat flour, rice, oatmeal. .. } Macaroni, dried peas & beans }	12 oz.	2 1-2 oz.	1-4 oz.	1 1-4 oz.
Animal fats .... } Butter .... } Oil............................ } Sugar............................ } Arrowroot................. ....)	14 oz.	A trace.	A trace.	2 oz.

ORDINARY CLASSIFICATION OF FOODS.

Foods are classified, in accordance with the preponderance of certain elements, as carbonaceous, or heat food; nitrogenous, or flesh food; and phosphatic, or brain and nerve food.

Heat foods include white flour, sugar, honey, molasses, butter, milk, corn starch, arrowroot, potatoes, beets, beans, turnips, carrots, parsnips, grapes, and all sweet fruits, and liver and fat meat.

Flesh food abounds in lean meat, oatmeal, whole wheat,

eggs, cheese, onions, cabbage, asparagus, salads, celery, cauliflower, and spinach.

Brain and nerve food is found in fresh fruit, unbolted flour, succulent vegetables, game, poultry, oysters, and in certain chemical compounds usually employed by physicians in special dietaries.

All nutritious and easily digested foods are included in these classes of nutrients.

LOCAL DISTRIBUTION OF FOODS.

Inland, throughout the United States, the food in general use is carbonaceous and nitrogenous, with the former somewhat in excess. Upon the seaboard and in the vicinity of lakes and rivers, the abundance and variety of fish give the diet a phosphatic character. Local dietaries in the Eastern States include too great a proportion of hot breakfast cakes, pickles, and pies, while the supply of fruit and vegetables is limited. Similar conditions are marked in the Middle States, but the abundance of fruit and vegetables and of excellent poultry modifies the diet considerably. In the West, except in some of the larger cities, the same kind of food is used as in the East, with the addition of pounded and fried meats; fruit and vegetables are abundant and early, but not sufficiently appreciated; the chief meats are beef and pork. In the South the supply of fruit and vegetables is somewhat limited, although several fine varieties of the latter are indigenous, but poultry is abundant and fine fish is plentiful near the seacoast. Two totally different kinds of cookery dispute for ascendancy: one derived from the genuine culinary ability of the early French and English inhabitants, and the other the abominable outgrowth of the dominion of grease. Bacon is the chief cured meat, and corn is abundantly used, both in a fresh and dried state.

GENERAL SUITABILITY OF LOCAL ALIMENTARY PRODUCTIONS.

In accordance with that impartial justice which demonstrates the eternal fitness of nature's laws, every locality seems to favor the production of such foods as are essential to the health of its inhabitants; this local abundance has led to the use of such alimentary combinations as serve to guide even the most inexperienced caterer.

Without understanding the rationale of the proceeding, the farm laborer relishes a bit of fat pork or bacon with his meal of vegetables or bread; the sailor, returning from a long voyage, during which his diet has been composed chiefly of salt or concentrated foods, instinctively feasts upon vegetables; the native of the tropics craves those juicy fruits with which bountiful nature provides him; and the tribes dwelling near either pole eagerly devour fats in their simplest form.

Despite these ruling facts, variations in the character of local dietaries are occasionally demanded by individual tastes and physical conditions; and they can readily be effected by any intelligent person, after a little study of the chemical composition and nutritive value of different alimentary substances.

INDEX.

Index of Dishes.

Soups.

Fish and Shell-fish.

Vegetables.

Salads and Sauces.

Dishes for Invalids.

Beverages.

General Index.

LIST OF

KITCHEN UTENSILS

REQUIRED FOR USE IN ALL THE COURSES OF LESSONS.

Soup kettle.
Fish   "
Ham   "
Frying "
6 sauce-pans, large and small.
3 dripping-pans   "   "
3 cake   "   "   "
2 *gratin*   "   "   "
2 frying   "   "   "
Omelette pan.
Bread   "
Biscuit   "
Dish   "
Vegetable cutters.
Biscuit   "
Pie plates, large and small.
Meat pie moulds, large and small.
Pudding   " plain and fancy.
Jelly   "   "   "   "
6 custard cups.
6 pudding cups.
6   " cloths, small.
1   " cloth, large.
Soup tureen and ladle.
Dishes of all kinds.
Meat saw.
Cleaver.
Apple corer.
Graters, large and small.
Dredging box.
Scale and weights from ½ oz. up.
Coal scuttle, shovel, and sifter.

Steak gridiron.
Fish   "
Oyster   "
Bean pot.
Coffee pot.
Tea pot.
Chocolate pot, with mill.
Sugar boiler.
Jelly bag.
Flour sieve.
Purée sieve (heavy wire.)
Colanders, large and small.
Strainers   "   "   "
Bolting cloth strainer.
Skimmers, large and small.
Egg whip.
Rolling pin.
Pastry board.
    " brush.
    " cutters.
Larding and trussing needles.
Mortar and pestle.
Potato masher.
Wooden and metal spoons.
Corkscrew.
Knives and forks.
Knife board.
Twine, emery paper.
Soap, soda, sand, borax.
Whiting, bathbrick, blacklead.
Towels, dish cloths, floor cloths.
Brooms, brushes, dustpan.

Lightning Source UK Ltd.
Milton Keynes UK
UKOW05f0410260717
306035UK00013B/324/P